The All-New
Vegetarian
PASSPORT

The All-New
Vegetarian
PASSPORT

350 Healthy Recipes Inspired by Global Cuisines

LINDA WOOLVEN

whitecap

The information in this book is true and complete to the best of
the author's knowledge. All recommendations are made without
guarantee on the part of the author or Whitecap Books Ltd. The
author and publisher disclaim any liability in connection with the
use of this information.

The material in this book relates to certain serious medical
conditions and their treatment. If you have any existing medical
conditions, you should check with your doctor or health care
professional before making changes to your diet.

Whitecap Books is known for its expertise in the cookbook
market, and has produced some of the most innovative and
familiar titles found in kitchens across North America. Visit our
website at www.whitecap.ca.

Design by Diane Robertson
Photography by Michelle Furbacher
Food styling by Michelle Furbacher, Ayesha Rashid and
Grace Yaginuma

Printed in Canada

Library and Archives Canada Cataloguing in Publication

Woolven, Linda
    The all-new vegetarian passport : 350 healthy recipes inspired
by global cuisines / Linda Woolven.

Includes index.

ISBN 978-1-77050-179-9

    1. Vegetarian cooking. 2. Cookbooks. I. Title.

TX837.W65 2013   641.5'636   C2012-905570-0

The publisher acknowledges the financial support of the
Government of Canada through the Canada Book Fund (CBF) and
the Province of British Columbia through the Book Publishing
Tax Credit.

13 14 15 16 17   5 4 3 2 1

Contents

Acknowledgements

I thank the countries and restaurants I visited, and all the people who invited me into their homes, for inspiring me to create the recipes in this book. I also thank my husband, Ted, for all his help with research, editing and tasting.

Preface

To me, there is little more exciting than trying and learning about new things. International travel offers opportunities to see new sights, hear new sounds, experience new scents, have new experiences and, of course, try new food. The thrill of trying new food can be experienced in several different places when you travel: in the markets, in restaurants and in people's houses, when you are lucky enough to get invited in for a meal. In the markets you can see the local foods and small stalls where fresh food is prepared, and buy ingredients and make some of the local dishes yourself if you have access to a kitchen. You might even get lucky enough to have a local person show you how to make local dishes their way. If they invite you to their house, you are in for a treat: a glimpse into their lives, how they live, what they are interested in and talk about and, of course, what they eat and how they eat it. When you get home, you can experiment with making your own versions of these local dishes. I always experiment—that's how I first got interested in international cooking.

I run a natural health clinic and write about how to be healthy and how to treat and prevent illnesses naturally. In my practice, I'm often asked "What should I eat to help treat or prevent [this or that illness], or to stay healthy?" In response, I've created this cookbook, one that is full of easy and fun recipes that contribute to general health and well-being.

I gathered the material for this book during years of travelling and eating international food. Whenever I return home from a trip, I try to create recipes using foods from the region I have just visited, modifying the recipes to make them healthier and easier to make (especially where an ingredient was hard to find). I have sometimes used ingredients that are not traditionally found in a region in order to make the recipe healthier, more interesting or a more complete meal. (For example, I sometimes substitute tofu for the meat or egg in a dish to make it vegetarian.)

I have put two passions of mine—travel and health—together in this book. I hope it helps you go on a healthy, culinary adventure of your own, "travelling" the world with recipes that contribute to great health.

Introduction

Healthy Eating

Every recipe in this book is vegetarian and is suitable for anyone trying to reach and maintain great health. The dishes are full of fibre, bursting with antioxidants and generally free of unhealthy fats. They can help reduce the risk of developing many of the health problems that are, unfortunately, so prevalent in our world today: cancer, candida, celiac disease, diabetes, gout, heart disease, multiple sclerosis, osteoarthritis and rheumatoid arthritis. The ingredients in these recipes make up a healthy diet. In addition, most of the recipes are appropriate for people following a vegan diet. Some of the recipes can even help with memory problems.

A healthily constructed vegetarian diet can promote optimal health in everyone. Factors such as stress, environment and genetics play roles in health and illness. However, the recipes in this book, because they are vegetarian, can help you to stay optimally healthy if you are already healthy or to become optimally healthy if you are following a special diet for health reasons.

INTERNATIONAL EATING

This cookbook is divided into regions of the world as follows: North Africa and the Middle East; the Mediterranean; Europe; India; Asia; Latin America and the Caribbean; and North America. These regions are culinary rather than geopolitical. So, for example, although Italy and Greece are technically part of Europe, they are placed in the Mediterranean section because of their similarities to each other and their unique Mediterranean character. I also put recipes from India all in their own section rather than in Asia because the cuisine of India is unique and distinct from the rest of Asia and it has a wealthy vegetarian tradition. Desserts and beverages appear at the end of the book, in their own section.

Within each region, I've organized the recipes by five types of dish: sides and starters, salads, soups, mains and barbecue. You can "travel" to a region and make a complete feast from that part of the world by picking different dishes, or you can design a culinary mosaic by choosing recipes from across the regions. Another option is to create your own healthy eating program by choosing recipes for their specific health benefits (see How to Use the Recipes in This Book, page 15). Any way you use it, *The All-New Vegetarian Passport* will help you deliver delicious, healthy meals to your kitchen table.

HOW TO BE AS HEALTHY AS POSSIBLE AND FEEL GREAT (OR, THE HEALTH BENEFITS OF A VEGETARIAN DIET)

To be as healthy as possible, it is best to eat a well-balanced vegetarian diet. A plant-based diet is one of the main factors in preventing numerous health problems. Why is a well-balanced vegetarian diet so beneficial? Compared to a meat-based diet, a well-balanced vegetarian diet is

- higher in fibre,

- richer in essential fatty acids,

- richer in antioxidants and

- lower in saturated fats.

A well-balanced vegetarian diet is also loaded with crucial nutrients. How do you eat a well-balanced vegetarian diet? Here are my recommendations:

- Avoid or restrict animal products.

- Eat foods that are high in fibre.

- Eat foods that are rich in essential fatty acids.

- Eat foods that are rich in antioxidants.

- Avoid saturated fats and hydrogenated fats.

- Avoid or restrict "empty foods."

AVOID OR RESTRICT ANIMAL PRODUCTS

Animal products are meat, poultry, fish and seafood, dairy products and eggs. Besides the moral issues surrounding choosing a vegetarian diet, there are health reasons to avoid meat as well. Animal products have less fibre than vegetarian items and can contribute to more health concerns. Fish, for instance, which is high in omega-3 fatty acids, can also contain varying degrees of lead and mercury, adding risks where vegetarian diets do not. And, like other animal products, fish is unnecessarily high in protein and low in fibre. Vegetarians can get enough protein and get complete proteins without eating animal products.

EAT FOODS THAT ARE HIGH IN FIBRE

Eating foods high in fibre is the key to good health. Fibre works for you in many ways: it balances blood sugar, lowers bad cholesterol (LDL), raises good cholesterol (HDL) and can help you normalize your weight.

High-fibre foods are whole grains, fruits and vegetables, and nuts, seeds and legumes.

Insoluble fibre is especially good for regulating the bowels. Good sources of insoluble fibre are whole grains and wheat bran.

Soluble fibre is especially good for lowering cholesterol and blood sugar, for helping with weight loss and for treating irritable bowel syndrome. Good sources of soluble fibre are oats, barley, legumes and most fruits and vegetables

EAT FOODS THAT ARE RICH IN ESSENTIAL FATTY ACIDS

Essential fatty acids (EFAs) can help treat many of the health problems that saturated fats cause. There are many ways that EFAs promote health in the body, including lowering blood pressure, reducing inflammation and strengthening the immune system. EFAs are not made in the body and must be consumed; without them life is not possible.

Essential fatty acids are polyunsaturated fats (such as flaxseed oil and hempseed oil). Though not an EFA, olive oil (a monounsaturated fat) is still a healthy oil. It can be used raw or for cooking, but flaxseed oil and hempseed oil should be eaten raw only. Cooking ruins these oils and makes them unhealthy. While flax and hempseed oils contain high levels of EFAs, you can also get smaller amounts in nuts, seeds, greens and grains.

EAT FOODS THAT ARE RICH IN ANTIOXIDANTS

An abundance of antioxidants in the diet rids the body of the free radicals that contribute to so many health problems. Free radicals are harmful unstable compounds that occur at the molecular level in the body and that have been linked to several diseases. Free radicals may also be the culprits in the cell degeneration that causes aging. Providing your body with enough antioxidants will help curb these radical cells from running amok.

Antioxidants include the following:

- Vitamin C and vitamin E

- Carotenes, some of which are converted in the body to vitamin A

- Selenium, which is a mineral found in Brazil nuts, wheat germ, oats, chard, brown rice and many other foods

- Flavonoids, which are found in blueberries, garlic, citrus fruit and green tea

AVOID SATURATED FATS AND HYDROGENATED FATS

A diet high in saturated fats and hydrogenated fats is one of the factors in many of today's health problems. Saturated fat occurs naturally in animal products, so a vegetarian diet avoids most saturated fats. Vegetarians still have to watch their hydrogenated-fat intake, however. Hydrogenated fat is a previously healthy unsaturated fat that has had hydrogen added to some of its carbon molecules. This may not sound bad, but it can lead to many health problems, including high cholesterol, cancer and immune suppression. Hydrogenated fats most often appear in items like margarine, some cooking oils and many processed foods. Depending on which country you live in, hydrogenated fat, or trans- fats, may not always be included on the food label. Wherever possible, use fresh, natural ingredients as opposed to processed foods.

AVOID OR RESTRICT "EMPTY FOODS"

Some foods—"junk" food—are simply "empty." They lack or are devoid of nutrients and are full of unhealthy fats as well as chemicals and additives. Eating them can be harmful to your health—they can suppress your immune system, raise your blood pressure and bad cholesterol and deplete other healthy nutrients from your body. Examples of empty foods are refined grains, sugar, caffeine and alcohol.

How a Vegetarian Diet Helps Health Conditions

🅒 CANCER

It comes as a surprise to many people that something as simple as diet can be so important for something as complicated and serious as cancer. People who want to avoid all of the most common cancers can benefit from the positive features of a vegetarian diet.

For example, changes in the diet could reduce the risk of breast cancer by as much as 80 percent. Vegetarian diets help combat breast cancer in a number of ways. Vegetarians have stronger immune systems and lower estrogen levels. Meat and saturated fat contribute to breast cancer, while whole grains, legumes and fruits and vegetables help prevent it.

Foods that are especially important for breast cancer include cruciferous vegetables and soy. Cruciferous vegetables include broccoli, cauliflower, cabbage, Brussels sprouts, kale, bok choy, collards, radish, watercress and others. Women who eat the most cruciferous vegetables have an almost twofold reduction in the risk of breast cancer.

Eating a lot of soy reduces the risk of breast cancer, of recurrence of breast cancer and of death from breast cancer. The very mild and gentle plant estrogens in soy block the binding of your body's stronger, harsher estrogens.

Men can also benefit from the cancer-fighting properties of a vegetarian diet. The greatest risk factor of all for prostate cancer is a diet high in animal fat. And the more bad fat you eat, the worse you do: men who

eat the most animal fat have a greater risk of developing a more advanced form of prostate cancer. Men who eat the most saturated fat have more than triple the risk of dying of prostate cancer than men who eat the least. On the positive side, eating more whole grains, fruits, vegetables and legumes, while cutting back on meat, dairy and refined carbohydrates, helps men with prostate cancer.

Foods that are especially important for prostate cancer include garlic, soy, tomatoes and strawberries. Men who eat more foods in the garlic family have a 50 percent lower risk of developing prostate cancer. And in countries where men eat a lot of soy, fewer men die of prostate cancer. Tomato is beneficial too. Tomatoes are loaded with a powerful anti-cancer carotene called lycopene, which can help lower the risk of developing prostate cancer and prevent its growth and spread. Pink grapefruit, watermelon, guava, papaya and apricot are also good sources of lycopene. As in breast cancer, cruciferous vegetables are beneficial as are strawberries. Cruciferous vegetables have also been shown to protect against lung, stomach, colon and rectal cancers.

Vegetarian diets in general help many kinds of cancer beyond breast and prostate, including the other two most common cancers: lung cancer and colon cancer.

Good cancer foods are high in fibre, rich in antioxidants and low in saturated and hydrogenated fats. They should also be rich in essential fatty acids. In addition to the foods we have already looked at, you should also include lots of antioxidant-rich spices like turmeric, basil, sage, thyme, ginger, oregano and rosemary. Deep leafy greens are also key foods to eat, as are carotene-rich foods like red peppers, squash and tomatoes. Really, all vegetables, fruits, legumes and whole grains are great anti-cancer foods. And so are raw, unsalted seeds and nuts, especially almonds, which have anti-cancer nutrients. And eat lots of sprouts. Avoid substances that are linked to cancer, like sugar, salt, animal products and chemicals.

CA CANDIDA

A candida diet is one that seeks to rid the body of foods that feed this unfriendly yeast overgrowth. The diet usually lasts from three to six months, sometimes longer. Most importantly, it avoids sugar in all its forms, including white sugar, brown sugar, maple syrup, honey, molasses, rice syrup and barley malt. Foods with moulds, like peanuts, peanut butter, cashews and melons, and live yeast foods (which can be found in some pâtés, packaged snack foods like popcorn, and alcoholic beverages) need to be avoided. Though sugars and simple carbohydrates should be avoided, complex carbohydrates and fibre are good. The candida diet should be high in fibre, as fibre helps to keep the bowels moving and clean out the yeast.

A healthy candida diet allows some fruit, usually only two to three fruits a day, but no dried fruit or fruit juice. Focus on apples, pears, plums, peaches and berries; avoid oranges, grapes, melons and tropical fruits.

You can eat whole grains like teff, amaranth, millet, quinoa, whole grain rice and buckwheat freely. This diet often restricts the glutenous grains like rye, barley, whole wheat, spelt and kamut—although some experts allow spelt and kamut. In terms of bread made with gluten-free grains (and breads made with spelt and kamut), some candida diets allow you to eat these breads made with yeast, while some will guide you to eat only yeast-free breads. In the baking recipes in this book, I allow breads made with yeast. (Note that sprouted grain bread is usually okay for candida, as the sprouting process begins to break down gluten, and this kind of bread is usually made without yeast.)

Animal products should be avoided, or at least greatly restricted. Dairy should always be avoided, and eggs are sometimes avoided as well. You can eat all the vegetables, legumes and raw seeds and nuts that you like. Some of the candida diets restrict soy foods for the first month of the diet. All food allergens should be identified and avoided. Also avoid alcohol and vinegar.

Recipes in this book have not been eliminated from the candida diet if they contain gluten, bread, yeast, potatoes, yam, fruit, small amounts of pure fruit juice, or chickpeas, so it is up to you to do so if you cannot eat these foods.

CD CELIAC DISEASE

People with celiac disease need to follow a diet that is entirely free from all gluten, the protein found in wheat, kamut, barley, spelt and rye.

Though most sources still say that people who have celiac disease need to avoid oats, most people who have celiac disease can tolerate moderate amounts. You need to be sure, though, that the oats you buy are not contaminated with gluten, a disturbingly common problem.

Also avoid gluten hidden in products like soy sauce and vegetable stock cubes; look for gluten-free versions. And read the ingredient labels of packaged foods and sauces carefully since packaged foods can contain gluten. Milk and dairy products should also be eliminated until your intestines are healed by the special diet and return to normal.

Enjoy gluten-free grains like teff, amaranth, buckwheat, whole-grain rice of all kinds, quinoa and millet.

D DIABETES

People who have diabetes can drastically improve their health by following a vegetarian diet. Vegetarians simply have less type 2 diabetes. High-fibre and vegan diets are extremely effective for controlling blood sugar. People who have diabetes should avoid simple sugars, refined carbohydrates and processed foods; they should eat lots of whole grains, complex carbohydrates and high-fibre foods and a wide variety of fruits and vegetables. Eating lots of nuts also helps.

The vegetarian diet helps people who have diabetes not only because of the fruits, vegetables, nuts and fibre that the diet adds, but also because of the saturated fat it eliminates. Saturated fats are bad for people who have diabetes, and essential fatty acids are good for people who have diabetes. If cell membranes are composed of too much saturated fat and not enough essential fatty acids, they lose their

fluidity and the cells become insensitive to insulin, leading to diabetes. So people who have diabetes need to reduce saturated fats by reducing meat and dairy and increase essential fatty acids.

Some foods are especially beneficial for people who have diabetes. In addition to nuts, garlic and onions are great for people who have diabetes. Adding lots of cinnamon to your food is also very helpful, as is incorporating fenugreek into your diet.

People who have diabetes can eat fruit because the fibre in the fruit helps to balance blood sugar. Eat two to three servings a day if you are diabetic, but don't drink sugary fruit juice, and avoid eating dried fruit.

G GOUT

Gout is a less discussed but very painful member of the arthritis family. It is primarily caused by diet and, for most people, can be cured by diet alone. Though common in meat eaters, gout is rare in vegetarians.

Too much uric acid in your body is the cause of gout. Uric acid is a breakdown product of purine. So getting rid of gout means getting rid of purine. This goal is accomplished by getting rid of red meat, organ meats, goose, gravy, broth, bouillon, consommé, shellfish (including shrimp, mussels and scallops), anchovies, sardines, mackerel, herring, fish roe, brewer's and baker's yeast, and peanuts. Foods moderately high in purines, like poultry, dried legumes, spinach, asparagus and mushrooms should be reduced.

If you have gout, you should also avoid alcohol (especially beer), refined sugar and refined carbohydrates. A vegetarian diet also helps because high protein increases the production of uric acid, and saturated fat decreases its elimination.

People with gout should eat lots of cherries. Pomegranate may also be helpful. Also eat foods rich in antioxidants like the proanthocyanidins found in berries, and eat foods rich in vitamin C, like citrus fruit, kiwi and cauliflower.

HD HEART DISEASE

A vegetarian diet is good for your heart because it has less cholesterol and saturated fat but lots of fibre, essential fatty acids and antioxidants. Vegetarians have lower cholesterol, lower blood pressure and less heart disease.

Heart-healthy foods are low in cholesterol, saturated fats, trans-fatty acids and sodium, and rich in unsaturated fats, fibre, antioxidants, calcium, magnesium and potassium. Foods like legumes, garlic, celery, onions and carotene-rich foods are especially good. So eat your deep leafy greens, red peppers, cauliflower, kiwi, cabbage and squashes. And add heart-healthy antioxidant-rich herbs and spices to your cooking such as: rosemary, ginger and cayenne. Also especially important are potassium- and magnesium-rich foods like deep leafy greens, avocado, lima beans, tomato, peaches, plums, carrots, tofu, legumes, nuts, seeds, whole grains and bananas. All vegetables, fruits, legumes, whole grains and raw seeds and nuts are great. People who eat eight or more servings a day of fruit and vegetables have a much lower risk of dying from heart disease.

Animal products should be avoided and salt needs to be minimized. Also avoid alcohol, packaged foods (they are often high in salt) and caffeine. And don't forget to eat your flaxseed and your flax, olive and hempseed oils; they can help prevent and reduce heart disease.

There are also some special foods for heart health. Both garlic and soy are great for lowering cholesterol and blood pressure. Despite the frequent and erroneous advice that nuts are fattening, they are not; in fact, they are good for the heart and improve cholesterol. Cruciferous vegetables are also good for your heart. Eating them lowers your risk of dying from cardiovascular disease.

M MEMORY LOSS

Eating for memory? That's not as commonly heard as eating for heart health. But vegetarian diets are just as important for your brain as they are for your heart—and sometimes for the same reasons. Vegetarian diets protect against high cholesterol, high blood pressure and atherosclerosis, all of which increase your risk of Alzheimer's disease.

Eating more fruit, vegetables and especially fibre improves brain function in elderly people. Drinking more fruit or vegetable juice lowers your risk of developing Alzheimer's.

Vegetarian diets are also good for your brain because the kind of fat you eat affects it. Eating more monounsaturated fat and less saturated fat improves cognitive function and memory.

The antioxidants that are packed into a vegetarian diet also protect your memory.

People who get the most betacarotene, vitamin C and especially vitamin E have a lower risk of developing Alzheimer's. Try adding antioxidant herbs and spices like sage and rosemary to your cooking; they are two of the best herbs for improving memory. Other antioxidant herbs and spices like oregano, thyme, basil and turmeric are also good choices.

Eat foods like whole grains, legumes and deep leafy greens that are rich in B vitamins and antioxidants, which are good for memory. The B vitamins B6, B12 and especially folic acid are great for protecting memory and preventing Alzheimer's. Foods high in the antioxidants vitamin C and E are very important. Again, try eating whole grains (and wheat germ), and also cabbage, kiwi, cauliflower, potatoes, oranges, lemons and grapefruit—really, all fruits and vegetables. Also be sure to eat your flaxseed oil; it's great for memory.

MS MULTIPLE SCLEROSIS

There is a correlation between diets that are high in animal and dairy products, and multiple sclerosis. The problem is the saturated fats found in animal products. People who eat foods that are high in saturated animal fat are more likely to develop multiple sclerosis, while diets high in fruits, vegetables and coldwater fish help to prevent it. Changing the diet may not only prevent the disease from progressing, it may also help prevent mortality from the disease. The more polyunsaturated fat in the diet and the less saturated fat, the less mortality there is from multiple sclerosis.

The diet should be rich in fruits and vegetables. It also allows coldwater fish, like mackerel, herring and tuna, that are rich in omega-3 fatty acids, but it is good to get your essential fatty acids from hempseed or flaxseed oil, as fish contains toxins and pollutants (for example, mercury) that are not healthy. The diet bans meat, dairy, margarine and other hydrogenated fats. The developer of this diet, Dr. Roy Swank, showed that if you were put on the diet before symptoms appeared, there could be little, if any, development of the disease and a greatly enhanced chance of long life. Even people who were more advanced in the disease did better on the diet, so it's never too late to start. Dietary changes and supplements may not only stop the deterioration but actually improve health in many newly diagnosed multiple sclerosis sufferers.

So, multiple sclerosis sufferers should avoid dairy, saturated fat, animal protein, hydrogenated fat and possibly gluten and other allergens, and eat foods rich in essential fatty acids like flaxseed and hempseed oil, and polyunsaturated fats. Eat fibre-rich, antioxidant-rich foods, like gluten-free whole grains, legumes, soy, fruits, vegetables, and raw seeds and nuts like walnuts.

You should also eat foods rich in selenium and vitamins C and E, like two Brazil nuts a day, red Swiss chard, orange juice, turnips, garlic, brown rice, kale, collard greens, guava, kiwi, watercress, cabbage, oranges, mangos, peppers, asparagus, green leafy vegetables, berries, raw seeds, gluten-free whole grains and polyunsaturated vegetable oils, as long as you are not allergic to these foods.

OA OSTEOARTHRITIS

If you suffer from osteoarthritis, a vegetarian diet may help you in part because it is the best and safest way to lose weight, and achieving a healthy weight is one of the most important steps in preventing osteoarthritis and in relieving the pain if you already have it.

The osteoarthritis diet should be bursting with fruits and vegetables because they are such rich sources of antioxidants. Eating lots of antioxidant-rich foods can slow down the deterioration of your joints. Eat lots of flavonoid-rich blueberries, blackberries, cranberries, cherries and dark grapes. You should also eat lots of sulfur-rich foods like garlic, onions, broccoli and cabbage.

Some osteoarthritis sufferers may benefit from avoiding the nightshade foods and dairy that rheumatoid arthritis sufferers leave out of their diet. You should also watch out for foods that you are allergic to.

RA RHEUMATOID ARTHRITIS

If you suffer from rheumatoid arthritis, then a vegetarian diet will bring you plenty of relief. Arthritis is an inflammatory disease and saturated animal fats are inflammatory. The unsaturated fats found in plants are anti-inflammatory. People with rheumatoid arthritis have been found to have more animal fat in their diet than people without the disease. When you remove the animal fats from your diet, you get better. Becoming a vegan can signifigantly improve your arthritis symptoms.

In addition to meat and dairy, if you have rheumatoid arthritis, it may be helpful to avoid the nightshade family of vegetables; that is, tomatoes, potatoes, eggplant, tobacco and peppers. Rheumatoid arthritis sufferers also need to identify and avoid common food allergens. The most common ones are dairy and wheat, but other common offenders are corn, beef and food additives.

Eat a diet rich in fibre and whole foods, like vegetables, fruits, whole grains, legumes and raw seeds and nuts. Eat plenty of antioxidant-rich foods and essential fatty acids. Antioxidant-and nutrient-rich foods include broccoli, Brussels sprouts, cabbage, citrus fruits, cauliflower, honeydew, carrots, kiwi, berries and squash. The antioxidant flavonoids found in dark grapes, blueberries, cranberries, blackberries and cherries are especially helpful. Avoid saturated and hydrogenated fats. Eat sulfur-rich foods like garlic, onions, legumes, Brussels sprouts and cabbage.

V VEGAN DIET

A vegan diet differs from a vegetarian diet in that, in addition to avoiding meat, poultry and fish, it eliminates *all* animal products, including dairy, honey and eggs. Vegans eat only plant foods, from vegetables, sea vegetables, fruits, seeds, nuts, legumes and grains. This diet is the healthiest one you can eat. It prevents and treats everything from heart disease, cancer and diabetes, to asthma, arthritis, allergies, premenstrual syndrome, fibroids, cysts, gout, multiple sclerosis and obesity—really, everything. And a vegan who eats little junk food, uses only whole grains instead of refined ones and eats a diet rich in essential fatty acids does even better.

How to Cook for Health

EAT A VARIETY OF HEALTHY FOODS DAILY

In general, each day, everyone should eat

- 6 to 8 servings of vegetables (1 or more of these servings should be a leafy deep-green vegetable, which is especially packed with nutrients),

- 2 to 3 servings of fruit,

- 4 to 9 servings of whole grains,

- 1 to 3 servings of legumes and

- a handful of raw, unsalted seeds and nuts.

Eat food with a wide variety of colours—orange, red, purple, white and green foods.

EAT RAW FOOD

Aim to make raw food 50 to 75 percent—or more—of your daily food intake. You can easily accomplish this by eating raw fruit and vegetables throughout the day as snacks and having a giant salad with lunch or dinner. I eat a huge bowl of salad every day (often two bowls) and add fruit to a smoothie whenever I have one.

Raw food helps provide the body with enzymes. Enzymes help digestion, which means that there will be less wear and tear on your digestive system. If your body is getting enzymes from raw food, it doesn't have to make as many of its own enzymes. This means that energy is freed up for other uses, such as repair and rejuvenation.

Also, raw food is higher in vitamins and minerals than cooked food, and it helps your body detoxify itself, making it more able to resist illness.

EAT "SUPER-VEGGIES"

"Super-vegetables" are literally packed full of nutrients, containing magnesium, calcium, potassium, boron and vitamins C, D, E, K and folic acid. Super-vegetables are leafy dark-green vegetables—kale, chard, watercress, mustard greens, spinach, arugula, beet greens and bok choy. Broccoli, Brussels sprouts, cabbage and cauliflower, although not dark green nor leafy, are also considered super-vegetables.

USE HERBS AND SPICES

Most herbs and spices are loaded with antioxidants, which is why many of them help boost immunity; prevent cancer and diabetes; and promote heart health by increasing circulation, lowering blood pressure and reducing cholesterol. Many herbs and spices also aid in digestion (which helps you feel better and helps you absorb nutrients better). As a master herbalist, I've known that incorporating international cooking into your lifestyle can help promote health because so many of the world's diets liberally use herbs and spices—think of the turmeric-rich curries of India.

Particularly good herbs for overall good health include basil, caraway, coriander, dill, fennel, fenugreek, oregano, parsley, rosemary, sage and thyme.

Particularly good spices for overall health include black pepper, cayenne, chili powder, cinnamon, cumin, curry powder (which is a mixture of spices) and turmeric.

Try to use fresh herbs rather than dried herbs in cooking and in raw dishes such as salads whenever possible. Fresh herbs generally provide more nutrients, and often taste stronger and flavour the dish better. If you do have to use dried herbs in a recipe, note that one teaspoon (5 mL) of dried herbs is equivalent to one tablespoon (15 mL) of fresh herbs. Add fresh herbs near the end of the cooking time.

DRINK GREEN TEA

Green tea is a tasty and valuable beverage, and the flavonoids in it are very powerful antioxidants. Green tea may help in the prevention and treatment of cancer and heart disease, and also leads to greater bone mineral density and significantly helps in the prevention of osteoporosis. Regular drinking of green tea, and regularly rinsing your mouth with green tea, may help stop plaque from forming on your teeth.

COOK WITH HIGH-QUALITY INGREDIENTS AND EQUIPMENT

Organic ingredients

Use organic ingredients if you can find them and afford them (they are coming down in price). Experiment with growing your own (I grow much of our own food in the summer months). Organic foods are free of chemicals, hormones and additives, and they are typically higher in nutritional value. They also taste better. When it comes to eggs, always use organic and free range.

Soup stock

Use organic vegetable stock cubes or liquid stock if you can find it. Many stores carry organic soup stock now. Organic stock is free of chemicals and has fewer additives and salt (it uses herbs for flavour).

Note that you can use water instead of oil or other fat when sautéing vegetables for soup, although technically, of course, this would no longer be sautéing. You can also add water as you cook if the ingredients seem dry or are sticking to the pan. When using stock cubes, always use the ones found in health food stores or health food sections of grocery stores. They tend to be made with less, or no, salt, and are made of dehydrated vegetables and herbs, so they have fewer additives. I always use low-sodium.

Experiment with making your own soup stock. Here is one version of a basic soup stock recipe. Most of the ingredients are optional; you can substitute or adapt however you like.

- 2 to 3 large onions, peeled and chopped

- 2 leeks, chopped (optional; leeks make for a stronger-tasting stock)

- 1 to 4 cloves garlic, peeled

- 2 potatoes, chopped

- 1 small zucchini, sliced (optional)

- 1 cup (250 mL) squash or yam, peeled and chopped (optional; squash or yam makes for a sweeter stock)

- 1 small apple, peeled, seeded and chopped (optional; apple makes for a sweeter stock)

- 2 sticks celery, chopped
- 2 carrots, chopped
- 1 teaspoon (5 mL) fresh parsley or dill (optional; add near the end of the cooking time)
- a ½- to 1-inch (1–2.5 cm) piece of dried kombu (optional; kombu makes for a stronger-tasting, consummé-like, salty stock, but it is loaded in minerals)
- 1 bay leaf
- a good grinding of black pepper
- ¼ teaspoon (1 mL) salt, or a salt alternative
- 10 cups (2.5 L) water

Put everything in a pot, cover and bring to a boil. Turn the heat down and simmer for 45 minutes. Strain and use as the base for cooking.

You can emphasize different flavours in a stock by adding tomato, dill, onion, mushrooms, and/or celery. For an Italian flavour, add basil, thyme and oregano. For an Asian flavour, add ginger, shiitake mushrooms, green onions and tamari sauce. For a thicker stock, add yellow split peas.

Store-bought sauces

When purchasing store-bought sauces like spaghetti sauce, ketchup and barbecue sauce, watch out for excess sugar and salt.

Non-stick cookware

Non-stick cookware makes cooking and cleaning easier, but it is controversial. The chemical used in its manufacture has been linked to cancer in animals and may be linked to elevated cholesterol, thyroid disease and infertility in humans. The question, still unresolved, is whether any of this chemical remains in your pots and pans after manufacture.

If you use non-stick cookware, use it on low or medium heat only. When brought to high temperatures, non-stick cookware release fumes that can make you feel sick. Health Canada says not to heat non-stick pots and pans to over 650°F (350°C); SickKids Hospital in Toronto gives the more cautious limit of 500°F (260°C).

If you are concerned about the chemicals used in the manufacture of non-stick cookware, or about the fumes that are released at high heat, I suggest you use stainless steel, cast iron, ceramic titanium or porcelain-enamelled cast-iron cookware instead. If you do use an alternative and find that the food sticks when you are cooking, grease or oil the pan before cooking—this will prevent food from sticking.

Cans and plastic

Though there are dangerous chemicals (BPAs) found in cans and plastic, the reality is that most home cooks occasionally use canned food or food that has been stored in plastic. For that reason, I have included canned foods (particularly beans) in some of the recipes in this book. If you do use canned beans, drain and rinse them well to get rid of the excess salt and other undesirable ingredients that might be in the can. You can always substitute dried or fresh beans for canned ones. Make large batches and store them in the fridge or freezer in BPA-free containers.

BEANS AND GRAINS COOKING CHART

On the following pages are charts of cooking times for beans and grains. They are guides only. Your stove may cook hotter—in which case you could add more liquid. As things are cooking, check them and add more liquid if needed. It is better to use a little too much water than too little, especially when you are cooking grains. The excess water can always be drained.

Wash and sort dried beans, peas and lentils, removing any unusable parts. It is better not to soak them before cooking, as this contributes to some nutrient loss. Cooked beans can be kept in the refrigerator for up to three days and in the freezer for longer. Store them in freezer-safe containers. I often store cooked beans in some of their cooking liquid, and when I'm ready to use them, I thaw them and drain off the liquid. The liquid has some nutritional value and can be used in making soups and other dishes.

Beans cooking chart

This chart is based on using 1 cup (250 mL) of dried beans.

BEANS	WATER AMOUNT	COOKING TIME	YIELD
ADZUKI	3½ cups (875 mL)	45 minutes	2 cups (500 mL)
BLACK BEANS	4¼–5 cups (1.125–1.25 L)	2½ hours	3 cups (750 mL)
BLACK-EYED PEAS	3¼ cups (800 mL)	1 hour	2 cups (500 mL)
CHICKPEAS	4½ cups (1.125 L)	3¼ hours	2 cups (500 mL)
KIDNEY BEANS *(see additional instructions below)*	3½ cups (875 mL)	1¼–1¾ hours	2¼ cups (560 mL)
LENTILS, GREEN	3 cups (750 mL)	45 minutes–1 hour	2 cups (500 mL)
LENTILS, RED	2 cups (500 mL)	20 minutes	1½–1¾ cups (325–435 mL)
LIMA BEANS	4 cups (1 L)	2½ hours	2 cups (500 mL)
PINTO BEANS	4 cups (1 L)	1½–3 hours	2½ cups (625 mL)
MUNG BEANS	3 cups (750 mL)	1 hour	2 cups (500 mL)
NAVY BEANS	4½ cups (1.125 L)	3½ hours	2¼ cups (560 mL)
SOY BEANS	3½ cups (875 mL)	2½–3 hours	2¼ cups (560 mL)
SPLIT PEAS, GREEN OR YELLOW	3 cups (750 mL)	45 minutes–1 hour	2¼ cups (560 mL)

Additional instructions:

1. Bring the water to a boil.

2. Add the legumes and allow to boil for a few minutes, then turn down to a very low boil. If you are cooking kidney beans, boil them on high for at least 10 minutes before turning the heat down. This prevents haemagglutinin, which can cause food poisoning, from forming.

3. Keep covered, at least partway, and stir if needed. Check water level from time to time as different stoves require different amounts of water. Cooking time can vary depending on the length of time things have been stored and the heat of the stove, so always taste everything before you assume it is done, starting from 15 minutes before the end of cooking time listed in the chart.

4. Drain before using, if needed.

Grains cooking chart

This chart is based on using 1 cup (250 mL) of dry grains.

GRAINS	WATER AMOUNT	COOKING TIME	YIELD
AMARANTH	3 cups (750 mL)	25 minutes	2 ½ cups (625 mL)
BARLEY	3 ½ cups (875 mL)	80 minutes	3 ½ cups (875 mL)
BROWN RICE	3 ¼ cups (810 mL)	50 minutes	3 cups (750 mL)
BULGUR *(see additional instructions below)*	3 cups (750 mL)	15–20 minutes	2 ½ cups (625 mL)
CORNMEAL	4 cups (1 L)	20 minutes	3 cups (750 mL)
COUSCOUS *(see additional instructions below)*	4 cups (1 L)	10–15 minutes	1 ½ cups (375 mL)
MILLET	3 ½ cups (875 mL)	40–50 minutes	3 ½ cups (875 mL)
QUINOA	2 ¼ cups (560 mL)	15 minutes	2 ½ cups (625 mL)
WILD RICE	4 ½–6 cups (1.125–1.5 L)	65–70 minutes	2 ½ cups (625 mL)

Additional instructions:

1. Bring the water to a boil.

2. Add the grains and allow to boil for a few minutes, then turn down to a very low boil. If you are cooking bulgur or couscous, simply put it in a bowl and pour boiling water over it. Cover and allow it to stand: 10 minutes for couscous, 20 minutes for bulgur.

3. Keep covered, at least partway, and stir if needed. Check water level from time to time as different stoves require different amounts of water. Cooking time can vary depending on the length of time things have been stored and the heat of the stove, so always taste everything before you assume it is done, starting from 15 minutes before the end of cooking time listed in the chart.

4. Drain before using, if needed.

How to Use the Recipes in This Book

A healthily constructed, well-balanced vegetarian diet can promote optimal health in everyone. The recipes in this book, because they are vegetarian, can help you to stay optimally healthy if you are already healthy or to become optimally healthy if you have to follow a special diet for health reasons.

Every recipe in this book is vegetarian and is therefore suitable for anyone trying to reach and maintain great health. Most of the dishes are full of fibre, free of unhealthy fats and bursting with antioxidants. Most of the recipes are suitable for anyone, and many of the recipes are appropriate for those following a vegan diet.

HOW TO INTERPRET THE ICONS IN THE RECIPES

Every recipe is accompanied by a set of icons. The full set of icons represents ten health concerns and one special diet. Here is the full set:

If an icon does not appear, the recipe contains ingredients that may not be suitable for the health concern or special diet.

ⓒ Cancer

This icon does not appear if the recipe uses higher amounts of dairy or eggs, or sugar in most forms (honey, fruit, fruit juice and dried fruit are okay). Reducing or eliminating dairy and eggs and eliminating sugar may help in the prevention and management of cancer. Substitute vegan soy, rice or hemp cheese for the dairy cheese in the recipes as often as possible. Because the recipes with salt are easily adaptable with salt-free alternatives (see page 18), the cancer icon is kept in for these recipes. However, those on a cancer diet should minimise salt intake and use substitutes as often as possible.

CA Candida

This icon does not appear if the recipe uses live yeast, refined wheat, peanuts, cashews, melon, honey, white or brown sugar, dried fruit or fruit juice, tropical fruits, oranges, grapes, high amounts of white vinegar or alcohol, or dairy, unless it is a probiotic (live culture) yoghurt. Some, but not all, health professionals do not allow mushrooms, but I do make an exception for the immunity-boosting, Candida-fighting shiitake mushroom. Though some health professionals ban eggs from a candida diet, the effect of eggs on candida is controversial. Recipes in this book that contain eggs have not been ruled out for candida, but because treatments vary, you can check with your health care provider before consuming egg-rich foods. Though sugars and simple carbohydrates should be avoided, complex carbohydrates and fibre are good. The candida diet should be high in fibre, as fibre helps to keep the bowels moving and clean out the yeast.

CD Celiac disease

This icon does not appear if the recipe uses any amount of dairy or food with gluten. Some celiacs, however, may be able to tolerate some dairy, especially if the diet has been followed for some time and the intestines have improved. I have allowed soy sauce and oats, but remember to check the labels; only use gluten-free soy sauce and oats that are not contaminated.

D Diabetes

This icon does not appear if the recipe uses dairy or eggs, refined wheat, or sugar in any form, including honey, dried fruit and fruit juice. Eliminating these ingredients may help in the prevention and management of type 2 diabetes and in the management of type 1 diabetes.

G Gout

This icon does not appear if the recipe uses any amount of alcohol, dairy, refined sugar in any form or purine-rich foods. Purines are compounds from which uric acid is produced. Uric acid crystallizes in the joints and causes inflammation. While you won't find them in these recipes, these ingredients are the most detrimental to gout sufferers: red meat, organ meats, shellfish (including shrimp, mussel and scallops), anchovies, sardines, mackerel, herring and fish roe. Brewer's and baker's yeast and peanuts are also detrimental. Though they have fewer purines than the meat items listed previously, some vegetarian foods can also have purines and must be eaten in moderation if you are trying to treat gout. Examples of purine-rich foods that should be eaten with care are asparagus, spinach, mushrooms and dried legumes (split peas and soy are okay). Reducing or eliminating these purine-rich foods, as well as alcohol, dairy and sugar (fruit and fruit juice are okay), can help control gout.

HD Heart disease

This icon does not appear if the recipe uses eggs or higher amounts of dairy or sodium. Reducing or eliminating dairy, eggs and sodium may help in the prevention and treatment of heart disease. Substitute vegan soy, rice or hemp cheese for the dairy cheese in the recipes as often as possible.

M Memory loss

This icon does not appear if the recipe uses higher amounts of dairy or eggs. These types of foods can lead to circulatory problems, causing poor cognitive function.

MS Multiple sclerosis

This icon does not appear if the recipe uses saturated animal fats such as dairy and eggs, or hydrogenated fats like regular margarine. Studies done by Dr. Roy Swank have shown that by banning meat, dairy, margarine and other hydrogenated fats from your diet, you may be able to slow the progress of multiple sclerosis. However, if you use only nonhydrogenated, dairy-free margarine, you can enjoy the recipes with margarine in them. Regular margarine usually contains *hydrogenated* oils, as well as dairy, and that makes it bad for multiple sclerosis.

OA Osteoarthritis

Some people with osteoarthritis may benefit from avoiding dairy and nightshade fruits and vegetables. Nightshades are eggplant, bell peppers, potatoes and tomatoes. If these ingredients are included in a recipe, it's up to you whether or not to make the recipe.

RA Rheumatoid arthritis

This icon does not appear if the recipe uses inflammatory satured fats, including dairy and eggs or nightshade vegetables. Nightshade vegetables are eggplant, bell peppers, potatoes and tomatoes. I have allowed chili peppers because their significant anti-inflammatory and pain-killing properties outweigh the possible negative effect of nightshade vegetables. Nightshade vegetables and dairy may aggravate rheumatoid arthritis.

ⓥ Vegan diet

This icon does not appear if the recipe uses dairy, eggs or honey. Because of the growing availability of vegan cheese, many recipes in this book can be made vegan by substituting the dairy with its vegan counterpart.

HOW TO ADAPT THE RECIPES

Almost every recipe in this book can be easily adapted and used even if the icon does not appear for a health concern or special diet. Experiment! Feel free to omit or replace ingredients however you like. See the chart of substitution ingredients on page 18. The ingredients that I have provided substitutions for are the ingredients that may have caused an icon to be omitted from a recipe because of a health concern or special diet. For example, a recipe will not have a heart disease icon if it uses a higher amount of sodium. If you have heart disease and want to make the recipe anyway, you can adapt the recipe. Here's how:

1. Look to see how sodium is used in the recipe (i.e., it may be used as soy sauce).

2. Find it on the substitution chart.

3. Choose a substitution ingredient that you think would work for the recipe (i.e., for soy sauce, you could choose a low-sodium soy sauce).

These substitutions are suggestions only. For some ingredients there are no practical substitutions. And for some ingredients you will make substitutions based on your own health concerns or special diet. For example,

if a recipe uses dairy, and you need to avoid dairy, you can use rice, hemp or soy milk or cheese.

A Glossary of Special Ingredients

AMARANTH

A seed used by the ancient Aztecs. Amaranth is rich in protein, calcium and magnesium, and is higher than other grains in the amino acid lysine. It is used as a grain in cooking. If you can't find it, use brown rice or quinoa instead.

ASAFOETIDA POWDER

A pungent spice. Asafoetida powder can usually be found in Indian markets, but if you can't find it, use cumin or fennel seed instead.

CUBANELLE PEPPER

A sweet pepper from the species *Capsicum annuum*, which is bright red when ripe. Cubanelle pepper can usually be found in specialty, or Latin American markets, but if you can't find it, use chili peppers, jalapeño peppers, bell peppers or smoked peppers, depending how hot you want the dish to be.

DULSE

A seaweed rich in minerals—a good source of iodine and iron. Dulse can usually be found in the macrobiotic or Asian section of stores. It often comes dried.

FILÉ POWDER

The powdered leaves of the sassafras tree. Filé powder is used in Cajun cooking, including gumbo.

Chart of substitution ingredients

INGREDIENT	INGREDIENT AS USED	SUBSTITUTION
ALCOHOL	red wine, sake	• water • soup stock • non-alcoholic red wine
DAIRY	butter	• dairy-free margarine • olive oil
	cheese	• non-dairy cheese (such as soy, rice or hemp cheese; in terms of vegan Parmesan, I prefer the taste of rice Parmesan)
	cream	• soy milk
	milk	• non-dairy versions of milk (such as hemp milk, rice milk, soy milk, almond milk)
	yoghurt	• non-dairy versions of yoghurt (such as soy yoghurt)
EGGS	eggs	• commercial egg-replacement products
FOODS WITH GLUTEN	kamut flour, rye flour, spelt flour, wheat flour	• rice flour • legume flours (chickpea and soybean) • sorghum flour • potato flour
	any food based on wheat flour or that contains wheat flour (e.g., soy sauce)	• commercial gluten-free food products (e.g., gluten-free soy sauce)
	barley	• quinoa, teff, millet, brown rice, etc.
	wheat or egg noodles	• rice noodles
PEANUTS	peanuts	• almonds
MUSHROOMS	mushrooms	• other vegetables as desired and practical
FOODS WITH PURINES	asparagus, peanuts, spinach, mushrooms, dried legumes	• other vegetables or legumes as desired and practical
NIGHTSHADE VEGETABLES	eggplant, peppers, potatoes, tomatoes	• other vegetables as desired and practical
SODIUM	salt, stock cubes, soy sauce	• other seasonings as desired • commercial salt-free seasoning blends • low-sodium stock cubes • low-sodium soy sauce
SUGAR	brown cane sugar, dates, fruit juice, honey, maple syrup, raisins	• stevia

GINSENG

A revered herb in Chinese medicine. An adaptogenic herb, ginseng helps the body deal with stress, energizes and balances the body and improves immunity.

KASHA

Kasha is toasted buckwheat.

KEFALOTIRI CHEESE

A heady cheese from Greece. Very strong and salty, and yellow with tiny holes. Kefalotiri cheese can usually be found in Greek markets.

KING MUSHROOMS

A delicacy in China. This slightly phallic looking mushroom can usually be found in most Asian markets. If you can't find them, use any other kind of mushroom.

KUDZU ROOT

A root from Japan that is rich in minerals. A healthy thickener, kudzu is often used in sauces. It can usually be found in the macrobiotic or Asian section of stores.

KOMBU

A seaweed in the kelp family. Very rich in minerals and nutritious. Kombu helps the digestion of beans. It usually comes in a dried form and can be found in the macrobiotic or Asian section of stores.

LONG BEANS

A long green bean with an edible pod native to Southeast Asia. Also known as snake bean or Chinese long bean.

LOUISIANA HOT SAUCE

Louisiana hot sauce is a spicy hot sauce that is a bit smoky with sweet undertones. Use a regular hot sauce that is slightly sweet, spicy and slightly smoky if you cannot find it.

MANGO POWDER

Ground dried mango. It is often found in Indian stores.

MUNG BEAN THREADS

A thin gluten-free pasta made from mung beans can be found in Asian markets. If you can't find it, use another light pasta, such as brown-rice pasta, instead.

MUTSU APPLE

Also known as a Crispin apple. Medium to large in size, and crisp and juicy with a sweet-tart flavour. The Mutsu apple is popular in Japan.

PURPLE POTATO

The purple potato is common in South America and found in some larger markets. Purple potatoes are rich in the valuable antioxidant anthocyanin. Use regular potato if you cannot find purple potato.

SPICY RED PEPPER OIL

Oil that has soaked red pepper flakes and has then been strained. Often found in specialty stores. You can make your own—crush 3 tablespoons (45 mL) of red pepper flakes, soak in one cup of pure extra-virgin olive oil in a glass jar and shake every day, twice a day. After three days, strain, keeping the liquid.

SUMAC

Sumac is used all over the Middle East, from Arabic countries to Turkey to Iran, and especially in Lebanese cuisine. This healthy berry is sun dried and ground into coarse reddish powder. Sumac has a tangy, citrusy taste.

SWEET BROWN RICE

A sweeter rice than other rice. Sweet brown rice is a shorter grain than long-grain brown rice. If you can't find it, use regular long-grain brown rice.

TANDOORI BARBECUE MASALA SPICE

A barbecue-flavoured Indian spice blend. If you cannot find it, use regular masala and add some barbecue sauce to it.

TARO POTATO

A root vegetable common in Hawaii and other tropical places. Available in some specialty markets. Use regular potato if you cannot find it.

TREE EAR FUNGUS

A firm, oddly shaped mushroom used in Chinese cooking. Sold dried in Asian markets.

UMEBOSHI PLUM

A salted, pickled and aged plum from Japan. Found supermarkets or the macrobiotic section of some markets. It has a salty-sour taste and is great for aiding digestion.

WHITE LENTILS

A white lentil—which sometimes looks yellowish—found in Indian markets. Use other lentils if you can't find them.

YAMS/SWEET POTATOES

A root vegetable found in most larger markets. When it comes to sweet potatoes, the colour indicates an abundance of beta carotene. Most items labelled yams in North America are actually sweet potatoes (a much healthier cousin to yams). What's the difference? Traditional wild yams originate in South Africa and are hairy and large, and have white flesh. Wild yams aren't really sold in North America, so chances are what you are looking at in a store is actually a sweet potato (although you can probably find a variety of yam at Latin American markets). Sweet potatoes are brown or tan on the outside and yellow or orange on the inside.

North Africa and
the Middle East

Recipes

North Africa and the Middle East

THIS REGION OFFERS A WEALTH of choice for vegetarians. The Middle East offers falafel, lentil soup, tabbouleh, baba ganoush, hummus, pickled foods, pita bread, salads, rice with lentils, shepherd's salad and eggplant dishes. The food is well flavoured, often with cumin, cayenne, oregano, hot sauce, lemon, garlic, sea salt and olive oil. Tomatoes, parsley, bulgur and mint enliven the food in this region. Thick coffee is often consumed.

North Africa offers couscous, stews, spicy bean soup, chilled cucumber soup and grilled vegetables—not to mention salads and fruit. Morocco's cuisine is influenced by the Arabs, the French, the Africans and the Berbers. Mint tea is served after a meal, and after three cups, it is politely considered time to go.

From Ethiopia, we have the flat pancake-like bread called *injera,* and cabbage, collard greens, lentils, split peas, chickpeas, potatoes and carrot dishes with a spicy, buttery red chili pepper flavour. People sit down around a table with the stews, or *watts,* served on injera and eat them using the injera instead of cutlery. It is said that if you share a meal with someone in this way you will be friends for life. Rice, legumes, greens and other vegetables take centre stage in these cuisines. A truly sensuous fest. Drinks are often made with fresh fruit or nuts and are more popular than alcoholic drinks.

One of my favourite memories is of sitting on a restaurant boat on the Nile, watching the red sun set over the river I had dreamed of seeing since I was a child and eating fresh salads, lentil soup, okra in tomato sauce, eggplant in lemon, and well-spiced *foul,* a staple in Egypt.

Eggplant Spread/Salad

MAKES	TIME
4 servings	1 hour 30 minutes

Good as a salad or on bread or crackers for a light lunch or snack.

1 large eggplant
4 green onions, chopped
3 large garlic cloves, minced
3 Tbsp (45 mL) chopped fresh dill
2½ Tbsp (37 mL) rice vinegar
1 Tbsp (15 mL) flaxseed oil
1 tsp (5 mL) ground cumin
sea salt and pepper (for **HD** use sodium substitute)

Preheat the oven to 375°F (190°C).

Pierce the eggplant with a fork in a few places and bake on a cookie sheet for 1 hour. Peel while it's still hot and discard the skin. Allow to cool a bit. Blend the flesh of the eggplant in a blender. Mix in a bowl with the green onions, garlic, dill, rice vinegar, flaxseed oil, cumin, and sea salt and pepper to taste.

Baba Ganoush with Nut Butter

C **CA** **CD** **D** **G** **HD** **M** **MS** **OA**   **V** | MAKES
4 servings | TIME
1 hour 20 minutes

A twist on an old favourite. Serve as is, or on crackers or bread.

1 medium eggplant
2 garlic cloves, minced
2 Tbsp (30 mL) hazelnut butter
2 Tbsp (30 mL) first cold pressed extra virgin
   olive oil
2 Tbsp (30 mL) fresh lemon juice
1–2 sprigs fresh dill
sea salt and pepper (for **HD** use sodium substitute)

Preheat the oven to 375°F (190°C).

Pierce the eggplant with a fork in a few places and bake on a cookie sheet for about 45 minutes to an hour, until soft. Peel while it's still hot and discard the skin. Allow to cool a bit. Place the flesh of the eggplant in a food processor with the garlic, hazelnut butter, olive oil, lemon juice, dill, and sea salt and pepper to taste and blend until smooth.

Turkish Eggplant

C **CA** **CD** **D** **G** **HD** **M** **MS** **OA**   **V** | MAKES | TIME
4 servings | 1 hour 50 minutes

A delicious side dish from Turkey. Serve with some of the other side dishes in this section for a Middle Eastern feast.

> 1 medium eggplant, chopped into 1-inch (2.5 cm) pieces
>
> 3 Tbsp (45 mL) first cold pressed extra virgin olive oil
>
> 2 large white onions, roughly chopped
>
> 2 large tomatoes, chopped
>
> 1 medium-size green bell pepper, bite-size pieces
>
> 1 small carrot, sliced thinly
>
> sea salt and pepper (for **HD** use sodium substitute)

Add 1 tsp (5 mL) of sea salt to a large bowl of water (enough water to cover the eggplant) and soak the eggplant pieces for 1 hour. Drain and rinse.

In a frying pan over medium-low heat, heat the oil and sauté the onions, stirring, for about 20 minutes. Add the eggplant, tomatoes, bell pepper, carrot, and sea salt and pepper to taste and cook, stirring, for 20 to 25 minutes. Serve hot or cold.

Mashed Eggplant

| | MAKES
4 servings | TIME
1 hour 5 minutes |

This dish is a rich-tasting treat. And it's loaded with super-healthy garlic!

1 small eggplant

3 Tbsp (45 mL) dairy-free nonhydrogenated margarine

1 Tbsp (15 mL) whole wheat flour

12 very large garlic cloves, minced

sea salt and pepper (for **HD** use sodium substitute)

Preheat the oven to 375°F (190°C).

Pierce the eggplant a few times all over with a fork. Place it on a cookie sheet and bake for 50 minutes to 1 hour until soft. Peel while it's still hot and discard the skin. Mash the flesh in a bowl.

Place the margarine in a frying pan on low heat and cook the flour, stirring, for a couple of minutes. Add the garlic and cook, stirring, for a couple more minutes. Add the cooked eggplant and stir around for about 5 minutes to heat through before serving. Add sea salt and pepper to taste before serving.

Turkish Green Beans

 **C** **CA** **CD** **D** **G** **HD** **M** **MS** **OA**   **V**   MAKES
4 servings   TIME
45 minutes

This simple dish is served all over the coast of Turkey.

> 3 Tbsp (45 mL) first cold pressed extra virgin
>   olive oil
> 2 small white onions, thinly sliced
> 2 large tomatoes, diced
> 1 cup (250 mL) chopped green beans
>   (1-inch/2.5 cm pieces)
> ½ small green bell pepper, bite-size pieces
>   (optional)
> ½–1 fresh hot chili, minced, or more to taste
> sea salt and pepper (for **HD** use sodium substitute)

In a frying pan over medium-low heat, heat the oil and sauté the onions, stirring, for about 20 minutes. Add the tomatoes, green beans, bell pepper, chili, and sea salt and pepper to taste, and cook, stirring, for about 20 minutes.

Turkish White Beans

			MAKES	TIME
			4 servings	40 minutes

You'll have a complete protein if you serve this great side dish with a grain of some kind. We often just ordered numerous side dishes and shared them all when we were in Turkey. They were all so good and so healthy.

¼ cup (60 mL) first cold pressed extra virgin olive oil

3 small white onions, thinly sliced

1¼ cups (310 mL) canned navy beans, drained and rinsed

1 cup (250 mL) vegetable stock

1 carrot, thinly sliced (optional)

sea salt and pepper (for **HD** use sodium substitute)

dash or 2 of hot sauce (optional)

In a frying pan over medium-low heat, heat the oil and sauté the onions, stirring, for about 20 minutes. Add the beans, stock, carrot, sea salt and pepper, and hot sauce (if using) and cook, covered, stirring occasionally, for 10 to 15 minutes.

Sunflower Pâté

MAKES	**TIME**
4 servings	5 to 10 minutes

A great Middle Eastern spread for crackers or little breads.

2 medium garlic cloves, minced

¼ cup (60 mL) tahini

3 Tbsp (45 mL) water

2 Tbsp (30 mL) fresh lemon juice (optional)

2 tsp (10 mL) sesame oil

¾ cup (185 mL) sunflower seeds

Blend the garlic with the tahini, water, lemon juice (if using) and sesame oil in a blender. You may need to add more water if it looks too thick, but remember that it's a pâté, so it shouldn't be too runny. Use a spatula to get it all out. Transfer to a bowl, stir in the sunflower seeds and mix well.

Okra in Tomatoes

 | MAKES 4 servings | TIME 35 minutes

I had versions of this wonderful dish all over Egypt.

2½ cups (625 mL) canned puréed tomatoes,
   or 4–5 fresh tomatoes, skin on and puréed

2 cups (500 mL) sliced (in rounds) fresh okra

2 Tbsp (30 mL) first cold pressed extra virgin
   olive oil

chili powder

ground coriander

sea salt and pepper (for **HD** use sodium substitute)

Place everything in a pot, cover and cook on medium heat for about 30 minutes, stirring now and then.

THE ALL-NEW VEGETARIAN PASSPORT

Purifying Parsley Salad

MAKES	TIME
4 servings	20 minutes

Parsley is one of the most nutrient-rich edible plants we have. It's not just a garnish on your plate. It can cleanse and rid the body of toxins—and it tastes great in this garlicky salad.

> 2 large garlic cloves, minced
> 1 large bunch fresh parsley, well chopped
> 1 large tomato, diced (optional; omit for **RA**)
> ¼ medium-size Vidalia onion, diced
> 1 Tbsp (15 mL) first cold pressed extra virgin olive oil
> 1 Tbsp (15 mL) balsamic vinegar
> sea salt and pepper (for **HD** use sodium substitute)
> pinch of ground cumin (optional)

Mix everything together in a large salad bowl and let stand for about 15 minutes to marinate before serving.

Parsley Salad with Cucumber and Tomato

 | MAKES 4 servings | TIME 5 to 10 minutes

Parsley combines very well with garlic, green onions, cucumber, lemon juice and tomato.

1 medium bunch fresh parsley, finely chopped

4 green onions, finely chopped

3 medium garlic cloves, minced

1 large tomato, diced (optional; omit for **RA**)

½ small English cucumber, scrubbed and diced

1½ Tbsp (22 mL) fresh lemon juice

1½ Tbsp (22 mL) first cold pressed extra virgin olive oil or flaxseed oil

sea salt and pepper (for **HD** use sodium substitute)

chopped pickled artichokes (optional)

Mix everything together in a large salad bowl and serve.

Quinoa Tabbouleh Salad

		TIME
MAKES		
4 servings		1 hour

A great-tasting Middle Eastern salad that uses quinoa, so it is perfect for those who can't eat gluten. And it is a complete-protein salad.

1¾ cups (435 mL) uncooked quinoa

4 cups (1 L) cold water

3 green onions, finely chopped

3 medium garlic cloves, minced

1 large bunch fresh parsley

½ green bell pepper, diced (optional; omit for **RA**)

2–3 Tbsp (30–45 mL) fresh lemon juice

2 Tbsp (30 mL) first cold pressed extra virgin olive oil or flaxseed oil

1½ Tbsp (22 mL) balsamic vinegar

sea salt and pepper (for **HD** use sodium substitute)

Place the quinoa in a pot, add the water and bring to a boil. Reduce the heat to low and simmer, uncovered, for about 15 minutes. Strain and rinse under cool running water. Allow to cool. Transfer to a large salad bowl and add the remaining ingredients. Mix everything well and let stand for 20 minutes before serving.

Lentil Salad

	MAKES	TIME
	4 servings	about 1 hour 10 minutes

I first had this gorgeous salad on the banks of the Nile in a floating restaurant. The sun was setting, making the Nile look magical, and all my dreams of this romantic place, filled with history, was totally real. The juicy, vibrant tomatoes looked like the setting sun that streaked the water red.

½ cup (125 mL) dried green lentils, washed

1½ cups (375 mL) water

1 small white onion, diced

1 large clove garlic, minced

2 Tbsp (30 mL) fresh lemon juice

2 Tbsp (30 mL) first cold pressed extra virgin
   olive oil

sea salt and pepper (for **HD** use sodium substitute)

fresh parsley, chopped

2 large tomatoes, thinly sliced

Place the lentils in a pot with the water. Bring to a boil on high heat. Reduce the heat to medium-low, cover and cook, stirring occasionally, for about 1 hour, until tender. Drain the lentils and mix them with the onion, garlic, lemon juice, olive oil, and sea salt and pepper to taste. Mix in some parsley to taste. Place the tomatoes on a large white platter, and spoon some of the mixture overtop. Use more parsley to garnish.

Bean Salad with Cauliflower

MAKES	TIME
4 servings	5 to 10 minutes

A great Middle Eastern meal-in-a-bowl salad that uses a healthy cruciferous vegetable—cauliflower.

1 can (19 oz/540 mL) red kidney beans, drained and rinsed

1¾ cups (435 mL) finely chopped cauliflower

1 small white onion, diced

3 Tbsp (45 mL) first cold pressed extra virgin olive oil or flaxseed oil

2 Tbsp (30 mL) chopped fresh dill

2 Tbsp (30 mL) chopped fresh parsley

1 Tbsp (15 mL) balsamic vinegar

1 tsp (5 mL) prepared yellow mustard

sea salt and pepper (for **HD** use sodium substitute)

Place everything in a large salad bowl and toss to combine.

Shepherd's Salad

MAKES 4 servings   **TIME** 5 to 10 minutes

This great refreshing salad has a nice bite to it. It is served all over the coast of Turkey and was wonderfully welcome when we were there. It's incredibly healthy too, since it is loaded with cleansing vegetables and lemon, and lycopene from the tomatoes. Serve with some dill pickles or olives if you like.

2 large tomatoes, chopped into large dice

1 medium-size English cucumber, scrubbed and cut into large dice

¼ medium-size red or white onion, roughly chopped

1–2 fresh hot green chilies or jalapeño peppers, seeded and diced

1½ Tbsp (22 mL) first cold pressed extra virgin olive oil

juice of 1 lemon

handful of fresh parsley, finely chopped

chopped fresh mint (optional)

sea salt and pepper (for **HD** use sodium substitute)

Place everything in a large salad bowl and toss to combine. Serve immediately.

Chard and Pomegranate Salad

MAKES
4 servings

TIME
5 minutes

This one comes from the ancient land of Persia and features the pomegranate, a fruit rich in healthy nutrients.

4 cups (1 L) red and green chard, bite-size pieces

1 large red bell pepper, cut into thin strips
(optional; omit for **RA**)

¼ cup (60 mL) grated carrot

¼ cup (60 mL) fresh pomegranate seeds

2 Tbsp (30 mL) pomegranate juice

1 Tbsp (15 mL) first cold pressed extra virgin
olive oil

¼ tsp (1 mL) honey (optional; omit for **CA** **D** **V**)

sea salt and pepper (for **HD** use sodium substitute)

Place the three veggies in a large serving bowl in the order listed. Scatter the pomegranate seeds overtop. Mix together the pomegranate juice, olive oil, honey (if using), and sea salt and pepper to taste. Pour over the salad.

CHARD AND POMEGRANATE SALAD

Lentil and Date Soup

MAKES
4 servings

TIME
55 minutes

Lentil soup with a hint of fruit. How very Middle Eastern.

1 Tbsp (15 mL) butter or dairy-free
  nonhydrogenated margarine (for Ⓜ ⒸⒹ ⓂⓈ ⓇⒶ Ⓥ
  use margarine)
1 large cooking onion, roughly chopped
4 large garlic cloves, minced
6 cups (1.5 L) vegetable stock
1½ cups (375 mL) dried red lentils, washed
4 dried dates, pitted and chopped
½ tsp (2 mL) ground cumin
sea salt and pepper (for ⒽⒹ use sodium substitute)

In a soup pot over medium-low heat, melt the butter or margarine and sauté the onion, stirring, for about 20 minutes. Add the garlic, then the stock, lentils, dates, cumin, and sea salt and pepper to taste and bring to a boil over high heat. Cover, reduce the heat to low and cook, stirring occasionally, for about 30 minutes. You may need to add more water. This is also good puréed.

Red Lentil and Apricot Soup

C CA CD D HD M MS OA RA V

MAKES	TIME
4 servings	50 minutes

Fruit often shows up in Moroccan cooking, and here it is again. The cinnamon makes this soup taste wonderful, almost hinting at a dessert.

1 Tbsp (15 mL) first cold pressed extra virgin olive oil
1 large cooking onion, roughly chopped
3 large garlic cloves, minced
5 cups (1.25 L) vegetable stock
1 cup (250 mL) dried red lentils, washed
1 large carrot, cut into rounds
3–4 fresh apricots, peeled and diced
½ tsp (2 mL) ground cinnamon
sea salt and pepper (for HD use sodium substitute)
dried sumac

In a soup pot over medium heat, heat the oil and sauté the onion until soft, about 15 minutes. Add the garlic and sauté for 1 minute. Add the stock, lentils and carrot and bring to a boil, stirring. Reduce the heat to medium. Add the apricots and cook, covered, for about ½ hour, stirring occasionally. Add the cinnamon and sea salt and pepper to taste, then purée. Heat through and serve with a pinch of sumac.

Cumin and Garlic Red Lentil Soup

	MAKES	TIME
	4 servings	55 minutes

This Middle Eastern soup is easy, fast and delicious with a touch of heat.

1 Tbsp (15 mL) butter or first cold pressed extra
   virgin olive oil (for **CA** **CD** **D** **M** **MS** **RA** **V** use oil)

1 large cooking onion, diced

3 large garlic cloves, minced

½ cup (125 mL) yam, peeled and diced

6 cups (1.5 L) vegetarian chicken-flavour stock

1½ cups (375 mL) dried red lentils, washed

1½ tsp (7 mL) ground cumin

¼ tsp (1 mL) chili flakes

sea salt and pepper (for **HD** use sodium substitute)

In a soup pot over medium heat, heat the butter or oil and sauté the onion, stirring, for about 20 minutes. Add the garlic then the yam and cook, stirring, for 1 minute. Add the stock, lentils, cumin, chili flakes, and sea salt and pepper to taste and bring to a boil. Reduce the heat to medium-low and cook, covered, for about ½ hour, stirring. You may need to add more stock. Purée and heat through before serving.

Celery, Cumin and Onion Lentil Soup

	MAKES	TIME
	4 servings	1 hour

A soup that is served in different versions all over the Middle East. Serve this as part of a Middle Eastern meal with rice, pita bread, greens, salads and other favourites.

1½ cups (375 mL) dried brown lentils, washed

8 cups (2 L) onion-flavour stock

3 Tbsp (45 mL) first cold pressed extra virgin olive oil

2 large cooking onions, roughly chopped

4 sticks celery with leaves, chopped

1 tsp (5 mL) ground cumin

sea salt and pepper (for **HD** use sodium substitute)

In a soup pot over medium heat, place the lentils in the stock, cover and bring to a boil. Reduce the heat to medium-low and cook, covered, for 50 to 55 minutes, stirring now and then, until the lentils are soft. You may need to add more stock.

Meanwhile, in a frying pan over medium heat, heat the oil and sauté the onions, stirring, for about 25 minutes. Add the celery, cumin, and sea salt and pepper to taste and cook for about 10 minutes, stirring. Add to the cooked lentils, purée and heat through before serving.

White Lentil, Spinach and Walnut Soup

MAKES	TIME
4 servings	1 hour 30 minutes

A wonderful combination of flavours: basil, spinach, walnuts, garlic and lentils.

3 Tbsp (45 mL) first cold pressed extra virgin olive oil, divided

1 very large white onion, diced

3 large garlic cloves, minced

8 cups (2 L) vegetarian chicken-flavour stock

1½ cups (375 mL) dried white lentils, washed

sea salt and pepper (for **HD** use sodium substitute)

1 tsp (5 mL) dairy-free nonhydrogenated margarine

1 large tomato, diced (optional; omit for **RA**)

2 cups (500 mL) torn-up fresh spinach

large handful of fresh basil, torn up

¼ cup (60 mL) walnut pieces

In a large soup pot over medium-low heat, heat 1 Tbsp (15 mL) of the olive oil and sauté the onion, stirring, for about 10 minutes. Add the garlic and cook, stirring, for 2 minutes. Add the stock, lentils, and sea salt and pepper to taste and bring to a boil. Reduce the heat to medium-low and cook, covered, for about 40 minutes. Add the remaining 2 Tbsp (30 mL) olive oil, margarine and tomato and cook, covered, stirring now and then, for 30 minutes. Add the spinach, basil and walnut pieces and cook for 3 minutes. Purée and heat through before serving.

Hearty Lentil and Rice Soup

 **C** **CA** **CD** **D** **HD** **M** **MS** **OA** **RA** **V** | MAKES 4 servings | TIME 1 hour

A rich soup served all over Turkey. Serve with lemon wedges so you can squeeze them over the soup.

> 2 Tbsp (30 mL) brown rice
> ⅓ cup (80 mL) water
> 2 Tbsp (30 mL) dairy-free nonhydrogenated margarine
> 1 large white onion, diced
> 1 large clove garlic, minced
> 1 Tbsp (15 mL) whole wheat flour (optional; omit for **CD**)
> 6 cups (1.5 L) vegetable stock
> 1½ cups (375 mL) dried red lentils, washed
> sea salt and pepper (for **HD** use sodium substitute)

Place the rice in a small pot with the water. Bring to a boil over high heat. Reduce the heat to medium-low, cover and cook, stirring occasionally, for about 50 minutes, until the rice is tender. Drain.

Meanwhile, in a large soup pot over medium-low heat, heat the margarine and sauté the onion, stirring, for about 20 minutes. Add the garlic and stir for 1 minute. Add the whole wheat flour and cook, stirring, for a minute or two. Add the stock and lentils and bring to a boil. Cover, reduce the heat to low and simmer for about 30 minutes. You may need to add more stock. Purée and then add the rice. Warm through before serving.

Chickpea, Greens and Walnut Soup

MAKES	TIME
4 servings	40 minutes

This Middle Eastern soup flavoured with basil and garlic is really a meal-in-a-bowl.

2 Tbsp (30 mL) first cold pressed extra virgin olive oil

1 large white onion, diced

3 large garlic cloves, chopped

1 large red bell pepper, diced (optional; omit for **RA**)

10 cups (2.5 L) vegetable stock

1 can (19 oz/540 mL) chickpeas, drained and rinsed

5 cups (1.25 L) chopped greens (red and green chard and kale are ideal)

pepper

1 cup (250 mL) torn-up fresh basil

½ cup (125 mL) walnut pieces

1 cup (250 mL) grated Parmesan cheese (optional; omit for **CA CD D MS RA V**, reduce amount for **C HD M**)

In a large soup pot over medium heat, heat the oil and sauté the onion, stirring, for about 15 minutes. Add the garlic and bell pepper and sauté, stirring, for about 2 minutes. Add the stock and chickpeas and bring to a boil over high heat. Reduce the heat to medium and simmer, covered, stirring occasionally, for about 15 minutes. Add the greens and pepper to taste and cook for about 3 minutes. Add the basil and walnuts and cook for about 1 minute. Sprinkle the Parmesan overtop, if using, and serve.

Spicy Red Lentil and Kidney Bean Stew

	MAKES	TIME
	4 servings	1 hour

A rich, filling stew. Just add a salad and crusty whole-grain bread and you've got a complete meal.

2 Tbsp (30 mL) first cold pressed extra virgin olive oil

1 very large white onion, roughly chopped

3 large garlic cloves, roughly chopped

1 fresh hot green chili, diced (with seeds for more fire if you like)

10–12 cups (2.5–3 L) water or vegetable stock

1 can (19 oz/540 mL) red kidney beans, drained and rinsed

1½ cups (375 mL) dried red lentils, washed

1 can (28 oz/796 mL) diced tomatoes, with juice

1 tsp (5 mL) ground cumin

In a large soup pot over medium heat, heat the olive oil and sauté the onion, stirring, for about 20 minutes. Add the garlic and chili and stir for 1 minute. Add the stock, kidney beans and lentils, cover and bring to a boil. Reduce the heat to medium-low and cook for about 20 minutes, stirring now and then. Add the tomatoes with their juice and the ground cumin and cook, covered, for 10 to 15 minutes, stirring. The stew should be thick, so thin it down with extra water or stock only if absolutely necessary.

FALAFEL/TAMIYA

Falafel / Tamiya

MAKES	TIME
4 servings	about 25 minutes

The tasty Middle Eastern dish we know as falafel is called tamiya in Egypt. It is sold from small stands in every market. Serve with hot sauce, tahini, pickles, pickled artichoke hearts, pita bread, and diced tomatoes and cucumber. Other possible choices are shredded cabbage, pickled cabbage, lettuce, chopped parsley and chopped mint.

1 can (19 oz/540 mL) chickpeas, drained and rinsed

1 small white onion, diced

1 Tbsp (15 mL) first cold pressed extra virgin olive oil

1 Tbsp (15 mL) water

1 Tbsp (15 mL) fresh lemon juice

2 tsp (10 mL) ground cumin

¼ tsp (1 mL) chili powder

sea salt and pepper (for **HD** use sodium substitute)

first cold pressed extra virgin olive oil for frying

In a food processor, place the chickpeas, onion, olive oil, water, lemon juice, cumin, chili powder, and sea salt and pepper to taste and purée until smooth. Using your hands, form the mixture into patties. Fry over medium heat on both sides, in batches, in olive oil.

Foul

MAKES	TIME
4 servings	7 hours if the beans are cooked from scratch; 20 minutes if you use canned beans

This is a staple that you will see people eating all over Egypt, often from large communal bowls or shared dishes. It's rich in protein and delicious. This is my version using easy-to-find ingredients. Just add some rice on the side, or use bread and grab the foul and pinch it between your fingers the way the Egyptians do.

3 cups (750 mL) canned fava beans, drained and rinsed; or 2½ cups (625 mL) uncooked fava beans, washed

3 Tbsp (45 mL) butter or dairy-free nonhydrogenated margarine (for **C** **CA** **CD** **D** **HD** **M** **MS** **V** use margarine)

3 large red onions, bite-size pieces

6 large garlic cloves, minced

4 green onions, chopped

½ cup (125 mL) spaghetti sauce

2 Tbsp (30 mL) dried sumac

½ tsp (2 mL) chili powder

¼ tsp (1 mL) cayenne pepper

1 tsp (5 mL) ground cumin

sea salt (for **HD** use sodium substitute)

If you are using dried beans, place them in a pot with 8 to 10 cups (2–2.5 L) water. Bring to a boil on high heat, reduce the heat to medium-low, cover and cook, stirring occasionally, for 6 to 7 hours, until tender. You may need to add more water. After cooking, drain the beans if necessary.

In a large frying pan over medium heat, heat the butter and sauté the red onions and garlic, stirring often, for 5 minutes. Add the green onions, spaghetti sauce, sumac, chili powder, cayenne, cumin and sea salt to taste. Sauté for 5 more minutes, stirring. Add the cooked or canned beans and heat through for a few minutes, stirring, before serving.

Chickpeas with Tahini and Onions

C CA CD D HD M MS OA RA V | MAKES 4 servings | TIME 35 minutes

A quick and easy dish from Israel. Serve hot or cold, stuffed into pita pockets (or rice paper sheets for a gluten-free alternative).

1 Tbsp (15 mL) first cold pressed extra virgin olive oil

2 large white onions, roughly chopped

1 can (19 oz/540 mL) chickpeas, drained and rinsed

½ cup (125 mL) vegetable stock

2 Tbsp (30 mL) fresh lemon juice

pinch of cayenne pepper

1 cup (250 mL) tahini

In a frying pan over medium heat, heat the oil and sauté the onions, stirring, until tender. Add the chickpeas, stock, lemon juice and a pinch of cayenne pepper and simmer for 5 minutes, stirring. Add the tahini and heat through before serving.

Cinnamon and Lentil Orzo Casserole

  | MAKES 4 servings | TIME 2 hours 45 minutes

This Middle Eastern dish emits a wonderful aroma while it is cooking, making the whole house smell great. The orzo is more commonly associated with the Mediterranean, but is very good here. You can use another kind of small pasta if you prefer. Try to cook this in a clay dish if possible. It really does make a difference.

6–7 cups (1.5–1.75 L) water

1 cup (250 mL) dried red lentils, washed

¾ cup (185 mL) orzo

¼ cup (60 mL) first cold pressed extra virgin olive oil

10 baby carrots, cut into rounds

2 medium-size red potatoes, skin on, diced

1 large cooking onion, roughly chopped

2 tsp (10 mL) ground cinnamon

1 vegetable stock cube

handful of Thompson raisins

handful of whole cashews

sea salt and pepper (for **HD** use sodium substitute)

Preheat the oven to 375°F (190°C).

Place everything in a clay dish, or other ovenproof dish, that holds 12 cups (3 L). Cover and bake for 2 ½ hours or until everything is tender. You may need to add more water as it cooks.

Simple Lentils

MAKES	TIME
4 servings	1 hour 15 minutes

An easy, tasty Middle Eastern dish, with healthy lentils, garlic and cayenne, that will add protein to a meal and fill you up.

I always cook extra brown rice and keep the leftovers in the fridge. That makes dishes like this one fast and easy to make, especially if you use canned or leftover lentils too. Serve hot as is or wrap in whole-grain pita or flour tortillas for a quick sandwich.

¼ cup (60 mL) brown rice

1 cup (250 mL) dried green lentils, washed

1 Tbsp (15 mL) first cold pressed extra virgin olive oil

8 large garlic cloves, minced

1 large tomato, chopped (optional; omit for **RA**)

1 tsp (5 mL) ground cumin

¼ tsp (1 mL) cayenne pepper

Place the rice in a pot with ⅔ cup (160 mL) of water. Bring to a boil on high heat. Reduce the heat to medium-low, cover and cook, stirring occasionally, until tender, about 50 minutes. Drain.

Place the lentils in a pot with 3 cups (750 mL) of water. Bring to a boil on high heat. Reduce the heat to medium-low, cover and cook, stirring occasionally, until tender, about 1 hour. Test them after about 45 minutes. Drain.

In a large frying pan over medium-low heat, heat the oil and sauté the garlic, stirring, for about 2 minutes. Add the tomato and cook for about 5 minutes, stirring. Add the cooked lentils and rice, cumin and cayenne pepper, and heat through before serving.

Red Lentils Cooked in a Clay Casserole Dish

	MAKES	TIME
	4 servings	about 1 hour

An easy Middle Eastern dish that you just pop in the oven and let cook. The clay cooking dish marries the flavours really well, so do try to use one if possible. Serve with cooked greens and a salad.

2 cups (500 mL) dried red lentils, washed

¼ cup (60 mL) amaranth

2 cups (500 mL) water

1¼ cups (310 mL) tomato juice

1 red bell pepper, roughly chopped

½ cup (125 mL) raisins

2–3 Tbsp (30–45 mL) first cold pressed extra virgin olive oil

1 tsp (5 mL) ground cinnamon

½ tsp (2 mL) ground cumin

sea salt and pepper (for **HD** use sodium substitute)

Preheat the oven to 375°F (190°C).

Place everything in a large ovenproof clay casserole dish that holds at least 12 cups (3 L) and cover. Bake for about 1 hour until the lentils are tender and everything has cooked down nicely and blended well. Check the liquid level as it cooks. You may need to add more water.

Spicy Millet with Red Lentils and Black Beans

MAKES	TIME
4 servings	1 hour 15 minutes

A completely gluten-free spicy dish from North Africa that is incredibly filling. Just add a salad for a complete meal.

1 tsp (5 mL) first cold pressed extra virgin olive oil

1 large sweet white onion, roughly chopped

1 fresh hot green chili, diced, with seeds

10 cups (2.5 L) vegetable stock

1 can (19 oz/540 mL) black beans, drained and rinsed

1¼ cups (310 mL) dried red lentils, washed

½ cup (125 mL) millet

5 dried dates, pitted and chopped

1 tsp (5 mL) chili powder

¼–½ tsp (1–2 mL) cayenne pepper

In a very large frying pan or soup pot over medium-low heat, heat the olive oil and sauté the onion and chili, stirring, for about 10 minutes. Add the stock, beans, lentils, millet, dates, chili powder and cayenne pepper and bring to a boil on high heat. Reduce the heat to medium-low and cook, covered, stirring occasionally, for about 45 minutes. You may need to add water as it cooks.

MOROCCAN BLACK
BEAN CASSEROLE

Moroccan Black Bean Casserole

    | MAKES 4 servings | TIME about 3 hours 30 minutes

The olives add a nice touch to this dish, and they make it very Moroccan. The clay dish marries the flavours together very well, so do use one if possible.

1 can (19 oz/540 mL) black beans, drained and rinsed

1 cup (250 mL) dried red lentils, washed

¼ cup (60 mL) canned chickpeas, drained and rinsed

2 medium-size cooking onions, quartered and thinly sliced

1 can (28 oz/796 mL) diced tomatoes, with juice

1½ cups (375 mL) button mushrooms, sliced

1 cup (250 mL) pickled artichokes, quartered

⅓ cup (80 mL) first cold pressed extra virgin olive oil

12 kalamata olives, pitted and chopped

2 tsp (10 mL) dried oregano

1 tsp (5 mL) dried basil

sea salt and pepper (for **HD** use sodium substitute)

Preheat the oven to 400°F (200°C).

Place everything in a clay ovenproof dish that holds at least 12 cups (3 L). Add enough water to cover the ingredients by 2 to 3 inches (5–8 cm). You will need about 5 cups (1.25 L) of water for this. Cover and bake for about 3 hours and 15 minutes or until everything is tender.

White Beans with Bulgur and Cranberries

MAKES	TIME
4 servings	35 minutes

The white beans and bulgur in this Middle Eastern dish combine very well with the garlic, cranberries, kale, tomatoes and walnuts to form a truly memorable taste.

1½ cups (375 mL) bulgur

1 Tbsp (15 mL) dairy-free nonhydrogenated margarine

1 large cooking onion, roughly chopped

3 large garlic cloves, minced

1 cup (250 mL) water

⅓ cup (80 mL) dried cranberries

¼ tsp (1 mL) chili flakes

sea salt and pepper (for **HD** use sodium substitute)

4 large kale leaves, chopped into small pieces

1 can (19 oz/540 mL) white kidney beans, drained and rinsed

1 can (19 oz/540 mL) diced tomatoes, with juice

2 Tbsp (30 mL) balsamic vinegar

20 walnut halves, broken up into small pieces

Soak the bulgur in boiling water and let it sit, covered, for 15 minutes. Drain and reserve.

In a frying pan over medium heat, heat the margarine and sauté the onion, stirring, for about 15 minutes. Add the garlic and cook, stirring, for 2 to 3 minutes. Add the water, cranberries, chili flakes, and sea salt and pepper to taste, and cook, stirring, for 3 minutes. Add the kale, beans and reserved bulgur and cook, stirring, for 3 minutes. Add the tomatoes with their juice and balsamic vinegar and cook, stirring, for 5 minutes. Add the walnuts and heat through before serving.

Middle Eastern Clay Pot Stew

MAKES 4 servings	**TIME** 3 hours 30 minutes to 4 hours	

A filling, healthy and delicious Middle Eastern meal. Great for entertaining: just bring the pretty clay pot right to the table. Add a green salad. Very few legumes are used in this one, so it is fine for people with gout.

8–10 cups (2–2.5 L) water

1 jar (19 oz/540 mL) spaghetti sauce

1 cup (250 mL) brown rice

¼ cup (60 mL) wild rice

3 medium-size cooking onions, diced

1 small red potato, skin on, diced

½ medium-size celeriac, peeled and diced

½ small yam, skin on, diced

3 Tbsp (45 mL) first cold pressed extra virgin olive oil

2–3 tsp (10–15 mL) ground cinnamon

¼ cup (60 mL) dried black beans, washed (for Ⓖ, use a small handful)

¼ cup (60 mL) dried red lentils, washed (for Ⓖ, use a small handful)

sea salt and pepper (for **HD** use sodium substitute)

Preheat the oven to 375°F (190°C).

Place all the ingredients in a large ovenproof clay pot that holds at least 12 cups (3 L). Cover and bake for 3½ to 4 hours or until everything is tender. You may need to add more water as it cooks.

Barbecued Cinnamon Potatoes

C CA CD D G HD M MS OA **V** | MAKES **4 servings** | TIME about 15 minutes

A sweet-tasting potato dish from Morocco, flavoured with fruit and cinnamon (of course).

3 medium-size red potatoes, skin on, thinly sliced

3 medium-size fresh apricots, peeled and diced

1 tsp (5 mL) ground cinnamon

sea salt (for **HD** use sodium substitute)

Preheat the barbecue grill to medium.

Place the potatoes and apricots on a piece of aluminum foil. Sprinkle with the cinnamon and sea salt to taste. Wrap tightly in the foil. Cook for 10 to 15 minutes. This is done when a fork can easily pierce the potatoes.

The Mediterranean

Recipes

BARBECUE

The Mediterranean

THIS IS ONE OF MY favourite regions in the world to travel in: it's beautiful, the people are friendly and the food not only tastes great but is also healthy. So much research has shown the Mediterranean diet to be one of the healthiest in the world—and that it can help make you happier. The reasons are really fairly simple. The Mediterranean diet is loaded with healthy oils from nuts and olive oil, antioxidant-rich fruits and vegetables, and high-fibre legumes and whole grains, while being low in meat and dairy.

Tomatoes, peppers, garlic, onions, artichokes, eggplant, zucchini and greens are just some of the goodies that figure prominently in this diet. They are always used fresh and bursting with flavour and colour, and are, of course, loaded with antioxidants like vitamin C, flavonoids and carotenes and with heart-friendly nutrients like folic acid. Pasta and grains like rice are a large part of the diet, and so are lentils and other legumes. The garlic and onions that turn up in so many dishes are not only delicious, making even the simplest dish extraordinary—they are also immunity-boosting superstars. And, of course, antioxidant- and nutrient-rich fruit like olives, lemons, dates, pomegranates, figs and oranges are a large part of the Mediterranean diet.

So often when I was in the Mediterranean, both in the homes I was invited to and in the restaurants, the herbs in the dishes came straight from the garden and bursting with antioxidants. So it is not surprising that the Mediterranean diet has been found to be good for memory, especially as it provides essential fatty acids.

But perhaps the thing I like most in this part of the world is the way the meal is eaten: it is a lengthy affair, with everyone sitting down to enjoy the food, the scents, the sounds and each other's company. It is visually appealing and the smells are invariably incredible. Think of the fresh garlic, olive oil, pine nuts, basil and Parmesan cheese in pesto, the smell of which most of us are familiar with. Pesto is simple and brilliant, ingredients perfectly combined to create something absolutely mouth-watering that can be used in so many ways. Or think of Greek food, with its simple blend of olive oil, lemon and oregano—and sometimes mint and cinnamon (its Eastern influences)—in so many dishes; the tastes linger on the tongue and keep you wanting more. Hotter spices can figure in the diet in some areas of the Mediterranean, especially farther south in some countries like Italy.

Many years ago I met an 85-year-old woman named Mona in Cephalonia, Greece. She was climbing a tree to cut down wood to build a fence and picking up hot coals with her bare hands and throwing them into the fire that she was cooking vegetables on. And she was doing all of this before she climbed up a pretty big mountain, which I, at 22, was having trouble with. So she must have been doing something right. She was energetic, and full of life and love for her family and her land. She cooked field greens for me, which all the elders ate. Field greens are loaded with folic acid and bone-building and disease-fighting nutrients. They taste bitter, but they stimulate and aid digestion.

In Italy, they eat many courses but often only a little bit of each. Of course you do not have to follow this custom: you can eat as many or as few dishes from this chapter at a time as you like. But be sure to only use the freshest ingredients if you truly want to taste the best the Mediterranean has to offer.

Dilled Hummus

MAKES	TIME
4 servings	5 minutes

The dill provides a sweet twist for an old favourite.

> 1 can (19 oz/540 mL) chickpeas or white beans,
>   drained and rinsed
> 2–3 Tbsp (30–45 mL) fresh lemon juice
> 1 Tbsp (15 mL) tahini
> 1 small bunch fresh dill
> ¼ cup (60 mL) warm water

Place the chickpeas in a food processor with the lemon juice, tahini and dill. Adding the water a little at a time, blend until smooth.

Garlicky Chickpea Spread

MAKES
4 servings

TIME
5 to 10 minutes

A delicious Italian spread that is great with crackers, bread and toast. It is also good as a dip for vegetables.

1 can (19 oz/540 mL) chickpeas, drained and rinsed

1½ cups (375 mL) walnut halves

5–6 medium-large garlic cloves, peeled

12 fresh basil leaves

1 Tbsp (15 mL) first cold pressed extra virgin
   olive oil

pepper

1–2 Tbsp (15–30 mL) flaxseed oil

Place the chickpeas in a food processor with the walnuts, garlic, basil, olive oil and pepper to taste. Adding the flaxseed oil a little at a time until you have the desired consistency, blend until smooth.

Mediterranean Tofu Spread

MAKES	TIME
4 servings	5 minutes

This is very good served with crackers, on little breads or as a sandwich filling. Try it with pasta. Or place some of it between thin slices of raw turnip and cover with a cold fresh tomato-basil sauce.

1 package (12 oz/350 g) extra-firm tofu

14 kalamata olives, pitted

6 sun-dried tomatoes, chopped

2 Tbsp (30 mL) first cold pressed extra virgin
   olive oil

1 bunch fresh basil

Blend everything well in a food processor.

MEDITERRANEAN
TOFU SPREAD

Garlicky Eggplant

C **CA** **CD** **D** **G** **HD** **M** **MS** **OA**   **V** | MAKES | TIME
4 servings | 1 hour 15 minutes

This spread is very good on black bread or crackers or as a dip for vegetables.

> 1 medium-size eggplant
> 4 large garlic cloves, minced
> ¼ cup (60 mL) fresh lemon juice
> 3 Tbsp (45 mL) spicy red pepper oil, or use olive oil and add chili flakes to taste
> 1 tsp (5 mL) mixed dried oregano and basil
> sea salt and pepper (for **HD** use sodium substitute)

Preheat the oven to 375°F (190°C).

Pierce the eggplant with a fork and bake on a cookie sheet for about 1 hour. Allow to cool, and remove the skin and place the flesh of the eggplant in a food processor. Add the remaining ingredients and blend until smooth.

Tomato and Cauliflower

	MAKES	TIME
	4 servings	20 minutes

A side dish you will find all over Greece. It tastes great and features the healthy cruciferous cauliflower.

> 2 cups (500 mL) cauliflower florets
>
> 4 large tomatoes, diced, with seeds
>
> 2 Tbsp + 1 tsp (30 mL + 5 mL) first cold pressed
>   extra virgin olive oil, divided
>
> 2 Tbsp (30 mL) fresh lemon juice
>
> sea salt and pepper (for **HD** use sodium substitute)
>
> a few fresh basil leaves, chopped (optional)

Steam the cauliflower in a steamer basket for about 4 minutes.

Cook the tomatoes and 1 tsp (5 mL) of the olive oil in a pot on medium heat, stirring frequently, for about 15 minutes. Mix in the lemon juice, sea salt and pepper to taste, basil leaves (if using) and then the cauliflower. Serve hot or let cool and serve cold.

ARUGULA
AND ARTICHOKE
SALAD

Arugula and Artichoke Salad

	MAKES	TIME
	4 servings	5 to 10 minutes

The bite of the arugula makes a wonderfully exciting salad. The artichokes and red beans add extra colour and flavour.

SALAD

2 large bunches arugula, bite-size pieces

2 large tomatoes, thinly sliced

3 balls bocconcini cheese, sliced (optional; omit for **C** **CA** **CD** **D** **HD** **M** **MS** **V**)

1¼ cups (310 mL) pickled artichokes, quartered

½ cup (125 mL) canned red beans or red kidney beans, drained and rinsed

4 green onions for garnish (optional)

DRESSING

2 Tbsp (30 mL) first cold pressed extra virgin olive oil or flaxseed oil

2 Tbsp (30 mL) balsamic vinegar

sea salt and pepper (for **HD** use sodium substitute)

For the salad, layer the first five ingredients in the order listed on four separate plates. Garnish with 2- to 3-inch (5–8 cm) thinly sliced lengths of the white part of the green onion.

Combine the oil and vinegar with sea salt and pepper to taste and pour over the salad before serving.

Spinach and Pear Salad

    OA

MAKES	TIME
4 servings	5 minutes

A brightly coloured salad that is delicious and full of antioxidants from the spinach and the red pepper. I first had this one on a cliff overlooking a valley in Italy. The view was superb and so was the salad.

4 cups (1 L) fresh spinach, bite-size pieces

1 medium-size red bell pepper, cut into thin strips

1 large pear, skin on, cored, seeds discarded,
   cut into thin strips

2 small balls bocconcini cheese, thinly sliced

2 Tbsp (30 mL) pine nuts

2 Tbsp (30 mL) first cold pressed extra virgin
   olive oil

1½ Tbsp (22 mL) balsamic vinegar

sea salt and pepper (for **HD** use sodium substitute)

Place everything in a large salad bowl, toss well and serve.

White Bean and Spinach Salad

C **CA** **CD** **D**   **HD** **M** **MS** **OA**   **V** | MAKES
4 servings | TIME
5 minutes

Another delicious meal-in-a-bowl salad, rich in healthy lycopene, lutein and other antioxidants.

1 can (19 oz/540 mL) white kidney beans, drained
  and rinsed

2 large tomatoes, diced

1½ cups (375 mL) torn-up fresh spinach leaves

1–2 balls bocconcini cheese, sliced (optional; omit
  for **CA** **CD** **D** **MS** **V**)

1 small bunch fresh basil, torn up

2 Tbsp (30 mL) first cold pressed extra virgin
  olive oil

2 Tbsp (30 mL) balsamic vinegar

2 tsp (10 mL) pine nuts (optional)

sea salt and pepper (for **HD** use sodium substitute)

Mix everything together on a large platter and serve.

Kidney Bean Salad

MAKES	TIME
4 servings	5 to 10 minutes

A filling salad full of carotenes. The beans make it almost a full meal. I first had this while overlooking the gorgeous Mediterranean sea.

3 cups (750 mL) torn romaine lettuce leaves

1 can (19 oz/540 mL) red kidney beans, drained and rinsed

2 inches (5 cm) English cucumber, diced

2 large handfuls of chives, finely chopped

1 large tomato, diced (optional; omit for **RA**)

1 stick celery, diced (optional)

1 carrot, diced (optional)

3 Tbsp (45 mL) first cold pressed extra virgin olive oil or flaxseed oil

1 Tbsp (15 mL) apple cider vinegar

1 tsp (5 mL) prepared yellow mustard (optional)

sea salt and pepper (for **HD** use sodium substitute)

Place everything in a large salad bowl, mix well and serve.

Mixed Bean Salad with Arugula

C **CA** **CD** **D** **HD** **M** **MS** **OA** **RA** **V**

MAKES	TIME
4 servings	20 minutes

A very filling high-fibre salad, and a great one for picnics. I first had a version of this in Italy, on one of the Aeolian Islands, sitting right next to a live volcano.

1 can (19 oz/540 mL) mixed beans, drained
and rinsed

2 large tomatoes, diced (optional; omit for **RA**)

1 medium-size green bell pepper, bite-size pieces
(optional; omit for **RA**)

1 small bunch arugula, bite-size pieces

2 Tbsp (30 mL) balsamic vinegar

2 Tbsp (30 mL) first cold pressed extra virgin
olive oil

sea salt and pepper (for **HD** use sodium substitute)

Place everything in a large salad bowl and mix well. Let stand for at least 15 minutes before serving.

Baby Lima Bean Salad

| | | MAKES
4 servings | TIME
5 minutes |

A great way of getting in those healthy lima beans.

1 cup (250 mL) canned lima beans, drained
and rinsed

2 green onions, chopped

2 ½ tsp (12 mL) first cold pressed extra virgin
olive oil

1 tsp (5 mL) balsamic vinegar

handful of fresh dill, finely chopped

sea salt and pepper (for **HD** use sodium substitute)

Place everything in a large salad bowl and mix well. Serve at room
temperature.

Tomato, Cucumber and Bocconcini Salad

C   **HD**   **OA**   MAKES **4 servings** | TIME **5 minutes**

I first had this Italian salad on a summer solstice. Very juicy, cooling and welcome on the longest day of the year.

1 very large tomato, perfectly ripe, sliced

⅓ English cucumber, sliced

2 balls bocconcini cheese, sliced

3 Tbsp (45 mL) first cold pressed extra virgin olive oil

2 Tbsp (30 mL) balsamic vinegar

sea salt and pepper (for **HD** use sodium substitute)

Arrange slices of tomatoes and cucumber, overlapping, on a platter, and top with slices of cheese. Mix together the olive oil, balsamic vinegar, and sea salt and pepper to taste and pour over the salad.

Cucumber and Scallion Salad

 **C CA CD D G HD M MS OA RA V** | MAKES **4 servings** | TIME **5 minutes**

A very simple light salad from Italy.

1 medium-size English cucumber, thinly sliced

6 green onions, chopped

2 Tbsp (30 mL) first cold pressed extra virgin
  olive oil

juice of 1 lemon

1½ Tbsp (22 mL) finely torn fresh basil

Place the cucumber and green onions in a bowl. Mix together the olive oil, lemon juice and basil and pour over the vegetables. Mix well before serving.

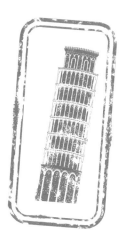

Black Bean Soup

 MAKES 4 servings | TIME about 4 hours 30 minutes

Filling and hearty with a great lemon and oregano flavour.

¼ cup (60 mL) first cold pressed extra virgin olive oil

1 large cooking onion, chopped

5 large garlic cloves, minced

12 cups (3 L) water

2 cups (500 mL) dried black beans, washed

10 baby carrots, diced

2 large sticks celery, diced

4–6 Tbsp (60–90 mL) fresh lemon juice

2 vegetable stock cubes

1½ tsp (7 mL) dried oregano

sea salt and pepper (for HD use sodium substitute)

In a large soup pot over medium heat, heat the olive oil and sauté the onion, stirring, for 20 minutes. Add the garlic and sauté for 2 minutes. Add the water, beans, carrots and celery. Cover, bring to a boil, stirring, and then reduce the heat to medium-low. Cook, covered, stirring occasionally, for about 4½ hours, or until the beans are soft, adding more water if necessary as the soup cooks. Add the lemon juice, stock cubes, oregano, and sea salt and pepper to taste and heat through for a few minutes. Purée three-quarters of the soup, then return to the pot and mix well to combine.

Black Bean and Chard Soup

MAKES	TIME
4 servings	about 3 hours 30 minutes

A great oregano-flavoured black bean soup that uses the green super-veggie chard.

2 Tbsp (30 mL) first cold pressed extra virgin
   olive oil

2 large white onions, chopped

3 large garlic cloves, minced

12 cups (3 L) vegetable stock

1½ cups (375 mL) dried black beans, washed

10 large chard leaves, cut up (red or green or a mix)

2 tsp (10 mL) dried oregano

1 cup (250 mL) diced feta cheese (optional; omit
   or use vegan feta for **CA CD D MS RA V**, reduce
   amount for **C HD M**)

In a large soup pot over medium heat, heat the oil and sauté the onions, stirring, for 10 minutes. Add the garlic and stir for 1 minute. Add the stock and beans, cover and bring to a boil. Reduce the heat to medium-low and cook, stirring from time to time, for about 3 hours, or until the black beans are soft. Add more stock if necessary as the soup cooks. Add the chard and oregano and cook for another 7 minutes. Add the cheese (if using) before serving.

Tomato and White Bean Soup

MAKES
4 servings

TIME
about 4 hours 15 minutes

A dill-scented soup with a hint of tomato served in various forms all over Greece. Dill grows wild in Greece, alongside the chamomile, and it all smells wonderful. Thick and filling, this is a whole meal when you add salad, bread and olives.

¼ cup (60 mL) first cold pressed extra virgin olive oil

2 large cooking onions, diced

20 baby carrots, diced

4 large sticks celery, diced

12 cups (3 L) water

1¾ cups (435 mL) dried large white beans, washed

¼ cup (60 mL) chopped fresh dill, or 2 tsp (10 mL) dried dill

2 Tbsp (30 mL) tomato paste (optional; omit for **RA**)

1 Tbsp (15 mL) balsamic vinegar

sea salt and pepper (for **HD** use sodium substitute)

In a large soup pot over medium heat, heat the olive oil and sauté the onions, stirring, for about 15 minutes. Add the carrots and celery and sauté for 1 minute. Add the water and beans and bring to a boil. Reduce the heat to medium-low, cover and cook for about 4 hours, stirring occasionally and adding more water if necessary. The beans should be soft. Toward the last 7 minutes of cooking time, add the dill, tomato paste, vinegar, and sea salt and pepper to taste. Serve hot.

NAVY BEAN AND ORZO SOUP

Navy Bean and Orzo Soup

MAKES	TIME
4 servings	about 4 hours

A fragrant, filling soup. The orzo are nice and slippery on your tongue, kind of like the soups you had as a kid—only healthier, thanks to the greens and antioxidant-rich tomatoes, peppers, garlic and basil.

10 cups (2.5 L) water

1¼ cups (310 mL) dried navy beans

2 cups (500 mL) orzo

4 large garlic cloves, minced

2 dried red chilies, crushed

2 onion-flavoured stock cubes

2 Tbsp (30 mL) first cold pressed extra virgin olive oil

sea salt and pepper (for **HD** use sodium substitute)

1 can (28 oz/796 mL) tinned crushed tomatoes

4 large handfuls of chopped fresh spinach or other green leafy vegetable

a few fresh basil leaves, torn up

Parmesan cheese, grated (optional; omit or use vegan Parmesan for **MS** **V**)

In a large soup pot, place the water and beans, cover and bring to a boil. Reduce the heat to medium-low and cook, covered, stirring occasionally, for about 2 ½ hours. Add the orzo and cook, covered, for another 1 hour or so until everything is tender. Add the garlic, dried chili, stock cubes, olive oil, and sea salt and pepper to taste and cook for a few minutes. Add the crushed tomatoes and cook for 15 minutes. Add the greens and basil and cook for a few more minutes. Sprinkle a little cheese on top of each bowl of soup before serving.

Greek Orzo and Bean Soup

	MAKES	TIME
	4 servings	about 3 hours 30 minutes

A filling, delicious soup that features white beans, oregano and orzo. A complete meal if you add a salad. Greek white beans are also called "gigantes."

2 cups (500 mL) dried large Greek white beans or large lima beans, washed

1 tsp (5 mL) dried oregano

1 vegetable stock cube

sea salt and pepper (for **HD** use sodium substitute)

2–3 Tbsp (30–45 mL) first cold pressed extra virgin olive oil

2 large cooking onions, diced

1 can (28 oz/796 mL) tomatoes, well-chopped, with juice

1 large stick celery, diced

½ cup (125 mL) orzo

In a large soup pot, cover the beans with 12 cups (3 L) water. Bring to a boil, then reduce the heat to medium-low and simmer, covered, for about 3 hours, or until tender, stirring occasionally and adding more water if necessary. Add the oregano, stock cube, and sea salt and pepper to taste near the end of cooking time.

Meanwhile, in a frying pan over medium heat, heat the olive oil and sauté the onions, stirring, for 25 minutes. Add the tomatoes with their juice and the celery and cook for 5 minutes. Set aside.

Cook the orzo according to the package instructions. Drain. Add the orzo and the onion-tomato mix to the cooked beans. Cook for another 20 minutes.

Navy Bean and Vegetable Soup

	MAKES	TIME
	4 servings	**about 4 hours**

A filling, flavourful soup.

¼ cup (60 mL) first cold pressed extra virgin olive oil

1 large cooking onion, chopped

6 baby carrots, sliced

4 sticks celery, chopped

1 medium-size yam, peeled and diced

10–12 cups (2.5–3 L) water

1½ cups (375 mL) dried navy beans, washed

10 cherry tomatoes, quartered

3 Tbsp (45 mL) chopped fresh dill

2 Tbsp (30 mL) salsa

2 Tbsp (30 mL) balsamic vinegar

4 tsp (20 mL) dried oregano

1 vegetable stock cube

pepper

In a large soup pot over medium heat, heat the oil and sauté the onion, stirring, for 20 minutes. Add the carrots, celery and yam and sauté for 3 minutes, stirring. Add the water and beans, cover and bring to a boil. Reduce the heat to low and cook for 2½ to 3 hours, stirring once in a while and adding more water if necessary. The beans should be tender. Add the tomatoes, dill, salsa, balsamic vinegar, oregano, stock cube and pepper to taste and cook, stirring now and then, for another ½ hour.

Fresh Romano Bean Soup

| | | MAKES
4 servings | TIME
about 2 hours |

One of my favourite soups—as long as Ted shells the beans. It's best at the height of summer, or early fall, when basil is at its freshest.

2 Tbsp (30 mL) first cold pressed extra virgin
olive oil

1 large white onion, chopped

3 large garlic cloves, chopped

1¾ cups (435 mL) shelled fresh romano beans

10 cups (2.5 L) water

1 vegetable stock cube

1 large red bell pepper, bite-size pieces

10 fresh basil leaves, torn up

pepper

Parmesan cheese, grated (optional; omit or use
vegan Parmesan for **CA** **CD** **D** **G** **MS** **V**)

In a large soup pot over medium heat, heat the oil and sauté the onion, stirring, for about 5 minutes. Add the garlic and sauté, stirring, for 1 minute. Add the beans and stir for 1 minute. Add the water and bring to a boil. Reduce the heat to medium-low and cover. Cook, stirring occasionally, for about 1½ hours or until the beans are soft. Add the stock cube and bell pepper and cook for about 20 minutes. Add the fresh basil and cook for 1 minute. Add pepper to taste, and serve with Parmesan sprinkled overtop, if desired.

Lentils and Greens Soup

MAKES	TIME
4 servings	about 1 hour 30 minutes

A great way of getting in healthy greens and a sea vegetable—and it tastes great. Sea veggies are a great source of vitamins and minerals, and they are good for your thyroid.

3 Tbsp (45 mL) first cold pressed extra virgin olive oil

1 very large white onion, chopped

6 large garlic cloves, chopped

2 large sticks celery, diced

1½ cups (375 mL) dried brown or green lentils, washed

12 cups (3 L) water

two 1-inch (2.5 cm) pieces dried kombu

2 large tomatoes, diced (optional; omit for **RA**)

2 tsp (10 mL) dried oregano

4 cups (1 L) mixed fresh greens (red and green chard, kale, bok choy), bite-size pieces

small handful of finely chopped fresh dill

3 Tbsp (45 mL) soy sauce

1 Tbsp (15 mL) balsamic vinegar

sea salt and pepper (for **HD** use sodium substitute)

In a large soup pot over medium heat, heat the oil and sauté the onion for 10 minutes. Add the garlic and celery and sauté for 1 minute. Add the lentils and stir for 1 minute. Add the water and bring to a boil. Add the kombu, cover and reduce the heat to medium-low to simmer for about 50 minutes, stirring occasionally. You may need to add more water.

Add the tomatoes and oregano and cook, covered, for about 20 minutes. Add the greens, dill, soy sauce, balsamic vinegar, and sea salt and pepper to taste and cook for about 4 minutes before serving.

Lentil and Yam Soup

	MAKES	TIME
	4 servings	1 hour 25 minutes

Versions of lentil soup are served all over Greece with a pretty strange-sounding name to our ear—kind of a swear-word sound. I'll say no more. This version is delicious, well flavoured with garlic. And it is good for your heart and immune system.

¼ cup (60 mL) first cold pressed extra virgin olive oil

2 large cooking onions, chopped

8 large garlic cloves, minced

1 medium-size yam, skin on, diced

8 cups (2 L) vegetable stock or water

2 cups (500 mL) dried green lentils, washed

½–1 tsp (2–5 mL) dried thyme

½–1 tsp (2–5 mL) dried savory

½–1 tsp (2–5 mL) dried sage

1 tsp (5 mL) apple cider vinegar

sea salt and pepper (for **HD** use sodium substitute)

In a large soup pot over medium heat, heat the oil and sauté the onions, stirring, for about 10 minutes. Add the garlic and yam and sauté, stirring, for about 3 minutes. Add the stock, lentils, thyme, savory and sage and bring to a boil. Reduce the heat to medium-low and cook, covered, for about 1 hour, stirring from time to time. Add the vinegar and sea salt and pepper to taste and cook for another 10 minutes.

Dill and Yam White Bean Soup

MAKES
4 servings

TIME
about 5 hours 20 minutes

A sweet-tasting, filling puréed soup. In Greece, dill grows wild on the islands, making the air smell sweet and fragrant. Dill is a great carminative herb, which makes it great for digestion.

2 Tbsp (30 mL) first cold pressed extra virgin olive oil

1 large sweet white onion, chopped

1 large clove garlic, minced

1 large yam, peeled and diced

1½ cups (375 mL) dried large Greek white beans (gigantes), washed

1 bay leaf

12 cups (3 L) vegetable stock

1 large bunch fresh dill, chopped

sea salt and pepper (for **HD** use sodium substitute)

In a large soup pot over medium heat, heat the olive oil and sauté the onion for 10 minutes. Add the garlic and the yam and sauté for 2 minutes. Add the beans and bay leaf and sauté, stirring, for 1 minute. Add the stock and bring to a boil. Reduce the heat to medium and simmer, covered, for 4 to 5 hours, stirring from time to time, and adding more stock as necessary, until the beans are soft. Add the dill and sea salt and pepper to taste and cook for 5 minutes. Remove the bay leaf, and purée and warm through before serving.

White Bean and Rice Soup

MAKES	TIME
4 servings	about 4 hours

A garlicky, dill-infused soup that has a strong flavour of celeriac and is made extra hearty by the rice. Just add a salad for a complete meal.

½ cup (125 mL) brown rice

1 Tbsp (15 mL) first cold pressed extra virgin olive oil

2 large cooking onions, chopped

4 large garlic cloves, minced

1 small-medium celeriac, peeled and chopped

1 white potato, peeled and diced

12 cups (3 L) vegetable stock

2 cups (500 mL) dried large Greek white beans (gigantes), washed

1 large bunch fresh dill

sea salt and pepper (for **HD** use sodium substitute)

lemon wedges (optional)

In a pot place the rice in 1 ¾ cups (435 mL) of water and bring to a boil over high heat. Reduce the heat to medium-low and simmer, covered, for about 50 minutes, stirring now and then.

Meanwhile, in a soup pot over medium heat, heat the oil and sauté the onions, stirring, for 20 minutes. Add the garlic, celeriac and potato and cook for 2 minutes, stirring. Add the stock and beans and bring to a boil. Cover, reduce the heat to medium-low and cook, stirring occasionally, for 3 to 3 ½ hours or until the beans are tender. You may need to add more stock. Add the dill and sea salt and pepper to taste and cook for more 5 minutes. Purée. Add the cooked rice and warm through before serving with lemon wedges if desired.

Dill and Potato Soup

C **CA** **CD** **D** **G** **HD** **M** **MS** **OA**   **V** | MAKES
4 servings | TIME
50 minutes

Makes great use of simple, readily available ingredients.

2 Tbsp (30 mL) first cold pressed extra virgin
   olive oil

1 very large white onion, chopped

5–6 larger-size new potatoes, peeled and diced

8–10 cups (2–2.5 L) vegetable stock

¾ cup (185 mL) finely chopped fresh dill

sea salt and pepper (for **HD** use sodium substitute)

In a large soup pot over medium heat, heat the oil and sauté the onion, stirring, for 5 minutes. Add the potatoes, stir for 1 minute, and then add the stock and bring to a boil, stirring. Reduce the heat to medium-low, cover and cook, stirring occasionally, for about 40 minutes. Add the dill, heat through and purée. Season to taste with sea salt and pepper. Heat through before serving.

Hearty Minestrone Soup

MAKES	TIME
4 servings	about 1 hour

A vegetarian version of the classic served all over Italy. This meal-in-a-bowl soup with tomato and basil smells like Italy.

2 Tbsp (30 mL) first cold pressed extra virgin olive oil

1 large cooking onion, chopped

2 large garlic cloves, minced

4 cups (1 L) water

1¾ cups (435 mL) canned mixed beans, drained and rinsed

1 cup (250 mL) diced fresh tomatoes

¼ cup (60 mL) peeled, diced potato

¼ cup (60 mL) peeled, diced yam

1 vegetable stock cube

handful of broken-up whole wheat spaghetti pasta (for **CD** use brown-rice spaghetti)

1 Tbsp (15 mL) dried basil or handful of fresh basil

1 tsp (5 mL) dried oregano

¼ tsp (1 mL) dried savory

sea salt and pepper (for **HD** use sodium substitute)

¼ cup (60 mL) frozen peas

¼ cup (60 mL) frozen corn

In a large soup pot over medium heat, heat the oil and sauté the onion, stirring, for about 20 minutes. Add the garlic and sauté for a couple of minutes, stirring. Add the water, beans, tomatoes, potato, yam, stock cube, pasta, basil, oregano, savory, and sea salt and pepper to taste. Cover and cook for about 20 minutes, stirring. Add the peas and corn and cook for 4 minutes.

Minestrone Soup with Broccoli and Cauliflower

MAKES
4 servings

TIME
about 40 minutes

This version of the Italian classic is loaded with antioxidants and immunity-boosting cruciferous vegetables, legumes and whole grains—and it tastes great. Use brown-rice spaghetti if you are following a gluten-free diet.

1 Tbsp (15 mL) first cold pressed extra virgin olive oil

1 medium-size white onion, diced

4 large garlic cloves, minced

8–10 cups (2–2.5 L) water or vegetable stock

small handful (2 oz/60 g) uncooked whole wheat spaghetti, broken up (for CD use brown-rice spaghetti)

1 can (19 oz/540 mL) mixed beans, drained and rinsed

1 cup (250 mL) finely chopped broccoli

1 cup (250 mL) finely chopped cauliflower

1 can (28 oz/796 mL) diced tomatoes, with juice

4–5 Tbsp (60–75 mL) tomato paste

½ cup (125 mL) frozen corn

½ cup (125 mL) frozen peas

4–5 Tbsp (60–75 mL) fresh basil

sea salt and pepper (for HD use sodium substitute)

handful of chopped fresh spinach or arugula (optional)

In a large soup pot over medium heat, heat the olive oil and sauté the onion for a few minutes. Add the garlic and stir. Add the water or stock and bring to a boil. Add the pasta and cook for 5 minutes back on medium heat, covered, stirring frequently. Add the beans, broccoli and cauliflower and cook for 3 minutes. Add the tomatoes with their juice, and heat through again. Add the tomato paste and stir before adding the corn and peas. Cook for 3 minutes. Add the basil, and sea salt and pepper to taste and spinach or arugula if you are using it. Heat through for 2 minutes before serving.

Tomato, Pesto and Vegetable Soup

  **V**

MAKES
4 servings

TIME
about 1 hour

A delicious meal-in-a-bowl from Italy, loaded with all kinds of vegetables and beans. This is high in fibre and rich in healthy lycopene and other antioxidants. You can use a regular potato if you can't find a purple one.

½ cup (125 mL) long-grain brown rice

3 Tbsp (45 mL) first cold pressed extra virgin olive oil, divided

1 large white onion, cut up

4 large garlic cloves, minced, divided

1 medium-size beet, skin on, diced

1 medium-size purple potato, skin on, diced

12 cups (3 L) water

1 can (19 oz/540 mL) red kidney beans, drained and rinsed

1 can (19 oz/540 mL) black beans, drained and rinsed

1 vegetable stock cube

1 jar (19 oz/540 mL) spaghetti sauce

10 fresh snow peas, cut up

1 cup (250 mL) torn-up fresh spinach

½ cup (125 mL) frozen corn

½ cup (125 mL) frozen peas

large handful of fresh basil

3 Tbsp (45 mL) grated Parmesan cheese (for **CA CD D MS V** use vegan Parmesan)

2 Tbsp (30 mL) pine nuts

¼ tsp (1 mL) cayenne pepper

pepper

In a pot place the rice in 1⅓ cups (330 mL) water and bring to a boil on high heat. Reduce the heat to low and simmer, covered, for about 40 minutes, stirring now and then. Drain and reserve.

Meanwhile, in a large soup pot over medium heat, place 1 Tbsp (15 mL) of the olive oil and sauté the onion for 15 minutes. Add a little water if it starts to stick. Add three-quarters of the garlic, the beet and the potato and cook, stirring, for about 3 minutes. Add the water, cover, and cook for about 15 minutes, stirring occasionally. Add the beans, cooked rice and stock cube and cook for 5 minutes, stirring. Add the spaghetti sauce and cook for 5 minutes. Add the snow peas, spinach, corn and peas, and cook, stirring, for 4 minutes.

Meanwhile, in a blender, blend the basil leaves with the remaining garlic, the Parmesan, pine nuts and remaining 2 Tbsp (30 mL) olive oil. You may need to add a little water. Add this to the soup, then add the cayenne and pepper to taste and heat through for 5 minutes.

Tomato and Pesto Soup

MAKES
4 servings

TIME
10 minutes

A delicious, easy soup from Italy, rich in lycopene and other antioxidants. This is a cooling soup that is great for summer.

8 large fresh basil leaves, or more to taste

3 large tomatoes, chopped

3 large garlic cloves, peeled

2 Tbsp (30 mL) pine nuts

2 Tbsp (30 mL) first cold pressed extra virgin olive oil

1–2 Tbsp (15–30 mL) grated Parmesan cheese (optional; omit or use vegan Parmesan for **CA** **CD** **D** **G** **MS** **V**)

Place everything in a blender and blend until smooth. Allow to stand for a few minutes. Reblend and serve at room temperature.

Greek Soup

	MAKES	TIME
	4 servings	5 to 10 minutes

Another easy cooling soup that's great for a hot summer's day. This one tastes like a cross between a Greek salad and gazpacho.

4 large tomatoes, chopped

¾ medium-size English cucumber, peeled and roughly chopped

½ green bell pepper, roughly chopped

⅓ small white onion

⅔ cup (160 mL) feta cheese

3 Tbsp (45 mL) first cold pressed extra virgin olive oil

2 Tbsp (30 mL) fresh lemon juice

1 tsp (5 mL) dried oregano

sea salt and pepper (for **HD** use sodium substitute)

Place everything in a blender and blend until smooth. Serve at room temperature.

Cold Cucumber Soup

Ⓒ ⒸⒶ ⒸⒹ Ⓓ Ⓖ ⒽⒹ Ⓜ ⒨Ⓢ ⓄⒶ ⓇⒶ Ⓥ | MAKES
4 servings | TIME
25 minutes

A light, refreshing soup that is another great recipe on a hot summer day.

1 large English cucumber, peeled and
   roughly chopped

2 cups (500 mL) cold vegetable stock

1 Tbsp (15 mL) fresh dill

1 Tbsp (15 mL) first cold pressed extra virgin
   olive oil

Place everything in the blender and blend until smooth. Serve chilled.

Tomato, Spinach and Basil Soup

		MAKES 4 servings	TIME 5 to 10 minutes

A great way to use garden-fresh tomatoes and basil. This Italian soup is rich in many antioxidants, including lycopene, beta carotene and octacosanol. For a peppery bite, try fresh arugula instead of spinach.

1½ lb (750 g) medium-large fresh tomatoes
   (about 6), skin on, chopped

2 large handfuls of fresh spinach or arugula
   (for **G** use arugula)

¼ cup (60 mL) fresh basil

1 sun-dried tomato (optional; omit for **CA** **D**)

2 Tbsp (30 mL) first cold pressed extra virgin
   olive oil

sea salt and pepper (for **HD** use sodium substitute)

Place everything in the blender and blend until smooth. Serve at room temperature.

Pesto Noodle Soup

MAKES
4 servings

TIME
15 to 20 minutes

A wonderful-tasting and delicious-smelling hot soup that is a full meal-in-a-bowl from Italy.

6 Tbsp (90 mL) first cold pressed extra virgin olive oil

1 clove garlic, minced (optional)

12 fresh basil leaves

¼ cup (60 mL) pine nuts

2 Tbsp (30 mL) grated Parmesan cheese, plus more for serving (for CA CD D G MS RA V use vegan Parmesan)

8 cups (2 L) vegetable stock

3 cups (750 mL) torn-up fresh young chard leaves

2 cups (500 mL) brown-rice spaghettini or vermicelli

30 g (1 oz) extra-firm tofu, cut in small cubes

1 tsp (5 mL) hot sauce

pepper

In a blender, blend the oil with the garlic (if using), basil, pine nuts and Parmesan. Add 1 to 2 Tbsp (15–30 mL) hot water and blend until smooth.

In a soup pot bring the stock to a boil then reduce the heat to medium. Add the chard leaves and noodles and cook for 4 minutes. The noodles should be done. Remove from the heat but keep the noodles in the stock.

In a frying pan over medium heat, heat through the tofu with the hot sauce, stirring for about 5 minutes. Add this to the soup, and then add the pesto from the blender. Season to taste with pepper and mix until well combined. Serve with extra Parmesan if desired.

MAINS

Rich and Fragrant Lentil and Bean Stew

MAKES	TIME
4 servings	about 3 hours

Very festive when it comes out of the clay pot. If you don't have a clay pot, don't worry. It's not essential but it does add a special touch. The whole house smells great when you're making this. The artichokes really make the dish, so do use them. Serve with a salad and steamed greens.

1 can (28 oz/796 mL) chopped tomatoes, with juice

1 can (19 oz/540 mL) white kidney beans, drained and rinsed

1 cup (250 mL) dried red lentils, washed

1 cup (250 mL) pickled artichokes, quartered

1 large Vidalia onion, quartered and thinly sliced

1 medium-size red potato, medium dice

⅓–½ cup (80–125 mL) first cold pressed extra virgin olive oil

2 tsp (10 mL) dried oregano

sea salt and pepper (for HD use sodium substitute)

Preheat the oven to 400°F (200°C).

In a clay ovenproof dish that holds at least 12 cups (3 L), place all the ingredients and cover them with water (approx. 5 cups/1.25 L). Cover and bake for 2 hours 45 minutes to 3 hours, or until everything is tender.

White Beans with Tomatoes and Spinach

	MAKES	TIME
	4 servings	1 hour

The garlic and basil add a wonderful flavour to this Italian dish. Another healthy, high-fibre, antioxidant-rich dish.

½ cup (125 mL) brown rice

1 Tbsp (15 mL) first cold pressed extra virgin olive oil

8 very large garlic cloves

1 can (19 oz/540 mL) red or white kidney beans, drained and rinsed

1 can (28 oz/796 mL) diced tomatoes, with juice

4 cups (1 L) fresh spinach

4–5 Tbsp (60–75 mL) fresh basil, or 1 tsp (5 mL) dried basil

pepper

Put the rice in a pot with 1 ¾ cups (435 mL) of water. Bring to a boil on high heat then reduce the heat to medium-low. Cover and cook, stirring occasionally, for about 50 minutes or until tender.

In a frying pan, heat the oil and add the garlic. Cover and cook, stirring occasionally, for a few minutes until done on all sides. Crush with a potato masher. Add the cooked rice and the beans and stir for a minute. Add the tomatoes with their juice and cook for a few minutes. Add the spinach and basil and cook, stirring, for 3 to 5 minutes. Season to taste with pepper.

Mediterranean-Style Romano Beans

MAKES	TIME
4 servings	15 minutes

A delicious use of kale, a healthy super-veggie.

> 2 Tbsp (30 mL) first cold pressed extra virgin
> olive oil
> 7 large garlic cloves, minced
> 2½ cups (625 mL) kale, chopped
> 1 can (19 oz/540 mL) romano beans, drained
> and rinsed
> 10 sun-dried tomatoes, roughly chopped
> 1 medium-size red bell pepper, cut in thin strips
> 8 kalamata olives, pitted and diced (optional)
> 1 Tbsp (15 mL) balsamic vinegar
> sea salt and pepper (for **HD** use sodium substitute)
> 1 cup (250 mL) feta cheese, crumbled (reduce
> amount or use vegan feta for **C** **HD** **M**; use
> vegan feta for **CD** **D** **MS** **V**)

In a frying pan over medium heat, heat the olive oil and cook the garlic, stirring, for 3 to 4 minutes. Add the kale, beans, sun-dried tomatoes, bell pepper, olives, balsamic vinegar, and sea salt and pepper to taste and cook, stirring, for 4 to 5 minutes. Add a little water if necessary to prevent sticking. Add the feta and heat through for a couple of minutes, stirring.

Kidney Beans and Greens with Feta

C   **HD** **M**   **OA**   MAKES | TIME
4 servings | 10 to 15 minutes

An easy Greek dish that combines beans, garlic and healthy greens. Serve with rice.

1 Tbsp (15 mL) first cold pressed extra virgin
  olive oil

6 large garlic cloves, minced

1 can (19 oz/540 mL) red kidney beans, drained
  and rinsed

6 baby bok choy, chopped

4 green onions, chopped

sea salt and pepper (for **HD** use sodium substitute)

½ cup (125 mL) feta cheese, crumbled

3 Tbsp (45 mL) balsamic vinegar

In a frying pan over medium heat, heat the olive oil and sauté the garlic, stirring, for 2 to 3 minutes. Add the beans, bok choy, green onions and sea salt and pepper to taste and sauté, stirring, for 4 minutes. Add the feta and balsamic vinegar and heat through, stirring, for 2 to 3 minutes.

Kale and Kidney Beans with Sun-Dried Tomatoes and Walnuts

	MAKES	TIME
	4 servings	30 minutes

A delicious use of kale, a super-veggie, and walnuts, which are rich in healthy oils. Serve this Italian dish with rice.

1 Tbsp (15 mL) first cold pressed extra virgin
   olive oil

1 large white onion, chopped

1 can (19 oz/540 mL) red kidney beans, drained
   and rinsed

6 large kale leaves, torn up

5 sun-dried tomatoes, roughly chopped

¼ cup (60 mL) chopped walnuts

4–5 Tbsp (60–75 mL) balsamic vinegar

sea salt and pepper (for **HD** use sodium substitute)

In a frying pan over medium heat, heat the oil and sauté the onion until tender, about 25 minutes. Add the beans, kale, sun-dried tomatoes, walnuts, vinegar, and sea salt and pepper to taste and heat through, stirring, for about 5 minutes.

Mediterranean Stew

        **V** | MAKES
4 servings | TIME
about 3 hours

A wonderful, easy stew that makes the house smell incredible thanks to the tomatoes, olives and herbs.

4 cups (1 L) water

1 can (19 oz/540 mL) diced tomatoes, with juice

1¼ cups (310 mL) dried green lentils, washed

½ cup (125 mL) brown rice

¼ cup (60 mL) wild rice

12 kalamata olives, pitted and chopped

1 medium carrot, sliced

1 large cooking onion, chopped

½ cup (125 mL) first cold pressed extra virgin
   olive oil

1 tsp (5 mL) dried oregano

1 tsp (5 mL) dried dill

sea salt and pepper (for **HD** use sodium substitute)

3 Tbsp (45 mL) chopped fresh dill

Preheat the oven to 350°F (180°C).

In a large casserole dish that can hold at least 12 cups (3 L), place the water, tomatoes with their juice, lentils, brown rice, wild rice, olives, carrot, onion, olive oil, oregano, dried dill, and sea salt and pepper to taste. Cover and bake for 2 ½ to 3 hours, until everything is tender. Add more water if necessary as it cooks. Add the fresh dill during the last 15 minutes of cooking.

Lentil, Black Bean and Orzo Casserole

		MAKES	TIME
		4 servings	about 3 hours

I first had a version of this Greek dish in a woman's home in Northern Greece. It was washed down with retsina and accompanied by olives, bread and wonderful feta cheese. Serve with steamed greens and a salad of tomatoes and cucumbers. You can always drink sparkling water if you wish to avoid the alcohol.

8–10 cups (2–2.5 L) water

1 can (19 oz/540 mL) tomato soup

1½ cups (375 mL) dried green lentils, washed

½ cup (125 mL) canned black beans, drained and rinsed

1¼ cups (310 mL) pickled artichokes

1 cup (250 mL) orzo

1 cup (250 mL) brown rice

½ cup (125 mL) spiced green or black olives, pitted

3 Tbsp (45 mL) first cold pressed extra virgin olive oil

sea salt and pepper (for **HD** use sodium substitute)

Preheat the oven to 375°F (190°C).

Place everything in a large ovenproof clay dish (or other ovenproof dish if you don't have a clay one) that holds at least 16 cups (4 L). Cover and bake for about 3 hours, until the lentils and rice are cooked, adding more water if necessary as it cooks.

Clay Pot Lentils and Red Pepper

MAKES	TIME
4 servings	2 hours 35 minutes

An easy Greek dish that makes the house smell wonderfully of tomato sauce and oregano. The clay pot is used for a lot of dishes in this book. It helps to make the dishes taste wonderful by marrying the flavours together really well.

4 cups (1 L) water

1½ cups (375 mL) dried green lentils, washed

1¼ cups (310 mL) spaghetti sauce

¼ cup (60 mL) first cold pressed extra virgin olive oil

3 medium-size red bell peppers, roughly chopped

1 very large red onion, sliced

1 tsp (5 mL) dried oregano

pepper

Preheat the oven to 375°F (190°C).

Place everything in a large ovenproof clay pot and cover. Bake for about 2 ½ hours until everything is tender and the onions and lentils are fully cooked. You may need to add more water to prevent it from drying out.

Potatoes, Lentils and Artichokes with Tomatoes

MAKES	TIME
4 servings	1 hour 10 minutes

A wonderful easy Italian dish that essentially bakes itself after you assemble it. Serve with a green salad.

1 can (28 oz/796 mL) diced tomatoes, with juice

¼ cup (60 mL) first cold pressed extra virgin olive oil

4 large garlic cloves, minced

2 tsp (10 mL) dried basil

sea salt and pepper (for **HD** use sodium substitute)

4 medium-size red potatoes, thinly sliced

1 large carrot, thinly sliced

1½ cups (375 mL) dried red lentils, washed

6 pickled artichokes, chopped

Preheat the oven to 375°F (190°C).

In a food processor or blender, blend the tomatoes with their juice and the olive oil, garlic, basil, and sea salt and pepper to taste.

In a large ovenproof casserole dish, layer the potatoes and carrot. Place the lentils overtop. Add the artichokes and pour the sauce from the blender over it all. Cover and bake for about 1 hour until everything is tender.

Chickpeas with Walnuts and Spinach

MAKES	TIME
2 servings	10 to 15 minutes

The chickpeas, garlic, spinach and walnuts combine to create a truly memorable flavour in this Italian dish.

1 tsp (5 mL) first cold pressed extra virgin olive oil

3 large garlic cloves, minced

1 can (19 oz/540 mL) chickpeas, drained and rinsed

1 cup (250 mL) vegetable stock

2 Tbsp (30 mL) fresh lemon juice

2 cups (500 mL) chopped fresh spinach

½ cup (125 mL) chopped walnuts

In a frying pan over medium heat, heat the olive oil and sauté the garlic, stirring, for 2 minutes. Add the chickpeas, stock and lemon juice, and cook for 4 to 5 minutes, stirring. Add the spinach and walnuts and cook for another 3 minutes, stirring.

Garlic and Chickpeas with Watercress

MAKES
2 servings

TIME
15 minutes

A great Italian way of getting in a healthy green and legume. The garlic and watercress pair perfectly with the chickpeas and the soy sauce (a bit of an Asian influence here too).

1 tsp (5 mL) first cold pressed extra virgin olive oil

5 large garlic cloves, minced

1 can (19 oz/540 mL) chickpeas, drained and rinsed

2 bunches fresh watercress

2 Tbsp (30 mL) soy sauce

In a frying pan over medium-low heat, heat the oil and sauté the garlic, stirring, for a few minutes. Add the chickpeas and cook for another 3 minutes. Add the watercress and cook for 3 minutes. Add the soy sauce and heat through before serving.

Vegetable and Split Pea Medley

	MAKES	TIME
	4 servings	1 hour 5 minutes

A great gluten-free dish that is good served with brown rice or millet.

1¾ cups (435 mL) green split peas

3 Tbsp (45 mL) first cold pressed extra virgin
   olive oil

2 large onions, finely chopped

10 large assorted mushrooms, finely chopped

7 baby carrots, finely chopped

1 red bell pepper, finely chopped

2 Tbsp (30 mL) fresh lemon juice

1 tsp (5 mL) dried thyme

sea salt and pepper (for **HD** use sodium substitute)

Put the split peas in a soup pot and cover with 5 cups (1.25 L) of water. Bring to a boil on high heat then reduce the heat to medium-low. Cover and cook, stirring occasionally, for about 1 hour or until tender, and drain if there is a lot of excess liquid.

In a large frying pan over medium heat, heat the oil and sauté the onions, stirring, for about 15 minutes. Add the mushrooms, carrots and bell pepper and sauté for about 10 minutes, stirring. Add a little water, if needed, to prevent sticking. Add the lemon juice, thyme, sea salt and pepper to taste and the cooked split peas and heat through for a few minutes before serving.

Mushroom, Tomato and Lima Bean Casserole

| | MAKES
4 servings | TIME
1 hour 10 minutes |

From Italy, a great way of using lima beans, even for those who don't like them. It is also loaded with protein-rich mushrooms.

3 cups (750 mL) frozen baby lima beans

1 jar (19 oz/540 mL) spaghetti sauce

20 chopped large button mushrooms

2 large portobello mushrooms, chopped

pepper

¼ cup (60 mL) grated vegan Parmesan

Cook the lima beans according to the package directions.

Preheat the oven to 375°F (190°C).

In an ovenproof casserole dish, place the lima beans, spaghetti sauce, mushrooms and pepper to taste. Mix and then sprinkle the cheese over-top. Cover and bake for about 1 hour.

Pasta Sauce

        **V**

MAKES	TIME
4 servings	about 30 minutes

An Italian classic, this is truly the best-tasting pasta sauce I've ever had, and it is so easy to make. Just be sure to get really good tomatoes. Serve over your favourite pasta. (Note that cooking the wine evaporates most of the alcohol, so it is fine for those with gout.)

1 Tbsp (15 mL) first cold pressed extra virgin
   olive oil

1 small fresh hot green chili, diced

10 ripe plum tomatoes, diced

⅓ cup (80 mL) red wine

12 fresh basil leaves, torn up

¼ tsp (1 mL) sea salt (for **HD** use sodium substitute)

In a pot over medium heat, heat the oil and sauté the chili, stirring, for 1 minute. Add the tomatoes and cook for about 15 minutes, then add the wine and continue to cook for another 5 to 10 minutes, stirring now and then. Add the basil and sea salt and heat through for 1 minute.

Red Lentil Pasta Sauce

	MAKES	TIME
	4 servings	25 minutes

A filling, easy Italian pasta sauce, made with lentils, tomatoes and basil. Serve over whole wheat pasta.

1⅓ cups (330 mL) dried red lentils, washed

2½ cups (625 mL) canned diced tomatoes, with juice

10 to 12 green olives, pitted and chopped (optional)

4 very large garlic cloves, minced

2 Tbsp (30 mL) fresh basil

1 Tbsp (15 mL) first cold pressed extra virgin olive oil

sea salt and pepper (for **HD** use sodium substitute)

Put lentils in a pot with 2⅔ cups (660 mL) of water, and bring to a boil on high heat. Reduce the heat to medium-low, cover and cook for 20 minutes, stirring occasionally, until tender, draining if too wet.

Place the tomatoes, olives, garlic, basil, olive oil, and sea salt and pepper to taste in a food processor or blender and blend until smooth. Add to the cooked lentils and mix. Heat through for a few minutes on medium heat, stirring, before serving with cooked pasta.

Zippy Kale and Feta Pasta

C　　**D**　**HD** **M** **MS** **OA** **RA** **V**　| MAKES | TIME |
| 4 servings | 15 to 20 minutes |

A different, delicious way of getting in your greens and beans. Thank you, Greece.

1½ cups (375 mL) uncooked whole wheat
    bow-tie pasta

2 Tbsp (30 mL) first cold pressed extra virgin
    olive oil

5 large garlic cloves, minced

3 cups (750 mL) various sliced fresh mushrooms

1 can (19 oz/540 mL) romano beans, drained
    and rinsed

2 cups (500 mL) chopped kale

3 Tbsp (45 mL) balsamic vinegar

¼ tsp (1 mL) chili flakes

sea salt and pepper (for **HD** use sodium substitute)

1 cup (250 mL) feta cheese, crumbled (for **C** **D** **HD**
    M **MS** **RA** **V** use vegan feta)

Cook the pasta according to the package instructions.

In a large frying pan over medium heat, heat the oil and sauté the garlic, stirring, for a couple of minutes. Add the mushrooms and sauté for 4 minutes. Add the beans, kale, vinegar, chili flakes, and sea salt and pepper to taste and cook, covered, for 5 minutes, stirring occasionally. Add the feta and cooked pasta and heat through before serving.

Romano Bean and Spinach Pasta

 **C CA CD D** **HD M MS OA** **V** | MAKES
4 servings | TIME
40 minutes

A mouth-watering Italian pasta loaded with lutein and lycopene. Use brown-rice pasta for a gluten-free option.

1 cup (250 mL) uncooked whole wheat rotini pasta
(for **CD** use brown-rice pasta)

½ cup (125 mL) dried red lentils, washed

1 can (28 oz/796 mL) tomatoes, with juice

2 Tbsp (30 mL) first cold pressed extra virgin
olive oil

1 large white onion, diced

1 can (19 oz/540 mL) romano beans, drained
and rinsed

¼ cup (60 mL) pine nuts

¼ cup (60 mL) walnut pieces

1 cup (250 mL) chopped spinach

pepper

Cook the pasta according to the package instructions.

Put the lentils in a pot with 1 cup (250 mL) of water and bring to a boil on high heat. Reduce the heat to medium-low, cover and cook for 20 minutes, stirring occasionally, until tender, draining if too wet.

Purée the tomatoes with their juice.

In a large frying pan over medium heat, heat the oil and sauté the onion, stirring, for about 25 minutes. Add the puréed tomatoes and beans and cook, stirring, for a few minutes. Add the pine nuts and walnuts and cook, stirring, for 2 minutes. Add the cooked pasta and lentils along with the spinach and lots of pepper and cook, stirring, for 3 minutes.

Zucchini Pasta

	MAKES	TIME
	4 servings	20 minutes

A quick favourite of mine that made good use of the wild dill that grows in Greece, an herb that scented the air with a delicious sweetness.
Serve this with olives and a salad. Use brown-rice pasta for a gluten-free version.

> 2 cups (500 mL) uncooked whole wheat rotini pasta (for **CD** use brown-rice pasta)
>
> 1–2 Tbsp (15–30 mL) dairy free nonhydrogenated margarine, or olive oil
>
> 4 large garlic cloves, minced
>
> 1½ medium zucchini, skin on, quartered lengthwise then sliced thinly
>
> 1 cup (250 mL) soy milk
>
> 2 Tbsp (30 mL) fresh dill, or 2 tsp (10 mL) dried dill
>
> sea salt and pepper (for **HD** use sodium substitute)

Cook the pasta according to the package instructions.

In a frying pan over medium heat, heat the margarine and sauté the garlic, stirring frequently, for 3 to 4 minutes. Add the zucchini and cook, stirring, for 4 to 5 minutes. Add the soy milk and heat through for 1 minute. Add the pasta, dill, and sea salt and pepper to taste. Heat through for a couple of minutes, stirring.

Corkscrew Pasta with Basil and Pine Nuts

		MAKES	TIME
		4 servings	15 minutes

This one easily adapts to a gluten-free diet. Just substitute brown-rice pasta for the whole wheat pasta.

2 cups (500 mL) uncooked whole wheat corkscrew
    pasta (for **CD** use brown-rice pasta)

3 Tbsp (45 mL) grated vegan Parmesan

2 Tbsp (30 mL) pine nuts

2 Tbsp (30 mL) fresh basil or 2 tsp (10 mL)
    dried basil

¼ tsp (1 mL) sea salt (for **HD** use sodium substitute)

pepper

½ cup (125 mL) first cold pressed extra virgin
    olive oil

2–3 Tbsp (30–45 mL) hot water from the pasta

Cook the pasta according to the package instructions on package. Reserve 2 to 3 Tbsp (30–45 mL) of the cooking water.

In a blender or food processor, blend the Parmesan, pine nuts, basil, sea salt and pepper to taste with the olive oil and reserved cooking water. Allow the flavours to blend for a couple of minutes then blend again. Toss with the hot pasta.

Kamut Pasta and Veggies

MAKES
4 servings

TIME
20 to 45 minutes

A delicious, easy pasta dish from Italy that is full of super-veggies. For gluten-free diets use brown-rice corkscrew pasta.

2 cups (500 mL) uncooked kamut corkscrew pasta
(for **CD** use brown-rice pasta)

1 Tbsp (15 mL) first cold pressed extra virgin
olive oil

1 cup (250 mL) broccoli florets

1 cup (250 mL) cauliflower florets

½ medium zucchini, sliced

1 small fresh jalapeño pepper, finely chopped,
with seeds

¾ cup (185 mL) grated cheddar cheese
(for **C** **CA** **CD** **D** **G** **HD** **M** **MS** **RA** **V** use
vegan cheddar)

½ cup (125 mL) grated Parmesan cheese
(for **CA** **CD** **D** **G** **MS** **RA** **V** use vegan Parmesan)

pinch of chili flakes

sea salt and pepper (for **HD** use sodium substitute)

Cook the pasta according to the package instructions.

In a frying pan over medium heat, heat the olive oil and sauté the vegetables including the jalapeño, stirring, for 4 to 5 minutes. Add the cooked pasta with both cheeses, a pinch of chili flakes, and sea salt and pepper to taste and heat through.

Alternatively, for a different flavour, preheat the oven to 350°F (180°C). Place everything in an ovenproof dish, cover and bake for ½ hour.

Pasta with Chard and Feta

MAKES	TIME
4 servings	20 minutes

A delicious blend of flavours inspired by Greece, combined with a super-veggie, chard. Use brown-rice spaghetti for a gluten-free version.

½ lb (250 g) uncooked whole wheat spaghetti
    pasta (for **CD** use brown-rice spaghetti)

2 Tbsp (30 mL) first cold pressed extra virgin olive
    oil, divided

4 large garlic cloves, minced

1 can (19 oz/540 mL) romano beans, drained
    and rinsed

2 cups (500 mL) shredded chard, red and green

¼ cup (60 mL) pitted chopped kalamata olives

2 Tbsp (30 mL) balsamic vinegar

¼ tsp (1 mL) chili flakes

sea salt and pepper (for **HD** use sodium substitute)

1 cup (250 mL) crumbled feta cheese (optional;
    omit or use vegan feta for **CA** **CD** **D** **MS** **RA** **V**,
    reduce amount for **C** **HD** **M**)

Cook the pasta according to the package instructions.

In a frying pan over medium heat, heat 1 Tbsp (15 mL) of the olive oil and sauté the garlic, stirring, for 2 to 3 minutes. Add the beans, chard, olives, vinegar, chili flakes, and sea salt and pepper to taste and then the remaining 1 Tbsp (15 mL) of olive oil. Cook, stirring, for 5 to 6 minutes. Add the cooked pasta and feta (if using) and heat through for 1 to 2 minutes, stirring.

PASTA WITH CHARD AND FETA

Garlic, Olive and Sun-Dried Tomato Corkscrew Pasta

MAKES	TIME
4 servings	20 minutes

A colourful, mouth-watering pasta dish that's loaded with garlic, the small but important vegetable that helps fight just about every illness and promotes good health. Use brown-rice pasta for a gluten-free version.

2 cups (500 mL) uncooked whole wheat corkscrew pasta (for **CD** use brown-rice pasta)

2 Tbsp (30 mL) first cold pressed extra virgin olive oil

8 large garlic cloves, minced

1¼ cups (310 mL) crumbled feta cheese (optional; omit or use vegan feta for **CD** **G** **MS** **V**, reduce amount for **C** **HD** **M**)

14 kalamata olives, pitted and chopped

12 sun-dried tomatoes, roughly chopped

6 kale leaves, torn up (optional)

1 medium-size red bell pepper, cut in strips

1 Tbsp (15 mL) balsamic vinegar

sea salt and pepper (for **HD** use sodium substitute)

Cook the pasta according to the package instructions.

In a frying pan over medium heat, heat the oil and sauté the garlic, stirring, for about 2 minutes. Add the feta cheese (if using), the olives, sun-dried tomatoes, kale (if using), bell pepper, balsamic vinegar, and sea salt and pepper to taste. Stir and heat through for 3 to 4 minutes. Add the cooked pasta and stir to heat through.

Garlic and Mushroom Pasta

MAKES	TIME
4 servings	20 minutes (for pasta option) or 1 hour 30 minutes (for barley option)

From Italy, a pasta dish flavoured with mushrooms, spinach and garlic. If you have celiac disease, use 1 cup (250 mL) uncooked brown-rice pasta or even just brown rice instead.

1 cup (250 mL) uncooked whole wheat fettuccine (for **CD** use brown-rice fettuccine) or 2 cups (500 mL) cheese ravioli (not for **CD** **D** **MS** **RA** **V**) or 1⅓ cups (330 mL) whole-grain barley (not for **CD**)

2–3 Tbsp (30–45 mL) first cold pressed extra virgin olive oil

12 whole garlic cloves

1 cup (250 mL) red wine

½-inch (1 cm) piece of kudzu root (optional)

4 cups (1 L) chopped mixed fresh mushrooms

sea salt and pepper (for **HD** use sodium substitute)

2 cups (500 mL) fresh spinach

1 cup (250 mL) canned chickpeas, drained and rinsed (optional)

If you are using pasta, cook according to the package instructions. If you are using barley, put it in a pot with 4¾ cups (1.2 L) of water and bring to a boil on high heat. Reduce the heat to medium-low, cover and cook for 1 hour 20 minutes, stirring occasionally, until tender.

In a large frying pan over medium heat, heat the oil and sauté the garlic, stirring, for 3 minutes. Add the wine and whole piece of kudzu (if using), and sauté for a few more minutes, stirring, and allowing the mix to thicken if you are using the kudzu root. Crush the garlic with a fork.

Add the mushrooms and sea salt and pepper to taste and sauté for 5 minutes or so, stirring. Add the spinach and chickpeas (if using). Sauté for 2 to 3 minutes, stirring. Serve over the pasta or barley.

Tomato, Cream and Cheese Pasta

MAKES	TIME
4 servings	20 to 25 minutes

A wonderful aromatic pasta from Italy. Serve with a large green salad. Depending on your health concern or the diet you are following, you can use whole wheat or gluten-free pasta, or 2 cups (500 mL) cheese ravioli, or dried tomato or artichoke pasta.

1 cup (250 mL) uncooked pasta (see above)

1 Tbsp (15 mL) dairy-free nonhydrogenated margarine

4 cups (1 L) sliced button and fresh chanterelle mushrooms

6 garlic cloves, minced

¼–½ tsp (1–2 mL) chili flakes

pepper

1½ cups (375 mL) canned tomatoes, puréed

¼ cup (60 mL) red wine

¼ cup (60 mL) soy milk

Parmesan cheese, grated (for CD D MS V use vegan Parmesan)

Cook the pasta according to the package instructions.

In a large frying pan over medium heat, heat the margarine and sauté the mushrooms, garlic, chili flakes and pepper to taste, stirring, for about 5 to 7 minutes. Add the tomatoes, wine and soy milk and cook for 7 to 10 minutes. Serve over the pasta and sprinkle with grated Parmesan.

Artichoke, Red Pepper and Spinach Pasta

C   **HD** **M**   **OA**

MAKES	TIME
4 servings	20 minutes

The artichokes, red pepper, garlic and spinach in this dish from Italy go very well with the wonderful wine and cream sauce. Colourful and delicious.

2 cups (500 mL) uncooked whole wheat rotini or
    corkscrew pasta

1 Tbsp (15 mL) first cold pressed extra virgin
    olive oil

5 large garlic cloves, minced

1¼ cups (310 mL) pickled artichokes, quartered

1 red bell pepper, cut in thin strips

1 bunch spinach

pepper

1 cup (250 mL) red wine

½ cup (125 mL) whipping cream

¼ cup (60 mL) grated Parmesan cheese

Cook the pasta according to the package instructions.

In a frying pan over medium heat, heat the oil and sauté the garlic, stirring, for 1 minute. Add the artichokes and bell pepper and sauté, stirring, for 4 to 5 minutes. Add the spinach and pepper to taste and sauté for 1 minute, stirring. Add the red wine and whipping cream and cook, stirring, for 1 to 2 minutes. Add the cooked pasta and cheese and heat through.

Pasta with Pesto

C **CA** **CD** **D** **G** **HD** **M** **MS** **OA** **RA** **V**

MAKES
4 servings

TIME
20 minutes

An Italian classic made with antioxidant-rich basil. Use brown-rice pasta for a gluten-free version.

6 oz (175 g) uncooked whole wheat spaghetti (for **CD** use brown-rice spaghetti)

1 bunch fresh basil

1 very large clove garlic, minced

¼ cup (60 mL) first cold pressed extra virgin olive oil

2 Tbsp (30 mL) reserved pasta water, more if needed

1 Tbsp (15 mL) pine nuts

1 Tbsp (15 mL) finely grated Parmesan cheese (for **CA** **CD** **D** **G** **MS** **RA** **V** use vegan Parmesan)

sea salt and pepper (for **HD** use sodium substitute)

Cook the pasta according to the package instructions. Reserve at least 2 Tbsp (30 mL) of the cooking water.

Place the basil and garlic in a blender with the olive oil, hot pasta water, pine nuts, Parmesan cheese, and sea salt and pepper to taste and blend until smooth. Add more cooking water if it's too thick. Toss with the hot cooked pasta and serve.

Pasta with White Bean, Spinach, Herbs and Garlic

MAKES	TIME
4 servings	20 minutes

A delicious combination of white beans flavoured with garlic, spinach and basil. An antioxidant-rich meal from Italy.

- 2 cups (500 mL) uncooked short gluten-free pasta, any shape
- 3 Tbsp (45 mL) first cold pressed extra virgin olive oil
- 7 large garlic cloves
- ¾ cup (185 mL) canned white beans, drained and rinsed (I use white kidney beans)
- 1 bunch fresh spinach
- 12 fresh basil leaves, torn up
- 1 Tbsp (15 mL) mixed dried herbs like thyme, oregano, dill and parsley (optional)
- sea salt and pepper (for **HD** use sodium substitute)
- Parmesan cheese, grated (for **CA** **CD** **D** **MS** **RA** **V** use vegan Parmesan)

Cook the pasta according to the package instructions.

In a frying pan over low heat, heat the oil and sauté the garlic for a few minutes. Mash the garlic then add the beans, spinach, basil, dried herbs if using, and sea salt and pepper to taste. Cook for 2 to 3 minutes. Mix with the cooked pasta and sprinkle with cheese.

Pasta Shells with Broccoli and Mushrooms in a Spicy Creamy Tomato Sauce

	MAKES	TIME
	4 servings	about 1 hour

This creamy sauce does not actually contain any cream; it's 100 percent vegan. A great way of getting more healthy tofu into your diet, Italian-style.

1½ cups (375 mL) brown-rice pasta shells

5 Tbsp (45 mL) first cold pressed extra virgin olive oil, divided

8 garlic cloves, minced

2 cups (500 mL) sliced button mushrooms (optional; omit for **CA** **G**)

1½ cups (375 mL) finely chopped broccoli

2 tsp (10 mL) dried basil, divided

½ tsp (2 mL) chili flakes

sea salt and pepper (for **HD** use sodium substitute)

1 package (12 oz/350 g) extra-firm tofu

1 can (28 oz/796 mL) whole tomatoes, with juice

2 tsp (10 mL) garlic powder

3 Tbsp (45 mL) grated Parmesan cheese (for **CA** **CD** **D** **G** **MS** **V** use vegan Parmesan)

Cook the pasta according to the package instructions.

In a frying pan over medium heat, heat 3 Tbsp (45 mL) of the oil and sauté the garlic for a few minutes. Add the mushrooms and sauté for 10 minutes. Add the broccoli, 1 tsp (5 mL) of the basil, chili flakes, and sea salt and pepper to taste and cook, stirring, for a few minutes.

Meanwhile, in a food processor, blend the tofu with the tomatoes and their juice and the garlic powder until smooth. Add to the frying pan, cover and heat through for 7 minutes, stirring occasionally.

Preheat the oven to 375°F (190°C).

Toss the cooked pasta with the remaining 2 Tbsp (30 mL) olive oil, the cheese and remaining 1 tsp (5 mL) basil, and place in a large glass baking dish. Cover with the sauce from the frying pan. Sprinkle more cheese overtop, if desired. Bake, covered, for ½ hour.

Broccoli and Pesto with Brown-Rice Pasta

	MAKES	TIME
	4 servings	45 minutes

This Italian dish is a great way of getting in healthy antioxidant-rich pesto and a super-veggie. And it tastes incredible. You won't even notice that it is gluten-free.

2 cups (500 mL) uncooked brown-rice pasta spirals

2 cups (500 mL) broccoli florets

½ cup (125 mL) first cold pressed extra virgin olive oil

¼ cup (60 mL) grated Parmesan cheese (for **CA** **CD** **D** **G** **MS** **RA** **V** use vegan Parmesan)

12 fresh basil leaves

1 large clove garlic, minced (optional)

1 medium tomato, chopped (optional; omit for **RA**)

2 Tbsp (30 mL) pine nuts

¼ tsp (1 mL) chili flakes

pepper

Cook the pasta according to the package instructions.

Place the broccoli in a steamer basket in a pot and steam for 12 to 15 minutes or until soft. Place the broccoli, oil, Parmesan cheese, basil, garlic (if using), tomato, pine nuts, chili flakes and pepper to taste in a food processor or blender, and blend until smooth. Add more oil if it seems too thick. Pour over the hot cooked rice pasta and toss to combine.

Preheat the oven to 350°F (180°C).

Place the sauce and pasta in an ovenproof casserole dish and cover. Bake for 15 to 25 minutes, until heated through.

PASTA SHELLS
WITH OLIVES,
ARTICHOKES
AND ASPARAGUS

Pasta Shells with Olives, Artichokes and Asparagus

MAKES
4 servings

TIME
35 minutes

Another gluten-free pasta dish from Italy. You might want to omit the asparagus if you have gout.

1½ cups (375 mL) brown-rice
   pasta shells

5 slender stalks asparagus

2 Tbsp + 1 tsp (30 mL + 5 mL) first cold
   pressed extra virgin olive oil, divided

1 medium-size cooking onion, diced

4 large garlic cloves, minced

¾ cup (185 mL) pickled artichokes,
   cut up

½ cup (125 mL) pitted, sliced
   kalamata olives

1 tsp (5 mL) dried basil

chili flakes

sea salt and pepper (for **HD** use
   sodium substitute)

2 cups (500 mL) garlic-flavoured
   spaghetti sauce

Cook the pasta according to the package instructions.

Steam the asparagus in a steamer basket and then cut in 1-inch (2.5 cm) pieces.

In a large frying pan over medium heat, heat 2 Tbsp (30 mL) of the olive oil and sauté the onion, stirring, for about 25 minutes. Add the garlic and sauté, stirring, for 1 minute. Add the artichokes and olives and sauté, stirring, for 1 minute. Add the basil, 3 pinches of chili flakes, and sea salt and pepper to taste and then the spaghetti sauce. Heat through, stirring, for about 5 minutes. Add the steamed asparagus and heat through.

Toss the cooked pasta shells with a pinch of chili flakes, a little dried basil and a little olive oil (1 tsp/5 mL). Serve with the sauce on top.

Penne Pasta with Mushrooms in a Spicy Tomato Cream Sauce

C **HD** **OA**

MAKES
4 servings

TIME
20 minutes

A memorable pasta from Italy that guests will love. Serve with a large green salad and some steamed broccoli or asparagus.

2 cups (500 mL) whole wheat penne

1 Tbsp (15 mL) butter or dairy-free nonhydrogenated margarine

8 large garlic cloves, minced

5 large portobello mushrooms, halved then sliced

1 can (28 oz/796 mL) diced tomatoes, with juice

¼–½ tsp (1–2 mL) chili flakes

sea salt and pepper (for **HD** use sodium substitute)

½ cup (125 mL) whipping cream

Cook the pasta according to the package instructions.

In a large frying pan over medium-low heat, heat the butter and sauté the garlic for 1 minute. Add the mushrooms and sauté for about 10 minutes. Add the tomatoes with their juice, chili flakes, and sea salt and pepper to taste and heat through, stirring, for about 5 minutes. Add the cream and heat through, stirring. Serve over the pasta.

Pasta with King Mushrooms and Chickpeas in a Pesto Sauce

MAKES
4 servings

TIME
25 minutes

A dish inspired by one from Italy that uses king mushrooms, considered a delicacy in China, and very worth the price. Just add a salad with lots of green in it for a complete meal.

¼ lb (125 g) long whole wheat pasta or 1 cup (250 mL) short pasta, any shape (for **CD** use brown-rice pasta)

4 Tbsp (60 mL) first cold pressed extra virgin olive oil, divided

8 large garlic cloves, divided

4–5 large king mushrooms, sliced

1 can (19 oz/540 mL) chickpeas, drained and rinsed

1 tsp (5 mL) dried oregano

2 Tbsp (30 mL) grated Parmesan cheese (for **CD** **D** **MS** **RA** **V** use vegan Parmesan)

1–2 Tbsp (15–30 mL) warm water

small bunch fresh basil

pepper

Cook the pasta according to the package instructions.

In a large frying pan over medium-low heat, heat 1 Tbsp (15 mL) of the olive oil. Mince 6 of the garlic cloves and sauté with the mushrooms, stirring, for about 10 minutes. Add the chickpeas and oregano and sauté for a few minutes.

Place the remaining 3 Tbsp (45 mL) olive oil in a blender with the remaining 2 cloves of garlic and the cheese, water and basil. Blend until smooth. Add to the frying pan with pepper to taste and the cooked pasta. Mix well to heat through.

Fall Vegetable Lasagna

	MAKES	TIME
	4 servings	2 hours 15 minutes

An intriguing twist on the old cheese-heavy classic. This dish is full of vegetables and is both gluten- and dairy-free.

9 brown-rice lasagna noodles

2 Tbsp (30 mL) first cold pressed extra virgin olive oil

2 medium-size cooking onions, roughly chopped

2 cups (500 mL) peeled, cubed pumpkin

1 red bell pepper, roughly chopped

1 yellow bell pepper, roughly chopped

1¼ cups (310 mL) vegetable stock

½ cup (125 mL) dried red lentils, washed

½ cup (125 mL) canned red kidney beans, drained and rinsed

1 can (19 oz/540 mL) diced tomatoes, with juice

sea salt and pepper (for **HD** use sodium substitute)

1 tsp (5 mL) dried herbs like basil or oregano (optional)

Cook the lasagna noodles according to the package directions.

Meanwhile, in a frying pan over medium heat, heat the olive oil and sauté the onions, stirring, for about 25 minutes. Add the pumpkin and bell peppers and sauté, stirring, until soft, about 12 minutes. You may need to add a little water as it cooks. Add the stock with the lentils and kidney beans. Cook, covered, for 20 minutes. Add the tomatoes with their juice and cook for a few more minutes.

Preheat the oven to 350°F (180°C).

In a 9- × 13-inch (23 cm × 33 cm) baking dish, layer a tiny bit of the sauce, 3 cooked noodles, half the remaining sauce, 3 more cooked noodles, the remaining sauce and the 3 remaining cooked noodles. Cover and bake for 1 hour. Uncover during the last 10 minutes of cooking.

Pasta Primavera

C CA CD D G HD M MS OA RA V

MAKES	TIME
4 servings	15 minutes

I think gluten-free pasta makes this dish taste even better because it is light enough to let the vegetables really shine.

¼ lb (125 g) uncooked brown-rice fettuccine

2 Tbsp (30 mL) first cold pressed extra virgin olive oil

5 large garlic cloves, minced

½ large red bell pepper, chopped (optional; omit for **RA**)

¼ large green bell pepper, chopped (optional; omit for **RA**)

2 large portobello mushrooms, sliced (optional; omit for **CA G**)

4 or 5 fresh chanterelle mushrooms, chopped (optional; omit for **CA G**)

1½ cups (375 mL) chopped broccoli florets

3 green onions, finely chopped

¼ tsp (1 mL) garlic salt

chili flakes

pepper

¼ cup (60 mL) frozen peas

2 Tbsp (30 mL) chopped fresh basil

vegan Parmesan, grated

Cook the pasta according to the package instructions.

In a large frying pan over medium heat, heat the olive oil and sauté the garlic, stirring, for 1 minute. Add the bell peppers, portobellos and chanterelles and sauté for 5 minutes. Add the broccoli and green onions with the garlic salt, chili flakes and pepper to taste, and sauté, stirring, for about 1 minute. Add the peas and fresh basil. Sauté, stirring, for about 3 minutes. Toss in the cooked pasta and mix well. Serve hot with vegan Parmesan.

Kale, Red Pepper and Feta with Rice

C   **OA**

MAKES	TIME
4 servings	55 minutes

I first had this on a hillside overlooking the Mediterranean. It was superb. This dish is good for picnics and includes the super-veggie kale.

¾ cup (185 mL) brown rice

2 Tbsp (30 mL) first cold pressed extra virgin olive oil

3 large clove garlic, minced

7 large kale leaves, stems removed, leaves shredded

1 large red bell pepper, cut into bite-size pieces

3–4 Tbsp (45–60 mL) balsamic vinegar

1 Tbsp (15 mL) fresh lemon juice

½ tsp (2 mL) chili flakes

¼ tsp (1 mL) sea salt (for **HD** use sodium substitute)

pepper

1 cup (250 mL) crumbled feta cheese (reduce amount for **C HD M**)

Put rice in a pot with 2 ½ cups (625 mL) of water and bring to a boil on high heat. Reduce the heat to medium-low, cover and cook for 50 minutes, stirring occasionally, until tender.

In a frying pan over medium heat, heat the oil and sauté the garlic, stirring, for 2 to 3 minutes. Add the kale and bell pepper and sauté, stirring, for 6 to 7 minutes. Add the vinegar, lemon juice, chili flakes, sea salt and pepper to taste. Stir and then add the cooked rice. Add the feta and heat through for a few minutes, stirring. Serve hot or cold.

Greek Potatoes with Rice and Artichokes

	MAKES	TIME
V	4 servings	3 hours 15 minutes

Rich and delicious. This is good with steamed broccoli, and tofu that has been crisped in a little oil.

1 cup (250 mL) brown rice

½–1 cup (125–250 mL) first cold pressed extra virgin olive oil

8–10 pickled artichokes, cut up

3 small potatoes, peeled and cut in chunks

¼–½ tsp (1–2 mL) sea salt (for **HD** use sodium substitute)

pepper

3 cups (750 mL) water

lemon wedges

Preheat the oven to 425°F (220°C).

Place the brown rice, olive oil, artichokes, potatoes, sea salt, pepper and water in a large ovenproof dish. I use a large clay dish. Cover and bake for 2 hours 15 minutes, then reduce the heat to 175°F (80°C) and bake for another hour. You may need to add some water as it cooks. Serve hot with lemon wedges.

Chickpeas and Rice with Pesto

C **CA** **CD** **D** **HD** **M** **MS** **OA** **RA** **V**

| MAKES | TIME |
| 4 servings | 1 hour |

Classic Italian flavours. Loaded with healthy garlic and antioxidant-rich basil.

⅔ cup (160 mL) brown rice

5 Tbsp (75 mL) first cold pressed extra virgin
olive oil

12 fresh basil leaves

2 garlic cloves, peeled

3 Tbsp (45 mL) pine nuts

3 Tbsp (45 mL) grated Parmesan
(for **CA** **CD** **D** **MS** **RA** **V** use vegan Parmesan)

1 Tbsp (15 mL) hot water

1 can (19 oz/540 mL) chickpeas, drained and rinsed

sea salt and pepper (for **HD** use sodium substitute)

Put rice in a pot with 2 ¼ cups (560 mL) of water and bring to a boil on high heat. Reduce the heat to medium-low, cover and cook for 50 minutes, stirring occasionally, until tender.

Meanwhile, in a blender, add the olive oil with the basil, garlic, pine nuts, Parmesan and water. Blend until smooth.

In a frying pan, heat the chickpeas with the cooked rice. Add the pesto from the blender and mix well. Season to taste with sea salt and pepper and serve immediately.

Rich Lentils and Rice or Barley in a Tomato and Onion Sauce

MAKES
4 servings

TIME
1 hour 5 minutes (for rice)
or 1 hour 25 minutes
(for barley)

An easy, healthy dish that is high in fibre and tastes great. If you like, you can use whole-grain barley instead of the rice, but do not make this substitution if you have celiac disease.

2 cups (500 mL) dried green lentils, washed

1¼ cups (310 mL) brown rice or 1 cup (250 mL) whole-grain barley (use brown rice for **CD**)

2 Tbsp (30 mL) first cold pressed extra virgin olive oil

3 large cooking onions, chopped

1 green bell pepper, cut into bite-size pieces

1 can (28 oz/796 mL) diced tomatoes with juice

sea salt and pepper (for **HD** use sodium substitute)

large handful of fresh basil, chopped

Put lentils in a pot with plenty of water (about 6 cups/1.5 L), and bring to a boil on high heat. Reduce the heat to medium-low, cover and cook for 1 hour, stirring occasionally and checking the water level, until tender, drain if too wet.

For the rice, put it in a pot with 4 cups (1 L) water and bring to a boil on high heat. Reduce the heat to low and cook, covered and stirring occasionally, for 50 minutes. For the barley, put it in a pot with 3 ½ cups (875 mL) water and bring to a boil on high heat. Reduce the heat to medium-low, cover and cook for 1 hour 20 minutes, stirring occasionally, until tender.

In a large frying pan over medium heat, heat the oil and sauté the onions, stirring, for about 30 minutes. Add the bell pepper and cook, stirring, for about 5 minutes. Add the tomatoes with their juice and sea salt and pepper to taste and cook, covered, stirring now and then, for about 10 minutes. Add the cooked lentils, cooked rice and fresh basil and heat through for about 5 minutes, stirring.

Simple Eggplant Parmesan

MAKES
8 servings

TIME
2 hours 15 minutes

A classic favourite at any dinner party, not least because you can serve it like a meat dish, with rice/potatoes and veggies on the plate. This one easily adapts to gluten-free cooking (use brown-rice flour), and for a more heart-friendly dish, you can leave out the eggs by using egg replacer or olive oil instead.

2 large eggplants, sliced in ¼-inch-thick (5 mm) rounds

4 eggs, beaten (for **HD** use egg replacer)

sea salt and pepper (for **HD** use sodium substitute)

2 cups (500 mL) whole wheat flour (for **CD** use brown-rice flour)

1 tsp (5 mL) dried oregano

first cold pressed extra virgin olive oil for frying

1 jar (19 oz/540 mL) spaghetti sauce

2½ cups (625 mL) grated mozzarella cheese (for **C** **CA** **CD** **G** **HD** **M** use vegan cheese)

½ cup (125 mL) grated Parmesan cheese (for **CA** **CD** **G** **HD** **M** use vegan Parmesan)

Soak the eggplant slices in a large bowl of salted water (use about 1 tsp/5 mL of sea salt and enough water to cover the eggplant) for 1 hour. Keep the eggplant submerged by weighing it down with a plate. Drain and rinse.

Beat the eggs in a bowl with sea salt and pepper to taste. In another bowl, place the flour, sea salt and pepper to taste and oregano and mix well. Dip each eggplant slice into the eggs and then the flour mixture, coating well.

Add about 2 Tbsp (30 mL) olive oil to a frying pan over medium-high heat and fry the eggplant in batches on each side until crispy and brown. Add more oil as necessary. Cook for a total of 5 to 10 minutes for each batch. Place the slices on paper towel to soak up the excess oil.

Preheat the oven to 375°F (190°C).

In two 9- × 13-inch (23 × 33 cm) ovenproof dishes, spoon 2 Tbsp (30 mL) spaghetti sauce and spread evenly across the bottom. Top with a layer of the eggplant then more sauce and sprinkle both cheeses on each layer. Repeat the layers, filling up the two dishes. Cover with aluminum foil and bake for about 40 minutes until melted and cooked.

Green Bean and Root Veg Stew

	MAKES	TIME
V	4 servings	1 hour 15 minutes

A filling, earthy kind of dish full of root vegetables. Serve hot with hearty crusty bread and a green salad.

⅓ cup (80 mL) first cold pressed extra virgin olive oil

1 large cooking onion, chopped

4 medium-size potatoes, peeled and diced

2 cups (500 mL) chopped green beans (1-inch/2.5 cm pieces)

½ very small turnip, peeled and diced

½ medium-size celeriac, peeled and diced

1 tsp (5 mL) dried parsley

sea salt and pepper (for **HD** use sodium substitute)

1 can (28 oz/796 mL) puréed tomatoes

In a large pot over medium heat, heat the olive oil and sauté the onion, stirring, for 20 minutes. Add the potatoes, green beans, turnip, celeriac, parsley, sea salt and pepper to taste and enough water to cover the vegetables by 1 inch (2.5 cm). Cover and cook, stirring occasionally, for about 30 minutes. You may need to add more water as it cooks. Add the tomatoes, cover and simmer for 10 to 12 minutes.

Mediterranean Stuffed Red Peppers

C   **HD**   **OA**

MAKES	TIME
2 servings	1 hour 45 minutes

A colourful dish that is great for entertaining. Serve with a salad and steamed greens.

1 cup (250 mL) brown rice

small handful of wild rice

4 cups (1 L) vegetable stock

¼ cup (60 mL) dried red lentils, washed

½ cup (125 mL) feta cheese, crumbled

¼ cup (60 mL) currants (optional)

1 Tbsp (15 mL) pine nuts

½ tsp (2 mL) ground cinnamon (optional)

sea salt and pepper (for **HD** use sodium substitute)

2 Tbsp (30 mL) fresh lime juice

1 Tbsp (15 mL) first cold pressed extra virgin olive oil

2 small- to medium-size red bell peppers, cut in half lengthwise, remove the seeds and white part

Cook the brown and wild rice in the stock. Bring to a boil, covered, and then reduce the heat to low and simmer, still covered, for 1 hour, stirring once in a while. You may need to add more stock. Add the lentils during the last 25 minutes. Drain the rice, if necessary, and mix with the feta cheese, currants (if using), pine nuts, cinnamon (if using), and sea salt to pepper to taste, then add the lime juice and oil and mix. Preheat the oven to 375°F (190°C).

Stuff the peppers with the rice mixture, place them in a baking dish and add 2 Tbsp (30 mL) water to the bottom of the dish. Cover and bake for 35 to 45 minutes or until tender.

Collards, Onions and Potatoes

C **CA** **CD** **D** **G** **HD** **M** **MS** **OA** **V** | MAKES
4 servings | TIME
1 hour 15 minutes

A delicious way of getting in those healthy greens. Collards go very well with potatoes, and even kids will often eat them this way.

4 large potatoes, peeled and chopped

2 cups (500 mL) chopped fresh collard greens

1 Tbsp (15 mL) first cold pressed extra virgin olive oil

1 large white onion, roughly chopped

¼ cup (60 mL) soy milk

¼ cup (60 mL) grated vegan Parmesan, plus more for topping

1 Tbsp (15 mL) dairy-free nonhydrogenated margarine

sea salt and pepper (for **HD** use sodium substitute)

Cook the potatoes in a pot until tender, about 20 minutes, then drain.

Place the collard greens in a steamer basket and cook for about 20 minutes, covered, until soft.

Preheat the oven to 350°F (180°C).

In a frying pan over medium-low heat, heat the oil and sauté the onion, stirring, for about 25 minutes. Add the boiled potatoes and steamed collard greens and mash them together. Mix in the soy milk, Parmesan, margarine, and sea salt and pepper to taste and place in an ovenproof dish. Top with a little more vegan cheese.

Bake for about 25 minutes, uncovered, until golden.

Zucchini Bake

MAKES	TIME
4 servings	1 hour 15 minutes

This dish is very good served with steamed greens, olives and a tomato-cucumber salad. In Greece, they use an earthenware dish and bring it right to the table for serving.

1¾ cups (435 mL) feta cheese, crumbled

3 eggs, beaten

2 cups (500 mL) milk

2 medium-size cooking onions, roughly chopped

1 large zucchini, sliced, skin on

1 cup (250 mL) whole wheat flour

1 tsp (5 mL) dried dill

sea salt and pepper

Preheat the oven to 375°F (190°C). Grease a large ovenproof dish.

Mix everything together well in a large bowl. Pour into the prepared dish. Bake for about 1 hour or until a toothpick inserted in the middle comes out clean.

Parmesan Zucchini

(V) | MAKES **4 servings** | TIME about 1 hour

A simpler, gluten-free, delicious version of the classic Italian Parmesan dish.

> 1 large zucchini, skin on, sliced thinly lengthwise
>
> 1 jar (19 oz/540 mL) spaghetti sauce
>
> 1 cup (250 mL) grated Parmesan cheese (for **C** **CA** **CD** **D** **G** **HD** **M** **MS** **V** use vegan parmesan)
>
> ½ cup (125 mL) grated mozzarella cheese (for **C** **CA** **CD** **D** **G** **HD** **M** **MS** **V** use vegan mozzarella)

Preheat the oven to 400°F (200°C).

In an ovenproof dish, place a layer of zucchini and cover with some sauce then some Parmesan cheese. Repeat the layers, ending with sauce and sprinkling with mozzarella. Cover and bake for 45 minutes to 1 hour, until tender.

SPANAKOPITA IN
RICE WRAPPERS

Spanakopita in Rice Wrappers

MAKES	TIME
4 servings	about 1 hour
6 to 8 wrappers	

I love Greek spinach and cheese pies, and I wanted to find a way to make them gluten-free, so I used rice paper sheets. Feta is traditional for this recipe but I prefer mozzarella.

2 Tbsp (30 mL) first cold pressed extra virgin olive oil

1 large cooking onion, roughly chopped

6 green onions, chopped

3 cups (750 mL) packed fresh spinach

2½ cups (625 mL) grated mozzarella cheese or crumbled feta cheese (for **C CA CD D HD M MS RA V** use vegan mozzarella)

2 tsp (10 mL) dried dill

sea salt and pepper

6–8 rice paper sheet, moistened with warm water

first cold pressed extra virgin olive oil for brushing

In a frying pan over medium heat, heat the oil and sauté the cooking onion for 25 minutes. Add the green onions and sauté for 5 minutes. Add the spinach and sauté for 1 minute. Remove from the heat and mix in the cheese, dill, and sea salt and pepper to taste. Place some filling in each of the rice wrappers and fold them closed, brushing with a little olive oil to help them be a little more pliable and become golden when baked.

Preheat the oven to 350°F (180°C). Lightly oil a cookie sheet.

Place the filled wrappers on the prepared cookie sheet and bake for about 20 minutes or until golden.

Alternatively, brush the wrappers with olive oil and layer them in a baking dish until you have a good base, and then place all the filling in the middle and cover with more oiled rice wrappers. Bake the same way until golden, 20 to 30 minutes.

Greek Feta, Kefalotiri and Kale Bake

OA

MAKES	TIME
4 servings	about 1 hour 15 minutes

A wonderful dish for entertaining. Various versions are served all over Greece in earthenware dishes that go straight to the table. You can find kefalotiri cheese in Greek markets. Serve with good hearty bread, sliced tomatoes, cucumbers and olives.

1 Tbsp (15 mL) first cold pressed extra virgin olive oil

3 very large kale leaves, chopped

4 green onions, chopped

2 cups (500 mL) soy milk

3 eggs, beaten

1 cup (250 mL) whole wheat flour

¾ cup (185 mL) finely crumbled feta cheese

¾ cup (185 mL) kefalotiri cheese, grated

2 tsp (10 mL) dried oregano

½ tsp (2 mL) sea salt

pepper

Preheat the oven to 375°F (190°C). Thoroughly grease a 9-inch (23 cm) pie plate (or use a non-stick one).

In a frying pan over medium heat, heat the olive oil and sauté the kale, stirring, for 5 minutes. In a large bowl, mix the green onions with the soy milk, eggs, flour, cheeses, oregano, sea salt and pepper to taste. Pour into the prepared pie plate and bake for 60 to 65 minutes or until a toothpick inserted in the centre comes out clean.

GREEK FETA, KEFALOTIRI
AND KALE BAKE

Gluten-Free-Crust Pizza

C **CA** **CD**　　**M**　　**OA** **RA**　| MAKES | TIME
| 4 servings | 1 hour

A great gluten-free pizza. Italy at its finest.

1¼ cups (310 mL) brown-rice flour

¼ cup (60 mL) tapioca flour

¼ cup (60 mL) bean flour

1 Tbsp (15 mL) baking powder

1 tsp (5 mL) sea salt

1 tsp (5 mL) dried basil

¼ tsp (1 mL) dried parsley

1 egg, beaten

1 Tbsp (15 mL) first cold pressed extra
virgin olive oil

Preheat the oven to 350°F (180°C). Grease a cookie sheet.

Mix together the flours, baking powder, sea salt, basil and parsley in a bowl, and then add the egg and mix well. Add the oil and enough water to make a dough. Mix well. Roll out thinly on the prepared cookie sheet. Bake for 10 minutes.

Top this with pesto sauce.

PESTO SAUCE

¼ cup (60 mL) first cold pressed extra
virgin olive oil

3–4 large garlic cloves, minced

a large handful of fresh basil

1 Tbsp (15 mL) chopped walnuts or
pine nuts

1 Tbsp (15 mL) grated Parmesan cheese
(optional; for **CA** **CD** **M** **RA** use vegan
Parmesan)

sea salt

Place everything in a blender and blend until smooth. Top the pizza with it, covering it right to the edge. Bake for another 5 minutes.

Add your choice of the following toppings:

pickled artichokes, cut up

thin red bell pepper strips
(omit for **RA**)

asparagus tops or broccoli florets

crumbled feta cheese
(omit for **CA** **CD** **RA**)

Bake for about 20 to 25 minutes at 375°F (190°C) or until cooked through.

BARBECUE

Grilled Asparagus

MAKES
4 servings

TIME
about 15 minutes

Lemon + garlic + grilled asparagus = delicious.

2 Tbsp (30 mL) first cold pressed extra virgin
   olive oil

2 Tbsp (30 mL) fresh lemon juice

½ tsp (2 mL) garlic powder

1 large bunch of young tender asparagus, thin tips,
   and tough end parts snapped off

Preheat the barbecue to medium-low.

Mix together the oil, lemon juice and garlic powder in a large bowl. Marinate the asparagus in this for 10 minutes. Barbecue, brushing the asparagus with the marinade as it cooks and flipping the asparagus once or twice. Cook until tender crisp, about 3 to 4 minutes.

Grilled Vegetables

	MAKES	TIME
	4 servings	about 15 minutes

A favourite in our house that gets in some super-healthy cruciferous veggies.

SAUCE

½ cup (125 mL) first cold pressed extra virgin olive oil

3 Tbsp (45 mL) balsamic vinegar

2 Tbsp (30 mL) fresh lemon juice

1 tsp (5 mL) dried oregano

sea salt and pepper (for **HD** use sodium substitute)

VEGGIES

1½ cups (375 mL) broccoli florets, cut long

1½ cups (375 mL) cauliflower florets, cut long

1 small red or white onion, sliced

1 small zucchini, cut in strips

1 medium-size red bell pepper, cut in strips

½ medium-size green bell pepper, cut in strips

½ medium-size yellow bell pepper, cut in strips

¾ cup (185 mL) feta, crumbled (use vegan feta for **CA CD D G MS V**; reduce amount for **C HD M**)

1 large tomato, diced (optional)

Preheat the barbecue to medium.

Mix together the sauce ingredients.

Grill the vegetables for 4 to 5 minutes or until done, brushing with some of the sauce as they cook. Remove from the grill and put back in the leftover sauce. Mix in the feta and the tomato (if using). Eat as is or wrap in whole wheat tortillas.

Grilled Vegetable Sandwich Filling

MAKES 2 servings	TIME 1 hour 25 minutes	

I first had a version of this in Italy. It was delicious and very welcome on a hot day at the beach. Eat as is, or stuff in pita pockets or roll in rice wrappers.

VEGGIES
¼ medium-size eggplant, cubed

2 small portobello mushrooms, medium slices (optional; omit for **CA G**)

1 large cooking onion, sliced

½ large red bell pepper, cut in medium strips

½ large yellow bell pepper, cut in medium strips

¼ small zucchini, medium slices (optional)

1 large tomato, sliced and quartered

MARINADE
3 large garlic cloves, minced

¼ cup (60 mL) first cold pressed extra virgin olive oil

2 Tbsp (30 mL) water

2 Tbsp (30 mL) apple cider vinegar or balsamic vinegar

sea salt and pepper (for **HD** use sodium substitute)

TO SERVE
2–3 Tbsp (30–45 mL) finely grated Parmesan cheese (optional; omit or use vegan Parmesan for **CA CD D G MS V**)

2 Tbsp (30 mL) fresh basil or 2 tsp (10 mL) dried basil

½ cup (125 mL) crumbled feta (optional; omit or use vegan feta for **CA CD D G MS V**)

pita pockets cut in half (optional; for **CD** use rice paper sheets)

Soak the eggplant in salt water for 1 hour (use 1 tsp/5 mL of salt), drain and rinse.

For the marinade, mix together the garlic, olive oil, water, vinegar, and sea salt and pepper to taste. Toss the eggplant, mushrooms, onion, bell peppers and zucchini in the marinade.

Preheat the barbecue to medium.

Remove the veggies from the marinade and grill in a vegetable grilling basket. Brush with the marinade as they cook. Grill, stirring, for 7 to 10 minutes. If you are using fresh basil, Parmesan or feta, add after barbecuing and toss with the veggies. Toss with the tomato and stuff into pita breads (if using).

Simple Kale on the Barbecue

		MAKES 4 servings	TIME 35 to 40 minutes

Enjoy this super-veggie al fresco.

> 2 cups (500 mL) chopped kale (remove any large
> or hard stalks)
>
> 2 Tbsp (30 mL) first cold pressed extra virgin
> olive oil
>
> 2 Tbsp (30 mL) balsamic vinegar
>
> sea salt and pepper (for **HD** use sodium substitute)

Toss the kale in the oil, vinegar, and sea salt and pepper to taste and marinate for about ½ hour.

Preheat the barbecue to medium-low.

Transfer the kale to a regular or non-stick grilling basket and grill, brushing with the remaining marinade and stirring occasionally, for about 5 minutes, or until soft.

Grilled Lemon Eggplant

MAKES	TIME
4 servings	1 hour 15 minutes

In Greece, they often grill on a large, open stone fireplace outside.

1 medium-size eggplant, sliced in ¼-inch-thick
(5 mm rounds)

½ cup (125 mL) first cold pressed extra virgin
olive oil

juice of 2 lemons

1½ tsp (7 mL) dried oregano

salt and pepper (for **HD** use sodium substitute)

feta slices (optional; omit or use vegan feta for **CA**
CD **D** **G** **MS** **V**)

lemon wedges

Soak the eggplant slices in enough hot salted water to cover the eggplant for 1 hour (use 1 tsp/5 mL of salt).

Drain and rinse. Mix together the oil, lemon juice, oregano, and sea salt and pepper to taste.

Preheat the barbecue to medium.

Place the eggplant slices on the grill and brush with the sauce as they cook, flipping them once or twice, with the barbecue lid open, for 7 to 10 minutes. The eggplant is done when soft and easy to cut through. Serve with sliced feta and lemon wedges.

Grilled Portobello Mushrooms

C   **CD** **D**   **HD** **M** **MS** **OA** **RA** **V** | MAKES 4 servings | TIME 55 minutes

This incredible-tasting mushroom dish from Italy will have meat eaters asking for more, thinking that it tastes a little like grilled meat. Serve with lots of salads, all different kinds.

¼ cup (60 mL) first cold pressed extra virgin
   olive oil

3 Tbsp (45 mL) balsamic vinegar

1 Tbsp (15 mL) soy sauce (optional)

1 tsp (5 mL) dried rosemary

chili powder (optional)

sea salt and pepper (for **HD** use sodium substitute)

4 medium-size portobello mushrooms,
   stems removed

Mix together the olive oil, balsamic vinegar, soy sauce (if using), rosemary, chili powder to taste (if using), and sea salt and pepper to taste. Let the mushrooms stand in the marinade for about ½ hour, basting occasionally. Some mushrooms absorb a lot of the marinade, so you might need to make a double batch.

Preheat the barbecue to medium.

Grill the mushrooms on both sides, basting with the marinade, until tender, about 15 to 25 minutes. This will depend on the size and how much marinade they have absorbed.

Grilled Stuffed Red Peppers with Feta

| | MAKES
2 servings | TIME
about 1 hour 5 minutes |

I had a version of this in a yard with grapes hanging down in true Greek style.

- 1⅓ cups (330 mL) brown rice
- 2 large tomatoes, diced
- 1½ cups (375 mL) crumbled feta (for **C** **CA** **CD** **D** **G** **HD** **M** **MS** **V** use vegan feta or other vegan cheese)
- 2 Tbsp (30 mL) first cold pressed extra virgin olive oil
- 1 Tbsp (15 mL) fresh lemon juice
- 1½ tsp (7 mL) dried oregano
- sea salt and pepper
- 2 medium-size red bell peppers, cut in half lengthwise

Preheat the barbecue to medium.

Place the rice in a pot with 4½ cups (1.125 L) of water. Bring to a boil on high heat then reduce the heat to medium-low, cover and cook, stirring occasionally, for about 50 minutes, until tender.

Mix together the cooked brown rice, tomatoes, feta, olive oil, lemon juice, oregano, and sea salt and pepper to taste in a large bowl.

Stuff the peppers with the rice mix and barbecue, with the lid closed, until soft, about 10 minutes. Check to make sure they are not burning.

Grilled Stuffed Red Peppers with Beans and Olives

	MAKES	TIME
	2 servings	15 to 20 minutes

A wonderful Italian treat that is great for company. Sun-dried tomatoes and olives combine very well with the white beans, and when they are stuffed into red peppers and grilled, the result is truly superb.

1 can (19 oz/540 mL) white kidney beans,
   drained and rinsed

12 kalamata olives, pitted

8 sun-dried tomatoes

2 Tbsp (30 mL) first cold pressed extra virgin
   olive oil

sea salt and pepper (for **HD** use sodium substitute)

2 medium-size red bell peppers, cut in
   half lengthwise

Preheat the barbecue to medium.

Blend the beans, olives, tomatoes, olive oil, and sea salt and pepper to taste in a food processor until smooth. Stuff the peppers and grill, with the lid closed, for about 10 minutes or until the peppers are soft and can be easily cut.

Italian-Flavoured Tofu

MAKES
2 servings

TIME
about 15 minutes

A simple, healthy way of preparing tofu.

¼ cup (60 mL) first cold pressed extra virgin
olive oil

3 Tbsp (45 mL) balsamic vinegar

1 tsp (5 mL) dried oregano, basil or thyme, or some
of each

sea salt and pepper (for **HD** use sodium substitute)

1 package (12 oz/350 g) extra-firm tofu, cut into
½-inch (1 cm) slices

Preheat the barbecue to medium-low.

Mix together the olive oil, balsamic vinegar, oregano, and sea salt and pepper to taste. Brush this over the tofu slices as they cook in a regular or non-stick grilling basket, turning occasionally as they cook, about 10 minutes. They should be slightly crispy.

Europe

Recipes

Europe

SO MANY COUNTRIES MAKE UP this region! And there are variations within this region too, of course, and lots of overlapping between culinary traditions. Some countries, like Spain, could be in the Mediterranean region, but I've placed them here.

When I travel in Europe, I often find that, although the guidebooks often promise easy-to-find vegetarian food, it's not always so, especially if you want vegan food.

You will find one or more of rice, potatoes, eggs, cheese and bread in the cooking of pretty much every European country, but these aren't always the healthiest of foods and certainly not always the most inspiring. However, many countries use a variety of vegetables in their cuisine, and there are some dishes that are quite wonderful and classic.

In the British Isles, the potato is ubiquitous, and if you pair it with a vegetable like kale or chard, it can make a tasty and healthy dish, full of super-veggies that are jam-packed with bone-building and immune-system-building nutrients and just about everything else that you need for good health. Scotland even offers a delicious vegan haggis in some places.

In England, you'll find a wealth of Indian and Pakistani foods in addition to jacket potatoes filled with cheese and other goodies. You'll also find vegetable-filled pasties that are quite lovely.

France is a land of many gorgeous salads (but often with cheese in them). And don't forget the crêpes and galettes, and lovely sauces, soufflés and quiches.

Spain offers a wonderful feast for vegetarians, especially with its North African and Mediterranean influences. Its cuisine features saffron, fruit, lemon juice, olive oil, oranges, artichokes (some of the best artichoke dishes I have ever had, in fact), paella (although not traditionally vegetarian it can easily adapted), potato omelettes, gazpacho and chickpea soups.

In Portugal, a North African influence also shows, with spices like cumin often being used. Cabbage, potatoes and greens show up in Portuguese soups. Olives, breads, fruit and vegetables combine to make some wonderful meals, and garlic is especially popular along the coastal region.

In Hungary, fruit and vegetables are sold in mounds in the markets. Paprika flavours many dishes, which tend to be relatively heavy. Bean and split pea soups and other heavy soups make filling meals. Cabbage rolls, latkes and salads made from one or two vegetables often show up. People tend to sit and talk for hours with family and friends about politics or other matters, and people gather in the streets to share a meal or drink or to just talk.

Russia's diet is rich in whole grains, potatoes, cabbage, millet, kasha, hearty dark rye and other breads, beets, parsnips and beans—vegetarian bliss. Typical dishes are borscht, potato or cabbage soup, perogies and eggplant dips, not to mention potato-centred dishes.

Germany offers potato-layered dishes and gorgeous salads filled with beets, asparagus, potatoes (again!) and greens. I had an incredible meal in Hildegard von Bingen's convent, where the nearby herb garden provided flavour for the meals served and an incredible array of vegetables, grains and legumes was turned into a vegetarian's delight. I was there in asparagus season, when white asparagus is featured in many dishes. And the wines in this region, the rieslings, are truly superb. People sit and have a meal in old squares with a glass of wine in their hands, and watch the Mosel or the Rhine go by, as people have done for years, or stare at the magnificent architecture.

Switzerland is home of the potato pancake dish rösti, and also the classic cheese fondue.

In Belgium, I had some of the best french fries I have ever had: of course, Belgium is thought by some to be the original home of the french fry. And they make excellent beers too.

Scandinavia offers the vegetarian a delicious array of breads, butter, cheeses and smörgåsborg-type meals.

Potatoes in Mustard-Tarragon Sauce

MAKES
4 servings

TIME
about 1 hour

The cranberry flavour gives these potatoes a unique taste. The mustard really reminds me of France. You'll need a clay ovenproof dish for this one.

10–12 mini red potatoes, skin on, halved

½ medium-size yam, skin on, diced

¼–½ cup (60–125 mL) orange juice or water (for **CA** use water)

2 Tbsp (30 mL) first cold pressed extra virgin olive oil

2 tsp (10 mL) dairy-free nonhydrogenated margarine

1½ tsp (7 mL) Dijon mustard

5 drops hot sauce

1 heaping Tbsp (15 mL) frozen cranberries

1 tsp (5 mL) dried tarragon

½ tsp (2 mL) ground cinnamon

Preheat the oven to 350°F (180°C).

In a large clay ovenproof dish, place the potatoes and yam. Mix together the juice or water, oil, margarine, mustard, hot sauce, cranberries, tarragon and cinnamon and add to the clay pot. Cover and bake for 45 minutes to 1 hour, adding more water if it starts to dry out. It should be tender. Uncover during the last few minutes of cooking and broil for a couple of minutes.

Mushrooms and Scalloped Potatoes

C | MAKES | TIME |
| 4 servings | 1 hour 30 minutes |

Portobellos give a classic English dish a twist.

4 large potatoes, peeled and thinly sliced

4 small onions, thinly sliced

3 cups (750 mL) portobello mushrooms, thinly
   sliced, gills intact

sea salt and pepper (for **HD** use sodium substitute)

1 tsp (5 mL) dried thyme

3–4 cups (750 mL–1 L) soy milk (start with
   3 cups/750 mL and add more if the potatoes
   get dry as they cook)

1 can (10 oz/284 mL) condensed cream of
   mushroom soup

Preheat the oven to 400°F (200°C).

Place the ingredients in a large ovenproof dish in the order listed, and then mix together and cover. Bake for 1 to 1 ½ hours, until the onions are tender. Check the liquid level at the 1-hour point and add more if necessary.

Potato Bake

 **C** **CA** **CD** | **G** | **M** | **OA**

MAKES	TIME
4 servings	about 1 hour

A great dish from England that kids love for its comfort food factor, and it slips in a healthy cruciferous veggie—kale.

2–3 cups (500–750 mL) chopped baby kale

3–4 large red potatoes, peeled and grated

1 large white onion, grated

1 small yam, peeled and grated

2 eggs, beaten

1 cup (250 mL) soy milk

sea salt and pepper

1 cup (250 mL) grated aged or medium cheddar
   cheese (for **C** **CA** **CD** **G** **M** use vegan cheese)

½ cup (125 mL) grated Parmesan cheese
   (for **CA** **CD** **G** use vegan Parmesan)

Preheat the oven to 350°F (180°C). Thoroughly grease an ovenproof dish big enough to hold all the ingredients.

Place everything in the prepared dish and mix well to combine. Sprinkle some more Parmesan overtop, cover and bake for 45 minutes to 1 hour, or until a toothpick inserted in the centre comes out clean. Uncover during the last 15 minutes of baking to let it turn a little golden on top.

Bean and Cabbage Salad

      | MAKES
4 servings | TIME
25 minutes

This Eastern European dish is a wonderful way of getting in a healthy cruciferous vegetable.

1 can (19 oz/540 mL) red kidney beans, drained
  and rinsed
4 cups (1 L) chopped green cabbage
1 small white onion, diced
3 Tbsp (45 mL) olive oil or flaxseed oil
1 Tbsp (15 mL) balsamic vinegar
1 tsp (5 mL) prepared yellow mustard
sea salt and pepper (for HD use sodium substitute)

Place everything in a large bowl, mix well and let stand for 20 minutes. Serve at room temperature.

Rich Split Pea Soup

C CA CD D G HD M MS OA RA V

MAKES	TIME
4 servings	1 hour 30 minutes

A hearty, delicious pea soup. Eastern Europe is known for hearty soups that are almost meals in themselves. Serve this with some crusty whole-grain bread and a salad.

1½ tsp (7 mL) dairy-free nonhydrogenated margarine

1 tsp (5 mL) first cold pressed extra virgin olive oil

2 large cooking onions, chopped

2 sticks celery, sliced

2 medium carrots, sliced

1¼ cups (310 mL) dried yellow split peas, washed

9–10 cups (2.25–2.5 L) water

2 chicken-flavoured vegetarian stock cubes

sea salt and pepper (for **HD** use sodium substitute)

10 green beans, finely chopped

In a large soup pot over medium heat, heat the margarine and oil and sauté the onion, stirring, for about 20 minutes. Then add the celery, carrots and split peas, followed by the water, chicken-flavoured stock cubes, and sea salt and pepper to taste. Bring to a boil then reduce the heat to medium and cook, covered, for about 1 hour or until everything is tender. Add the beans during the last 10 minutes of cooking.

Green Split Pea Soup

MAKES	TIME
4 servings	1 hour 15 minutes

Healthier than the traditional Eastern European version, this uses olive oil rather than saturated fats and adds red chard, a super-veggie.

2 Tbsp (30 mL) first cold pressed extra virgin olive oil

1 large cooking onion, chopped

3 large garlic cloves, minced

2 medium potatoes, peeled and diced

1 small yam, peeled and diced

2 cups (500 mL) dried green split peas, washed

pinch of dried marjoram

pinch of dried sage

pinch of dried thyme

1 bay leaf

8 cups (2 L) vegetable stock

2 large leaves red chard, chopped

2 sprigs fresh parsley

1 Tbsp (15 mL) fresh dill, finely chopped

sea salt and pepper (for **HD** use sodium substitute)

In a large soup pot on medium heat, heat the oil and sauté the onion, stirring, for 5 minutes. Add the garlic, potatoes and yam, and sauté, stirring, for a few minutes. Add the split peas, marjoram, sage, thyme and bay leaf, then the stock. Bring to a boil. Reduce the heat to medium-low and simmer, covered, for about 1 hour, stirring from time to time. Add the chard, parsley, dill, and sea salt and pepper to taste and cook for a few minutes. Remove the bay leaf, and purée and heat through before serving.

Split Pea Soup

MAKES	TIME
4 servings	2 hours

A hearty, filling soup from Eastern Europe that's a meal in itself. Serve with a green salad.

1 Tbsp (15 mL) first cold pressed extra virgin olive oil

1 large cooking onion, diced

3 cups (750 mL) chopped green cabbage

1 small red bell pepper, bite-size pieces (optional; omit for **RA**)

3 medium sticks celery, sliced

2 large carrots, sliced

1 small zucchini, skin on, sliced

12 cups (3 L) vegetable stock

1½ cups (375 mL) dried yellow split peas, washed

¾ cup (185 mL) pearl barley (for **CD** use brown rice)

1 Tbsp (15 mL) soy sauce

pepper

In a large soup pot on medium heat, heat the oil and sauté the onion, stirring, until tender. Add the cabbage and bell pepper and sauté, stirring, for 3 minutes. Add the celery, carrots and zucchini and sauté for 1 minute, stirring. Add the stock, split peas, barley and soy sauce and bring to a boil. Reduce the heat to medium-low and cook, covered, stirring occasionally, for about 1 ½ hours, or until the peas and barley are tender. Add more stock if necessary as the soup cooks.

Yellow Split Pea and Celeriac Soup

MAKES
4 servings

TIME
1 hour 25 minutes

A well-flavoured, rich-tasting pea soup with a twist on the original Eastern European recipe thanks to the celeriac.

1 Tbsp (15 mL) dairy-free
   nonhydrogenated margarine

1 very large white onion, diced

1 large potato, red or white, peeled and diced

1 large carrot, diced

1 medium-size celeriac, peeled and diced

1 cup (250 mL) dried yellow split peas, washed

12 cups (3 L) vegetable stock

pepper

In a large soup pot on medium heat, heat the margarine and sauté the onion, stirring, for about 20 minutes. Add the potato, carrot and celeriac and sauté for 1 minute. Add the split peas and then the stock and bring to a boil. Reduce the heat to medium-low and cook, covered, for about 1 hour. Stir now and then, adding more stock as needed as the soup cooks. Add pepper to taste, and purée and heat through before serving.

Hungarian Lentil Soup

MAKES	TIME
4 servings	1 hour 20 minutes

A warm, filling meal that tastes of Hungary. Most people from Hungary don't really feel that a meal is complete without soup to start.

2 Tbsp (30 mL) first cold pressed extra virgin olive oil

2 large white onions, diced

3–4 large red bell peppers, chopped

3 large garlic cloves, peeled and chopped

1½ cups (375 mL) dried red lentils, washed

12 cups (3 L) vegetable stock, onion-flavour is best

3–4 Tbsp (45–60 mL) medium-hot paprika, or more to taste

pepper

1 tsp (5 mL) dairy-free nonhydrogenated margarine

In a large soup pot on medium heat, heat the oil and sauté the onions, stirring, for 10 minutes. Add the peppers and sauté for 5 minutes, stirring. Add the garlic then the lentils and stir for 1 minute. Add the stock, paprika and pepper to taste, and bring to a boil. Reduce the heat to medium-low and cook, covered, for about 1 hour, stirring from time to time. Add the margarine, and purée and heat through before serving.

Red Lentil and Rice Soup

MAKES	TIME
4 servings	1 hour 30 minutes

A filling, delicious soup from Hungary that just needs a mixed green salad to make a complete meal.

1 Tbsp (15 mL) first cold pressed extra virgin olive oil

1 large white onion, diced

6 large garlic cloves, minced

2 small red bell peppers—the long thin ones, diced

1 medium-size fresh hot red chili, diced, with seeds

1½ cups (375 mL) dried red lentils, washed

½ cup (125 mL) brown rice

12 cups (3 L) vegetable stock

1 cup (250 mL) spaghetti sauce

1 Tbsp (15 mL) medium-hot paprika

sea salt and pepper (for **HD** use sodium substitute)

In a large soup pot on medium heat, heat the oil and sauté the onion, stirring, for about 20 minutes. Add a little water if necessary to prevent sticking. Add the garlic, peppers and chili and sauté for 1 minute. Add the lentils and rice and then the stock. Bring to a boil, stirring, and then reduce the heat to a low simmer and cook, covered, stirring now and then, for about 1 hour. Add more stock if needed. Add the spaghetti sauce, paprika, and sea salt and pepper to taste and cook for about 10 minutes to blend the flavours.

Yam and Cabbage Soup

      V

MAKES	TIME
4 servings	about 3 hours

A rich, warming soup from Eastern Europe that makes the most of fall produce.

1 Tbsp (15 mL) first cold pressed extra virgin olive oil

2 large cooking onions, diced

12 large button mushrooms, quartered (optional; omit for **CA** **G**)

3 cups (750 mL) chopped green cabbage

1 small beet and leaves, skin on, diced

1 medium yam, skin on, diced

½ yellow bell pepper, diced

⅛ turnip, peeled and finely chopped

10 cups (2.5 L) vegetable stock

1½ cups (375 mL) diced canned tomatoes, with juice (optional)

1½ cups (375 mL) spaghetti sauce

2½ tsp (12 mL) dried dill

1 tsp (5 mL) medium-hot paprika

sea salt and pepper (for **HD** use sodium substitute)

In a large soup pot on medium heat, heat the olive oil and sauté the onions, stirring, for about 10 minutes. Add the mushrooms, cabbage, beet, yam, bell pepper and turnip, and sauté for a few minutes, stirring. Add the stock. Cover, bring to a boil then reduce the heat to medium-low and simmer, stirring now and then, for about 2 hours. Add the tomatoes with their juice (if using), spaghetti sauce, dill, paprika, and sea salt and pepper to taste. Cook, covered, for about ½ hour, stirring now and then.

Collard and Potato Soup

V | MAKES **4 servings** | TIME **1 hour**

A superb and tasty way of eating collard greens, a super-veggie. And it makes use of what England uses most—the potato.

2 Tbsp + 1 tsp (30 mL + 5 mL) dairy-free nonhydrogenated margarine, divided

2 large cooking onions, diced

2 large garlic cloves, minced

10–12 cups (2.5–3 L) vegetarian chicken-flavour stock

3–4 very large white potatoes, peeled and chopped

1 large bunch collard greens, chopped

sea salt and pepper (for **HD** use sodium substitute)

In a large soup pot, heat 2 Tbsp (30 mL) margarine on medium heat and sauté the onions, stirring, for about 25 minutes. Add the garlic and sauté for 1 minute, stirring. Add the stock and potatoes and bring to a boil. Reduce the heat to medium-low and cook, covered, stirring now and then, for about 30 minutes. Meanwhile, steam the collard greens in a steamer basket in another pot until they are soft. Add to the soup. Add 1 tsp (5 mL) margarine, and sea salt and pepper to taste and heat through. Purée and heat through before serving.

Cold Cherry Soup

		MAKES	TIME
		4 servings	40 minutes

Loaded with antioxidants and great for anyone with arthritis or gout. This Hungarian soup loses its alcohol content when heated.

two ½-inch (1 cm) pieces of kudzu root

2 cups (500 mL) red wine

2 cups (500 mL) stoned red cherries

soy sour cream (optional)

Heat the pieces of kudzu root in the red wine for a few minutes until it's dissolved and thickened. Allow to cool then transfer to a blender with the cherries. Blend well, thinning with more wine if desired. Chill and serve with a little soy sour cream swirled in it if desired.

Hungarian Stew

MAKES	TIME
4 servings	3 hours 30 minutes

A delicious, rich, filling stew with paprika, which is of course used in many Hungarian dishes. Serve over pasta.

3 Tbsp (45 mL) first cold pressed extra virgin olive oil

2 large cooking onions, chopped

4 large garlic cloves, minced

1 small green banana pepper, diced

1 medium-size red bell pepper, bite-size pieces

1 small yam, peeled and diced

10 medium-size button mushrooms, chopped

8–10 cups (2–2.5 L) water

½ cup (125 mL) dried navy beans, washed

4 mini red potatoes, diced

1-inch (2.5 cm) piece dried kombu

1¾ tsp (8 mL) medium-hot paprika

sea salt and pepper (for **HD** use sodium substitute)

½ small zucchini, skin on, sliced in rounds

1 can (5.5 oz/156 mL) tomato paste

In a large soup pot, heat the olive oil and sauté the onions on medium heat, stirring, for about 20 minutes. Add the garlic, both peppers, yam and mushrooms, and sauté, stirring, for about 5 minutes. Add the water, navy beans, potatoes, kombu, paprika, and sea salt and pepper to taste and bring to a boil. Cover, reduce the heat to medium-low and simmer, stirring, for 2 ½ to 3 hours, or until the beans are tender. Add more water if necessary. Add the zucchini during the last 15 minutes of cooking time. Add the tomato paste and heat through for 5 minutes before serving.

Cabbage and White Beans

MAKES | 4 servings | TIME | 3 hours 30 minutes to 4 hours

A hearty peasant-style dish from Eastern Europe with the extremely healthy cabbage as the star.

- 1 cup (250 mL) dried white beans, washed
- 2 Tbsp (30 mL) first cold pressed extra virgin olive oil, divided
- 1 large cooking onion, diced
- 2 cups (500 mL) chopped green cabbage
- 1 can (28 oz/796 mL) diced tomatoes, with juice
- 1 Tbsp (15 mL) soy sauce
- 1 tsp (5 mL) chili flakes, or 2 tsp (10 mL) dried thyme
- sea salt and pepper (for **HD** use sodium substitute)

Place the beans and 1 Tbsp (15 mL) of the olive oil in a pot with 8 cups (2 L) of water. Bring to a boil, then reduce the heat to medium-low, cover and cook, stirring occasionally, for about 3 ½ hours or until the beans are soft. Add more water if necessary. Drain, reserving 1 cup (250 mL) of the cooking liquid, and set aside.

In a frying pan on medium heat, heat the remaining 1 Tbsp (15 mL) olive oil and sauté the onion, stirring, for about 25 minutes. Add the cabbage and sauté for 5 minutes, stirring. Add the beans with the reserved cooking liquid. Cook for about 5 minutes, stirring. Add the tomatoes with their juice, soy sauce, chili flakes, and sea salt and pepper to taste, and cook for 10 minutes, stirring.

Oregano-Flavoured Black Beans in Red Cabbage

	MAKES	TIME
	4 servings	35 minutes

A rich, filling dish from Portugal. Cabbage shows up in a lot of vegetarian dishes in Portugal, and that is mostly what I ate when I was there. But it tends to be a softer, lacier cabbage than we have here, which makes the dishes a little lighter and more delicately flavoured.

1 Tbsp (15 mL) first cold pressed extra virgin olive oil

1 large red onion, chopped roughly

5 cups (1.25 L) chopped red cabbage

1 can (19 oz/540 mL) black beans, drained and rinsed

2 cups (500 mL) water

1 can (5.5 oz/156 mL) tomato paste

2 tsp (10 mL) dried oregano

sea salt and pepper (for **HD** use sodium substitute)

In a large frying pan on medium heat, heat the oil and sauté the onion, stirring, for 10 minutes. Add the cabbage and sauté for 10 minutes, stirring. Add the black beans, water, tomato paste, oregano, and sea salt and pepper to taste and cook, stirring, for 10 minutes.

Sage and Brandy-Flavoured Baked Beans and Savoy Cabbage

MAKES
4 servings

TIME
50 minutes

A hearty, peasant-type dish from Eastern Europe, rich in vitamin C–packed cabbage. Serve hot with good crusty bread and a salad.

1 Tbsp (15 mL) first cold pressed extra virgin olive oil

1 large white onion, chopped

4 cups (1 L) chopped Savoy cabbage

½ cup (125 mL) brandy or cooking sherry

1 can (14 oz/398 mL) vegetarian baked beans

¼ tsp (1 mL) chili flakes

1 can (5.5 oz/156 mL) tomato paste

2 Tbsp (30 mL) soy sauce

1 tsp (5 mL) dried sage

pepper

In a large frying pan on medium heat, heat the oil and sauté the onion, stirring frequently, until soft and translucent, about 25 minutes. Add the cabbage and brandy and cook for 5 minutes. Add the beans and then fill the empty can with water, add the water to the frying pan and cook for 2 minutes. Add the chili flakes, tomato paste, soy sauce, sage and pepper to taste and cook for 15 minutes, stirring.

Beans with Cooked Cornmeal and Cabbage

MAKES	TIME
4 servings	45 minutes to 1 hour

This stew comes from Hungary where paprika is heavily used. Unlike many Eastern European dishes, though, it's healthy, without all the bad fats. The beans and veggies make it a heart-healthy, immune-system-boosting dish.

1 Tbsp (15 mL) first cold pressed extra virgin olive oil

1 large white onion, diced

3 large garlic cloves, minced

1 red bell pepper, bite-size pieces

½ small green cabbage, chopped roughly

1 can (28 oz/796 mL) diced tomatoes, with juice

1 can (19 oz/540 mL) red kidney beans, drained and rinsed

1 tsp (5 mL) medium-hot paprika

pepper

½ cup (125 mL) stone-ground raw cornmeal

In a large frying pan, heat the oil on medium-low heat and sauté the onion, stirring. After 10 minutes, add the garlic and bell pepper and cook, stirring, for about 2 minutes. Add the cabbage and cook, stirring, for about 10 minutes. Add the tomatoes with their juice, beans, paprika (add more to taste) and lots of pepper to taste, and cook, covered, stirring now and then, for about 15 minutes.

Meanwhile, cook the cornmeal according to the package instructions. Spoon some cornmeal into bowls, and spoon some of the stew overtop.

White Bean and Barley Stew

MAKES	TIME
4 servings	about 4 hours

A hearty, filling stew that you just pop in the oven and let cook while it fills your house with the smell of the kitchens of Eastern Europe.

8 cups (2 L) water

1 cup (250 mL) whole-grain barley

½ cup (125 mL) dried navy beans, washed

¼ cup (60 mL) first cold pressed extra virgin olive oil

20 baby carrots, chopped

2 large cooking onions, chopped

2 sliced button mushrooms (optional; omit for **CA**)

1 chicken-flavoured vegetarian stock cube

2 tsp (10 mL) dried thyme

sea salt and pepper (for **HD** use sodium substitute)

Preheat the oven to 375°F (190°C).

In a large ovenproof dish that holds at least 12 cups (3 L), place all the ingredients. Cover and cook for about 4 hours, or until the beans are soft, checking the water level as it cooks and adding more if necessary.

Barley and Lentil Casserole

MAKES	TIME
4 servings	2 hours 30 minutes

A wonderful dill-infused casserole from Eastern Europe. Just serve with a green a salad or steamed greens. Do try to use a clay dish if possible. It adds to the final flavour.

1¼ cups (310 mL) whole-grain barley

¾ cup (185 mL) dried green lentils, washed

3–4 red chard leaves, cut up

1 large cooking onion, chopped

1 large red potato, skin on, diced (optional; omit for **RA**)

½ medium-size celeriac, peeled and diced

5 dried dates, pitted

1 vegetable stock cube

1 tsp (5 mL) dried dill

1 tsp (5 mL) first cold pressed extra virgin olive oil

pepper

Preheat the oven to 375°F (190°C).

Place everything in a large ovenproof clay dish and cover with approximately 6 cups (1.5 L) of water. Cover and bake for about 2 ½ hours, or until tender. Check every ½ hour, and add more water if it is drying out. When it is done, it should be juicy but not soup-like.

Hungarian Spicy Stew

        **V**   MAKES
4 servings   TIME
1 hour 40 minutes

Serve this filling paprika-infused gluten-free stew over sweet brown rice.

3 Tbsp (45 mL) first cold pressed extra virgin
   olive oil

2 large white onions, chopped

3 large garlic cloves, minced

1 large yellow bell pepper, chopped

1 large red bell pepper, chopped

3 cups (750 mL) water

1 cup (250 mL) dried red lentils, washed

1-inch (2.5 cm) piece dried kombu

1 cup (250 mL) spaghetti sauce

2 ½ Tbsp (37 mL) medium-hot paprika

sea salt and pepper (for **HD** use sodium substitute)

In a large pot, heat the oil on medium heat and sauté the onions, stirring, for 10 to 15 minutes. Add the garlic and bell peppers and sauté, stirring, for about 4 minutes. Add the water, lentils and kombu. Cover and bring to a boil, then reduce the heat to medium-low and cook for 1 hour. Add more water if necessary as it cooks, and stir from time to time. It should be juicy but not swimming in liquid. If it is, uncover during the last few minutes of cooking, and boil the excess liquid away.

Add the spaghetti sauce, paprika, and sea salt and pepper to taste and cook for 15 minutes, covered, stirring occasionally.

Kasha

MAKES	TIME
4 servings	30 minutes

A traditional Jewish dish from Russia that my mom loved. The thyme is my addition—it's a good source of antioxidants—and buckwheat is a gluten-free grain, so it's great for celiacs.

1½ cups (375 mL) uncooked kasha (buckwheat)

1–2 Tbsp (15–30 mL) dairy-free nonhydrogenated margarine, or first cold pressed extra virgin olive oil

2 large white onions, diced

4 cups (1 L) sliced button or fresh shiitake mushrooms (for **CA** use shiitake)

1 cup (250 mL) vegetable stock

1 tsp (5 mL) dried thyme

sea salt and pepper (for **HD** use sodium substitute)

Place the kasha in a pot with 3 cups (750 mL) water. Bring to a boil on high heat. Reduce the heat to medium-low and cook, covered, for about 15 minutes or until tender.

In a large frying pan, heat the margarine on medium heat and sauté the onions, stirring, for about 15 minutes. Add the mushrooms and sauté for about 7 minutes. Add the cooked kasha, stock, thyme, and sea salt and pepper to taste. Cook, stirring, for about 5 minutes.

Oatmeal, Flax and Celery Burgers

MAKES	TIME
4 servings	30 minutes

A healthy version of a burger with super-healthy flaxseeds, a rich source of essential fatty acids. It tastes good too. And, of course, oats play a huge part in the traditional Scottish diet. Serve with Dijon mustard and pickles, in or not in buns. You can also serve this with sliced tomato, lettuce leaves or pieces of chard leaves and sprouts.

> 2 cups (500 mL) quick-cooking oats
> 3 eggs
> 2 medium sticks celery, finely chopped
> 3 Tbsp (45 mL) flaxseeds
> 1 Tbsp (15 mL) dried thyme
> sea salt and pepper
> first cold pressed extra virgin olive oil for cooking
> 2 cups (500 mL) vegetable stock

In a food processor, blend the oats with the eggs, celery, flaxseeds, thyme, and sea salt and pepper to taste.

Over medium-high heat, place a little oil into each of two or three hot frying pans. Using your hands, form patties, using 2 to 3 Tbsp (30–45 mL) of the mixture. Brown on both sides. Pour vegetable stock over the patties and cook on each side for about 5 minutes or until the liquid is absorbed.

Buckwheat Mushroom Crêpes (Galettes)

C **CD** **M** **OA**

MAKES	TIME
4–6 servings	25 to 30 minutes

This dish is served all over the Brittany region of France. The red wine makes it smell and taste wonderful—and it contains some antioxidants.

FILLING

1 tsp (5 mL) butter, or dairy-free nonhydrogenated margarine (for **CD** **M** use margarine)

4 cups (1 L) mix of cremini, button and chanterelle mushrooms, sliced

1 large clove garlic, minced

3 Tbsp (45 mL) red wine

1 tsp (5 mL) dried thyme

sea salt

dash of vegan Worcestershire sauce (for **CD** use gluten-free Worcestershire)

BATTER

2 eggs, beaten

1¼ cups (310 mL) soy milk

1¾ cups (435 mL) buckwheat flour

1 tsp (5 mL) vanilla extract

sea salt

For the filling, in a large frying pan, heat the margarine or butter on medium heat and cook the mushrooms, stirring, for 5 to 7 minutes. Add the garlic and cook, stirring, for 1 minute. Add the red wine, thyme, sea salt to taste and a dash of Worcestershire sauce and cook for 2 minutes.

For the batter, mix the eggs and milk with the flour, vanilla and a pinch of sea salt in a large bowl. Beat until smooth. Lightly oil a large frying pan over medium heat. Pour a thin, even layer of the batter in the pan, and cook on one side until bubbles form, and then gently turn over and cook the other side, about 2 minutes on each side. Continue until you've used all the batter—you should have 6 to 7 crêpes. Fill each one with some of the filling and roll to eat.

Mushroom and Onion Crêpes (Galettes)

	MAKES	TIME
	4 servings	40 to 45 minutes

A wonderfully nutty-tasting crêpe, called a galette, from Brittany. In France, they traditionally serve this with a fried egg and salad right on top. Use whole-grain buckwheat flour for a healthier version.

FILLING

2 tsp (10 mL) butter
(for **C** **CD** **M** **MS** use dairy-free nonhydrogenated margarine)

2 medium-size white onions, chopped

4 cups (1 L) sliced button mushrooms or mixed mushrooms

1 tsp (5 mL) dried thyme

sea salt and pepper

pinch of dried savory

BATTER

2 eggs, beaten

1¼ cups (310 mL) 2% milk (for **C** **CD** **M** **MS** use soy or other vegan milk)

¾ cup + 2 Tbsp (215 mL) buckwheat flour

¼ tsp (1 mL) sea salt

first cold pressed extra virgin olive oil

For the filling, in a large frying pan on medium heat, warm the butter and sauté the onions, stirring, for about 15 minutes. Add the mushrooms and cook, stirring, for about 15 minutes. Add the thyme, sea salt and pepper to taste and a pinch of savory. Cook for 1 minute. Remove from the heat.

For the batter, in a large bowl, mix together the eggs, milk, buckwheat flour and sea salt. Lightly oil a clean frying pan over medium heat. Pour a very thin layer of batter evenly into the pan. Allow to cook on one side, until bubbles form on the top, and then gently flip it over to cook on the other side, about 2 minutes on each side. Continue until you've used all the batter. This should make 4 crêpes. Fill each with some of the mushroom mix and fold over to eat.

MUSHROOM
AND ONION
CRÊPES
(GALETTES)

Vegetables with Rice

C **CA** **CD** **D** **G** **HD** **M** **MS** **OA**   **V**   MAKES 4 servings | TIME 1 hour

A colourful, filling dish that I first had in a tiny little mountain village in Spain called Cazorla. I went into a restaurant asking for vegetarian food, and the woman took me into her kitchen and showed me a veritable feast. And it was all vegetarian. I could not believe my good luck. Here is a version of one of the dishes.

1 cup (250 mL) brown rice

2 Tbsp (30 mL) first cold pressed extra virgin olive oil

1 large white onion, chopped

3 large portobello mushrooms, sliced (optional; omit for **CA** **G**)

1 large red bell pepper, chopped

1 large yellow bell pepper, chopped

10 pickled artichokes, quartered

2 large tomatoes, diced

sea salt and pepper (for **HD** use sodium substitute)

Put the rice in a pot with 3 ¼ cups (810 mL) of water. Bring to a boil on high heat. Reduce the heat to medium-low and cover. Cook, stirring occasionally for about 50 minutes or until tender.

Meanwhile, in a frying pan on medium heat, heat the oil and sauté the onion, stirring, for about 10 minutes. Add the mushrooms and peppers and cook, stirring, for 5 or 6 minutes. Add the artichokes and tomatoes and cook for about 5 minutes. Add the cooked rice and sea salt and pepper to taste, and heat through for a few minutes.

Chanterelle Mushroom Sauce for Pasta

	MAKES	TIME
	4 servings	20 minutes

There is nothing like eating fresh chanterelle mushrooms you picked during a walk in the woods. But if you are not lucky enough to have that experience, you can still enjoy them fresh from the grocery store. They truly make this French pasta dish, so try not to substitute them. Red wine contains antioxidants and adds to the nutritional benefits. Serve over whole wheat or gluten-free pasta.

1–2 Tbsp (15–30 mL) dairy-free nonhydrogenated margarine

2–3 cups (500–750 mL) chanterelle mushrooms, sliced (the more, the better)

3 large garlic cloves, minced

1 cup (250 mL) red wine

sea salt and pepper (for **HD** use sodium substitute)

In a large frying pan, heat the margarine on medium-low heat, and sauté the mushrooms and garlic, stirring, for about 5 minutes. Slowly add the wine and cook, covered, stirring occasionally, for about 10 minutes. Add sea salt and pepper to taste and mix well.

Paprika Noodles with Vegetables

C

MAKES	TIME
4 servings	about 45 minutes

A wonderfully scented, filling noodle dish from Hungary that's full of antioxidant-rich herbs and vegetables.

½ lb (250 g) egg noodles (for **HD** **MS** use brown-rice fettuccini noodles)

2 Tbsp (30 mL) dairy-free nonhydrogenated margarine

4 large garlic cloves, minced

4 cups (1 L) button mushrooms, sliced

1 very small zucchini, skin on, sliced

1 cup (250 mL) canned chickpeas, drained and rinsed

1½–2 Tbsp (22–30 mL) medium-hot paprika

1 tsp (5 mL) dried basil

1 tsp (5 mL) dried thyme

pepper

2 cups (500 mL) chopped fresh spinach

1 cup (250 mL) spaghetti sauce

vegan Parmesan, grated (optional)

Cook the egg noodles according to the package instructions.

In a frying pan on medium heat, heat the margarine and sauté the garlic with the mushrooms, zucchini, chickpeas, paprika, basil, thyme and pepper to taste, stirring, for about 10 minutes. Add the spinach and cook for 2 minutes.

Preheat the oven to 350°F (180°C).

Place the cooked egg noodles in an ovenproof dish and cover with the spaghetti sauce. Sprinkle with vegan Parmesan cheese, if using, and cover with the vegetables. Cover and bake for 20 to 25 minutes.

India

Recipes

India

INDIA IS A VEGETARIAN HAVEN. Nutritious vegetarian food is easy to find all across the country. The dals, curries, rices, breads and appetizers offer an exciting array of choice. Although some of the food tends to be spicy, there are also mild options, and the spicy dishes can be toned down to suit pretty much anyone's taste. If you need something to tone down the spice, you can mix some plain yoghurt or soy yoghurt with either sliced cucumber or lettuce to make raita, which will clean and cool your palate when eaten by the small spoonful.

I personally love the spicy, well-flavoured dishes from this country. Indian cuisine uses herbs and spices like cinnamon, cardamom, ginger, turmeric, clove, fennel, fenugreek, cumin, coriander, chili and cayenne, and spice blends like masala and curry powder. You can find these in Indian markets as well as most grocery stores. I've heard that some dishes contain up to 53 spices, and each chef will specially design his or her own unique blend. When I use a curry powder, I try to find the best ones from Indian markets that have a nice, sweet, rounded taste behind the hot spicy taste. These blends can be mild or hot, and when you make your own, you can vary the spiciness by adding more or less cayenne pepper, chilies or chili powder. If you have celiac disease and are buying curry powder, make sure there is no gluten hidden in it.

Other common ingredients used in India are lentils, chickpeas, split peas, kidney beans (and other beans), rice, wheat and a variety of vegetables. The farther south you go, the more rice is used and the spicier the food tends to be. Apparently spicier food cools you off in the heat, and spices help keep the food from spoiling. Drinks often feature fruit and fruit is sometimes offered after meals.

India is a country of colour—brilliant yellows, reds and earth colours—and the colours show up in the cooking. A full meal usually comprises breads and/or a rice dish, two or three vegetable curries, raita, mango-type pickles, sauces like hot sauce or tamarind sauce, soups and, often, dessert. Everything tends to be placed on the table all at once, and everyone digs in with their hands, using the bread to pick up the food, although forks and spoons are used as needed. It is truly a sensuous experience: taste, touch, smell and sight.

Spicy Potatoes

MAKES
4 servings

TIME
about 1 hour

India is famous for transforming plain, boring potatoes into something delicious. This can also be a main dish if you double the recipe. Serve this hot with mango pickle, raw veggies and Indian bread and/or with other Indian dishes.

4 large potatoes, peeled and quartered

2 Tbsp (30 mL) dairy-free nonhydrogenated margarine

2 large cooking onions, roughly chopped

2 fresh jalapeño peppers, diced, with seeds

2 tsp (10 mL) ground cumin

sea salt and pepper (for **HD** use sodium substitute)

In a pot, boil the potatoes on medium heat until tender, about 20 minutes. Reserve 1 ½ cups (375 mL) of the cooking water. Allow the potatoes to cool, and then cut into bite-size pieces.

In a frying pan, heat the margarine and sauté the onions on low heat, stirring often, for 25 to 30 minutes, until soft. Add a little water if they start to stick. Add the jalapeño peppers and sauté for 4 to 5 minutes, stirring often. Add the cumin and sea salt and pepper to taste, and sauté for 2 to 3 minutes, stirring often. Add the potatoes and reserved cooking water, and cook, stirring, for 5 more minutes.

Indian Potatoes

C **CA** **CD** **D** **G** **HD** **M** **MS** **OA** **V** | MAKES **4 servings** | TIME **40 minutes**

There are endless variations of this classic dish. This is mine. Eat with greens.

1 Tbsp (15 mL) first cold pressed extra virgin olive oil or dairy-free nonhydrogenated margarine

1 large cooking onion, chopped

3 large red potatoes, skin on or peeled, chopped roughly

1–2 fresh hot green chilies, diced, with seeds

1 Tbsp (15 mL) black mustard seeds

1 tsp (5 mL) curry powder

1 tsp (5 mL) ground cumin

1 tsp (5 mL) ground coriander

¼ tsp (1 mL) chili flakes

3 cups (750 mL) water

1 Tbsp (15 mL) fresh lemon juice

In a large frying pan over medium heat, heat the oil and sauté the onion, stirring, for 20 minutes. Add the potatoes, chilies, mustard seeds, curry powder, cumin, coriander and chili flakes and cook, stirring, for 1 minute. Add the water, cover and cook for about 15 minutes or until the potatoes are cooked, stirring occasionally. Add the lemon juice and heat through before serving.

Curried Long Green Beans, Potatoes and Peas

C   **HD** **M**   **OA**   MAKES | TIME
4 servings | 30 minutes

The long green beans make this authentic. Use Indian cheese (paneer) to continue the authenticity, or add an international touch with brie or mozzarella. Serve with chapattis.

2–3 Tbsp (30–45 mL) first cold pressed extra virgin olive oil

3–4 medium potatoes, peeled and diced

8–10 long green beans, cut into 1-inch (2.5 cm) pieces

2 dried red chilies, crushed

1 Tbsp (15 mL) curry powder

1 can (28 oz/796 mL) well-chopped tomatoes, with juice

1 cup (250 mL) frozen peas

½ cup (125 mL) cubed soft white cheese

sea salt and pepper (for **HD** use sodium substitute)

Place the olive oil in a frying pan over medium heat and sauté the potatoes for about 10 minutes, stirring. Add the beans, dried chilies and curry powder. Sauté for 3 to 5 minutes. Add the tomatoes with their juice and cook, covered, for 10 minutes, stirring occasionally. Add the peas and cheese and cook for 4 to 5 minutes. Season to taste with sea salt and pepper.

Spicy Indian Vegetables

MAKES
4 servings

TIME
about 55 minutes

A classic Indian side dish that can also stand alone. Just serve with chapattis or gluten-free Indian bread to make a main meal.

1 Tbsp (15 mL) dairy-free nonhydrogenated margarine or first cold-pressed extra virgin olive oil

2 medium-size cooking onions, chopped

2 large red potatoes, peeled and diced

4 tsp (20 mL) curry powder

½ tsp (2 mL) whole cumin seeds

½ tsp (2 mL) cayenne pepper (less if you prefer)

sea salt and pepper (for **HD** use sodium substitute)

1 can (28 oz/796 mL) diced tomatoes, with juice

2 cups (500 mL) cauliflower florets

1 cup (250 mL) frozen peas

In a frying pan over medium heat, heat the margarine and sauté the onions, stirring, for about 25 minutes, adding a little water if they start to stick. Add the potatoes and sauté, stirring, for 5 minutes. Add 1 cup (250 mL) of water, cover and cook, stirring occasionally, for about 10 minutes or until the potatoes are soft. Add the curry powder, cumin seeds, cayenne pepper (add this gradually to control the spiciness) and sea salt and pepper to taste and stir for 1 minute. Add the tomatoes with their juice and heat through for 5 minutes, stirring. Add the cauliflower and peas. Heat through, stirring, for 5 minutes. The cauliflower will still be crunchy, but that's the way we want it.

Kale with Mushrooms and Peas

	MAKES	TIME
	4 servings	20 minutes

The kale is a great addition as it's a super-veggie. This is good over brown rice or with Indian bread.

1 Tbsp (15 mL) dairy-free nonhydrogenated margarine

4 cups (1 L) button mushrooms, quartered

2 tsp (10 mL) curry powder

1½ tsp (7 mL) ground cumin

¼–½ tsp (1–2 mL) cayenne pepper, according to taste

2 cups (500 mL) roughly chopped kale

1 cup (250 mL) spaghetti sauce

1 cup (250 mL) frozen peas

2 Tbsp (30 mL) fresh lemon juice

sea salt and pepper (for **HD** use sodium substitute)

In a frying pan, on medium heat, heat the margarine and sauté the mushrooms, stirring, for 10 minutes. Add the curry powder, cumin and cayenne and then the kale. Cook, stirring, for 2 to 3 minutes. Add the spaghetti sauce, peas, lemon juice and sea salt and pepper to taste. Cook, stirring, for 4 to 5 minutes.

Spicy Cauliflower and Portobello

MAKES
4 servings

TIME
15 minutes

Cauliflower is used is many Indian dishes. Garam masala is sold in Indian groceries and most supermarkets.

1 Tbsp (15 mL) first cold pressed extra virgin
olive oil

1½ tsp (7 mL) garam masala

¼ tsp (1 mL) sea salt (for **HD** use sodium substitute)

pepper

pinch of chili flakes

pinch of fenugreek seeds, crushed with a mortar
and pestle (optional)

1 fresh hot green chili, diced, seeded if you like it
less hot

2 large portobello mushrooms, chopped

2 large tomatoes, chopped

2 cups (500 mL) chopped cauliflower florets

In a large frying pan on medium heat, heat the olive oil and add the garam masala, sea salt, pepper to taste, chili flakes and fenugreek seeds. Add the fresh chili and then the mushrooms and sauté, stirring, for 2 minutes. Add the tomatoes and sauté, stirring, for about 7 minutes, covered. Add the cauliflower and cook, stirring, for about 4 minutes.

Spicy Chapattis

		MAKES	TIME
		4 servings	15 to 20 minutes

Some kind of bread is almost always featured in Indian meals. I love asafoetida powder for its unique flavour, which lingers for quite some time on the tongue. You can find it in Indian grocery stores. If you're on a gluten-free diet, you can substitute chickpea flour or lentil flour for the whole wheat flour. It changes the kind of bread this is, but it's still delicious anyway.

2 cups (500 mL) whole wheat flour
   (for **CD** see above)
1 tsp (5 mL) asafoetida powder
½ tsp (2 mL) sea salt (for **HD** use sodium substitute)
½ tsp (2 mL) ground cumin

Mix together the flour, asafoetida, sea salt and cumin. Slowly add enough water to make a slightly dry dough. Mix well and knead on a well-floured work surface. Pinch off 1-inch (2.5 cm) balls of dough and roll each one on a floured counter into a very thin round—as thin as possible but without it being so thin that it breaks when you transfer it to the pan. They should end up being 6 to 8 inches (15–20 cm) in diameter.

Cook one at a time in a lightly oiled frying pan over medium-high heat, pressing down with a kitchen towel to form air pockets. The bread should puff up. Cook on both sides and remove from the heat as soon as it's done, about 3 to 4 minutes on each side.

Fenugreek Bread

MAKES	TIME
4 servings	10 to 15 minutes

A spicy little bread that offers the extra nutrition of legumes by way of chickpea flour. It is also gluten-free and dairy-free. You can use asafoetida powder instead of fenugreek, if you prefer.

2 cups (500 mL) chickpea flour

1 tsp (5 mL) poppy seeds

¼–½ tsp (1–2 mL) sea salt
(for **HD** use sodium substitute)

¼ tsp (1 mL) fenugreek seeds, crushed with a
mortar and pestle

¼ tsp (1 mL) cayenne pepper

¼ tsp (1 mL) garam masala

Mix the flour with the poppy seeds, sea salt, fenugreek seeds, cayenne pepper and garam masala and add enough water to make a thin batter. Lightly oil a frying pan over medium-high heat and pour some of the batter in a large thin circle into the frying pan. It should take up the whole pan. Cook for a few minutes on each side and gently flip. It should be golden and cooked. Press down with a paper towel while it cooks to get it to puff up a little. Don't worry if you have trouble flipping it and it falls apart. Just make smaller circles.

SALADS

Raita

 C **CA**   **HD**   **OA** | MAKES
4 servings | TIME
25 minutes |

A cooling accompaniment to Indian food that can also be eaten on its own as a salad. Use a yoghurt with live cultures (acidophilus and bifidus) in it for good digestion and health.

> 1 cup (250 mL) plain yoghurt
>
> 2 inches (5 cm) English cucumber, peeled
>   and grated
>
> 1 small clove garlic, minced (optional)
>
> pinch of cayenne pepper (optional)
>
> sea salt and pepper (for **HD** use sodium substitute)

Mix the yoghurt with the cucumber, garlic (if using), cayenne (if using) and sea salt and pepper to taste. Refrigerate, covered or uncovered, for at least 20 minutes. Serve cold.

MANGO SALAD
WITH INDIAN
DRESSING

Mango Salad with Indian Dressing

 | MAKES
4 servings | TIME
10 minutes

A sweet, spicy, colourful salad. The curry flavour makes it uniquely Indian. Serve this with wedges of gluten-free poppadum around the salad.

4 large romaine lettuce leaves, torn up

2 large mangos, peeled, pitted and sliced into thin strips

1 small red bell pepper, cut into thin strips (optional; omit for **RA**)

2 Tbsp (30 mL) first cold pressed extra virgin olive oil

1 Tbsp (15 mL) rice vinegar

¼ tsp (1 mL) chili flakes

¼ tsp (1 mL) ground cumin

sea salt and pepper (for **HD** use sodium substitute)

pinch of curry powder

Lay the lettuce on a large platter and place the mango and bell pepper strips on top of it. Mix together the olive oil, rice vinegar, chili flakes, cumin, and sea salt and pepper to taste, and pour over the salad. Dust with curry powder.

Sweet Lentil Soup with Fennel Seed

	MAKES	TIME
V	4 servings	55 minutes

A delicious soup spiced with fennel, which helps with digestion.

1 Tbsp (15 mL) first cold pressed extra virgin olive oil

1 cooking onion, chopped

3 garlic cloves, minced

6 cups (1.5 L) vegetarian chicken-flavour stock

1½ cups (375 mL) dried red lentils, washed

5 dried dates, pitted and chopped

1 large carrot, diced

1 tomato, diced

1½ tsp (7 mL) curry powder

¼ tsp (1 mL) whole fennel seeds

sea salt and pepper (for **HD** use sodium substitute)

In a soup pot on medium-low heat, heat the oil and sauté the onion, stirring often, for 25 minutes. Add the garlic and sauté for 1 minute. Add the stock, lentils, dates, carrot, tomato, curry powder, fennel seeds, and sea salt and pepper to taste. Bring to a boil then reduce the heat to medium-low and cook, stirring now and then, for about 25 minutes. If needed, add more stock as the soup cooks. Everything should be soft. Purée and heat through again before serving.

Squash and Apple Soup

		MAKES	TIME
		4 servings	1 hour

Healthy and full of delicious curry flavour and the best of fall foods. This is rich in beta-carotenes and other antioxidants. Cinnamon is especially good for diabetics as it helps to balance blood sugar.

1 Tbsp (15 mL) butter, or dairy-free nonhydrogenated margarine (for **CA** **CD** **D** **G** **MS** **RA** **V** use margarine)

2 cooking onions, chopped

2 large McIntosh apples, peeled, cored and diced

1 large acorn squash, peeled and diced

8–9 cups (2–2.25 L) vegetable stock

2 tsp (10 mL) curry powder

¼ tsp (1 mL) ground cinnamon

sea salt and pepper (for **HD** use sodium substitute)

In a large soup pot over medium heat, heat the margarine and sauté the onions, stirring frequently, until soft, about 15 minutes. Add water if they start to stick. Add the apples and squash and sauté, stirring, for a few minutes. Add the stock, curry powder, cinnamon, and sea salt and pepper to taste. Cover and bring to a boil, stirring occasionally. Reduce the heat to medium-low and cook, covered, for 35 to 40 minutes or until everything is soft. Purée and heat through before serving.

Spicy Pumpkin Soup

MAKES
4 servings

TIME
1 hour 40 minutes

A great soup rich in carotenes with a nice curry spice to it.

2 Tbsp (30 mL) dairy-free nonhydrogenated
   margarine
4 large cooking onions, chopped
4 cups (1 L) peeled, cubed pumpkin
12 cups (3 L) vegetable stock
1 tsp (5 mL) curry powder
¼ tsp (1 mL) cayenne pepper, or more to taste
pepper

In a large soup pot over low heat, heat the margarine and sauté the onions, stirring, for about 25 to 30 minutes, until the onions are soft and translucent. Add the pumpkin and stir for a few minutes. Add the stock, curry powder, cayenne pepper and lots of pepper to taste and bring to a boil. Reduce the heat to medium-low and cook, stirring now and then, for about 1 hour. Purée, and then heat through for a few minutes before serving.

MAINS

Indian Pumpkin Stew

             **V**

MAKES	TIME
4 servings	**1 hour**

A spicy stew loaded with healthy antioxidants like beta-carotene from the pumpkin and lycopene from the tomatoes.

3 Tbsp (45 mL) first cold pressed extra virgin olive oil

4 medium-size cooking onions, chopped

3 cups (750 mL) peeled, cubed pumpkin

2 tsp (10 mL) curry powder

1½ tsp (7 mL) ground coriander

¼–½ tsp (1–2 mL) cayenne pepper

sea salt and pepper (for **HD** use sodium substitute)

1½ cups (375 mL) water

12 button mushrooms, quartered (optional; omit for **CA** **G**)

1 red bell pepper, bite-size pieces

1 cup (250 mL) chopped green beans (1-inch/2.5 cm pieces)

1 can (28 oz/796 mL) crushed tomatoes

1 can (5.5 oz/156 mL) tomato paste

In a large soup pot over medium heat, heat the oil and sauté the onions, stirring, for 10 minutes. Add the pumpkin and sauté, stirring, for a few minutes. Add the curry powder, coriander, cayenne (start with ¼ tsp/ 1 mL and work up from there), and sea salt and pepper to taste. Cook, stirring, for 1 minute. Add the water, cover and cook, stirring occasionally, for about 25 minutes. Add the mushrooms, bell pepper and green beans and sauté, stirring occasionally, for a few minutes. Add the crushed tomatoes and tomato paste. Cover and cook, stirring occasionally, for 15 minutes on low heat.

Easy Eastern Stew

A spicy, simple dish that's good with Indian bread and raita.

1 Tbsp (15 mL) dairy-free nonhydrogenated
   margarine
2 large garlic cloves, minced
1 large carrot, bite-size pieces
1 large potato, peeled, bite-size pieces
½ large yam, peeled, bite-size pieces
2 cups (500 mL) water
2 cups (500 mL) crushed tomatoes
4 tsp (20 mL) curry powder
1 Tbsp (15 mL) ground cumin
⅛ tsp (0.5 mL) cayenne pepper
pepper

MAKES 4 servings
TIME 30 minutes

In a frying pan over medium heat, heat the margarine and sauté the garlic, stirring, for 2 minutes. Add the carrot, potato and yam. Sauté for 1 minute, stirring. Add the water and cook, covered, for 15 to 20 minutes, stirring occasionally. Add the tomatoes, curry powder, cumin, cayenne and pepper to taste and cook for 5 minutes, stirring.

Indian Casserole

MAKES	TIME
4 servings	2 hours

A spicy and slightly sweet dish.

1½ cups (375 mL) mango or orange juice

1 cup (250 mL) water

2 cooking onions, sliced

¼ cup (60 mL) first cold pressed extra virgin olive oil

½ cup (125 mL) dried red lentils, washed (optional; remove for Ⓖ)

2 large garlic cloves, minced

2 large white potatoes, peeled and sliced

4 mini red potatoes, peeled and sliced

1 medium-size yam, peeled and sliced

1-inch (2.5 cm) piece fresh ginger, minced (optional)

2 bay leaves

1 tsp (5 mL) ground cumin

1 tsp (5 mL) black mustard seeds

½ tsp (2 mL) ground cinnamon

pepper

Preheat the oven to 375°F (190°C).

Place everything in an ovenproof casserole dish, mix well and cover. Bake for about 2 hours.

Tofu and Peas in Tomato Sauce

 **V** | MAKES
4 servings | TIME
30 minutes

Spicy and filling. Serve with rice and or Indian bread.

first cold pressed extra virgin olive oil

1 package (12 oz/350 g) extra-firm tofu, cut into
  1-inch (2.5 cm) cubes

3–4 tsp (15–20 mL) curry powder

1 can (19 oz/540 mL) crushed tomatoes

1 cup (250 mL) frozen peas

sea salt and pepper (for **HD** use sodium substitute)

In a frying pan over medium heat, heat a little oil and sauté the tofu on all sides until browned. Stir in the curry powder. Add the tomatoes and cook, stirring, for 5 minutes. Add the peas, and sea salt and pepper to taste, and cook, stirring, for 4 to 5 minutes.

Spicy Tofu

MAKES
4 servings

TIME
30 minutes

Easy and very good. Serve with cooked greens and a salad.

1 tsp (5 mL) first cold pressed extra virgin olive oil

1 package (12 oz/350 g) extra-firm tofu, cut into
½-inch (1 cm) slices

1½ tsp (7 mL) curry powder

½–1 tsp (2–5 mL) tandoori barbecue masala spice

¾ cup (185 mL) puréed tomatoes or
barbecue sauce

1 tsp (5 mL) fresh lemon juice

In a large frying pan over medium heat, heat the oil and brown the tofu lightly on all sides. Sprinkle curry powder and masala spice on each side of the tofu slices. Cook for 1 minute on each side. Brush both sides of each slice with the puréed tomatoes or barbecue sauce and cook for 4 to 5 minutes on each side. Sprinkle lemon juice overtop before serving.

Mixed Vegetable and Tofu Curry

MAKES 4 servings | **TIME** 1 hour

A spicy complete meal when served with rice or chapatti.

2 Tbsp (30 mL) first cold pressed extra virgin olive oil or dairy-free nonhydrogenated margarine, divided

⅓ package (4 oz/115 g) extra-firm tofu, cut into 1-inch (2.5 cm) cubes or smaller

2 large cooking onions, chopped

2 large garlic cloves, minced

3 cups (750 mL) small- to medium-size button mushrooms, halved

1 Tbsp (15 mL) ground coriander

1½ tsp (7 mL) ground cumin

¼ tsp (1 mL) ground ginger

1 bay leaf

sea salt and pepper (for **HD** use sodium substitute)

1 can (19 oz/540 mL) diced tomatoes, with juice

1½ cups (375 mL) cauliflower florets

1 cup (250 mL) frozen peas

In a frying pan over medium heat, heat 1 tsp (5 mL) of the olive oil and fry the tofu on all sides until browned, about 20 minutes. Remove the tofu and set it aside.

In the same frying pan, add the rest of the olive oil (1 Tbsp + 2 tsp/25 mL) and sauté the onions, stirring, for about 25 minutes or until soft. Add the garlic and sauté for 2 minutes, stirring. Add the mushrooms and cook, stirring, for 5 minutes. Add the coriander, cumin, ginger, bay leaf, and sea salt and pepper to taste. Then add the tomatoes with their juice, cauliflower and peas and cook, stirring, for 3 to 4 minutes. Add the tofu and heat through. Remove the bay leaf before serving.

Vegetable Curry

MAKES
4 servings

TIME
12 to 15 minutes

A staple served all over India. Loaded with healthy spices and vegetables, this is good with Indian bread and over rice.

2 Tbsp (30 mL) dairy-free
 nonhydrogenated margarine

2 ½ tsp (12 mL) black mustard seeds

2 ¼ tsp (11 mL) ground coriander

1 ½ tsp (7 mL) garlic powder

1 tsp (5 mL) ground cumin

1 tsp (5 mL) ground ginger

¼ tsp (1 mL) chili powder

pepper

1 large carrot, sliced

1 cup (250 mL) chopped green beans
 (1-inch/2.5 cm pieces)

1 small red or green bell pepper, bite-size pieces
 (optional; omit for **RA**)

1 cup (250 mL) cauliflower florets, chopped

1 small to medium zucchini, skin on, sliced

In a frying pan over medium heat, heat the margarine and add the mustard seeds. Cover and shake the pan for 1 minute. Add the coriander, garlic powder, cumin, ginger and chili powder, and pepper to taste. Add the carrot and cook for a few minutes, stirring. Add the green beans and bell pepper and cook for 7 minutes, stirring. Add a little water as needed to keep everything from sticking. Add the cauliflower and zucchini and cook for 4 to 5 minutes, stirring.

Fiery Curry

MAKES 4 servings	TIME 25 minutes

A fiery one. Serve with brown rice or Indian bread.

2 Tbsp (30 mL) first cold pressed extra virgin olive oil

2 large garlic cloves, minced

¼-inch (5 mm) piece fresh ginger, finely grated

14 large button mushrooms, quartered

10 long green beans, cut in 1-inch (2.5 cm) pieces

1 medium-size carrot, diced

2 whole cardamom pods

4 tsp (20 mL) curry powder

1 tsp (5 mL) ground cumin

½–1 tsp (2–5 mL) chili flakes

1 cup (250 mL) soy milk

1 red bell pepper, bite-size pieces (optional; omit for **RA**)

1 cup (250 mL) frozen peas

½ cup (125 mL) canned lima beans, drained and rinsed

sea salt and pepper (for **HD** use sodium substitute)

In a frying pan over medium heat, heat the olive oil and sauté the garlic and ginger with the mushrooms, stirring, for 5 minutes. Add the green beans, carrot, cardamom pods, curry powder, cumin and chili flakes and sauté, stirring, for 10 minutes. Add the soy milk, bell pepper, peas and lima beans, and sea salt and pepper to taste, and cook for 5 minutes. Remove the cardamom pods before serving.

Rice with Beans, Corn and Cabbage

	MAKES	TIME
V	4 servings	60 minutes

A complete meal spiced up with the flavours of India. I like it with lots of black pepper. A high-fibre dish that is good for overall health and well-being.

½ cup (125 mL) brown basmati rice

2 Tbsp (30 mL) first cold pressed extra virgin olive oil

1 large cooking onion, chopped

1 can (28 oz/796 mL) diced tomatoes, with juice

1 can (19 oz/540 mL) red kidney beans, drained and rinsed

2 cups (500 mL) chopped green cabbage

1 cup (250 mL) water

¼ cup (60 mL) dried red lentils, washed

2 tsp (10 mL) ground coriander

½ tsp (2 mL) ground cinnamon

¼–½ tsp (1–2 mL) cayenne pepper

sea salt and pepper (for **HD** use sodium substitute)

¼ cup (60 mL) frozen corn

Place the rice in a pot with 2 ¼ cups (560 mL) water and bring to a boil. Reduce the heat to low, cover and cook for about 50 minutes or until soft.

In a large frying pan over medium heat, heat the oil and sauté the onion, stirring, for 20 minutes. Add the tomatoes with their juice, beans, cabbage, water, lentils, coriander, cinnamon, cayenne, and sea salt and pepper to taste. Cover and cook, stirring occasionally, for ½ hour, adding more water if necessary as it cooks. Add the corn and cooked rice, and heat through, stirring, for 5 minutes.

Curried Vegetable Rice

C **CA** **CD** **D**   **HD** **M** **MS** **OA** **RA** **V** | MAKES **4 servings** | TIME **1 hour**

Full of healthy carotenes including lycopene.

1⅓ cups (310 mL) brown rice

3 cups (750 mL) vegetable stock

2 cups (500 mL) acorn squash, peeled and cubed

1 Tbsp (15 mL) dairy-free nonhydrogenated margarine

1 large cooking onion, chopped

1 can (19 oz/540 mL) chickpeas, drained and rinsed

2 tsp (10 mL) curry powder

1 tsp (5 mL) ground cumin

sea salt and pepper (for **HD** use sodium substitute)

2 cups (500 mL) torn-up fresh spinach (you can use baby spinach)

Put the rice in a pot with 4 cups (1 L) of water. Bring to a boil on high heat. Reduce the heat to medium-low, cover and cook, stirring occasionally, for about 50 minutes or until tender, and drain if needed.

Meanwhile, place the stock in a pot and add the squash. Cover and bring to a boil, then reduce the heat and simmer, covered, on medium heat for about 20 minutes or until soft. Purée. Add more stock if necessary.

In a large frying pan over medium heat, heat the margarine and sauté the onion, stirring, for about 25 minutes, or until soft. Add the squash-stock mixture, chickpeas, curry powder, cumin, and sea salt and pepper to taste and cook for 10 minutes, stirring. Add the spinach and cook, stirring, for another 3 minutes. Serve over the rice.

Spicy Mung Beans and Rice

MAKES
4 servings

TIME
1 hour

A spicy meal that offers a complete protein source. I love the various flavours and textures in this dish: the pop of the black mustard seeds; the earthy-tasting sunflower seeds; the sweet, rich cashews; the soft, exotic-tasting mung beans; and the soft rice.

1 cup (250 mL) dried mung beans, washed

⅔ cup (160 mL) brown basmati rice

1 Tbsp (15 mL) dairy-free nonhydrogenated margarine

3 garlic cloves, minced

1 Tbsp (15 mL) black mustard seeds

1 tsp (5 mL) ground coriander

½–1 tsp (2–5 mL) chili powder

pepper

1 large carrot, diced

3 Tbsp (45 mL) soy sauce

3 Tbsp (45 mL) raw, unsalted sunflower seeds

3 Tbsp (45 mL) raw, unsalted whole cashews

Place the mung beans in a pot with 3 cups (750 mL) water and bring to a boil. Reduce the heat to low, cover and cook for about 1 hour or until soft.

Place the rice in a pot with 2¼ cups (560 mL) water and bring to a boil. Reduce the heat to low, cover and cook for about 50 minutes or until soft.

Meanwhile, in a large frying pan over medium heat, heat the margarine and sauté the garlic, stirring, for a few minutes. Add the mustard seeds, coriander and chili, and pepper to taste. Add the carrot and cook for a few minutes, stirring. Add the cooked beans, cooked rice and soy sauce and cook, stirring, for a few minutes more. Add the sunflower seeds and cashews before serving.

Mung Beans and Tomato Rice

MAKES	TIME
4 servings	1 hour 5 minutes

This well-flavoured and filling dish is a great immunity-boosting meal with the cabbage and tomatoes.

½ cup (125 mL) dried mung beans, washed

½ cup (125 mL) brown rice

1 Tbsp (15 mL) first cold pressed extra virgin olive oil or dairy-free nonhydrogenated margarine

¼ medium-size cabbage, chopped

10 plum tomatoes, diced

4 tsp (20 mL) curry powder

¼ tsp (1 mL) cayenne pepper

sea salt (for **HD** use sodium substitute)

Place the mung beans in a pot with 1½ cups (375 mL) of water and bring to a boil. Reduce the heat to low, cover and cook for about 1 hour or until soft.

Place the rice in a pot with 1⅔ cups (410 mL) of water and bring to a boil. Reduce the heat to low, cover and cook for about 50 minutes or until soft.

Meanwhile, in a frying pan on medium heat, heat the oil and cook the cabbage, stirring, for about 10 minutes. Add the tomatoes and cook, stirring, for about 20 minutes. Add the cooked beans and cooked rice, curry powder and cayenne pepper. Cook for about 5 minutes. Season to taste with sea salt before serving.

Mango and Chickpeas over Rice

| | | MAKES
4 servings | TIME
1 hour |

A spicy and slightly sweet rice dish with a bit of sweetness that comes loaded with healthy beta-carotene.

1 cup (250 mL) brown basmati rice

2 Tbsp (30 mL) first cold pressed extra virgin
   olive oil

2 cooking onions, chopped

1 can (19 oz/540 mL) chickpeas, drained and rinsed

2 tsp (10 mL) hot curry powder

sea salt and pepper (for **HD** use sodium substitute)

½ cup (125 mL) canned bamboo shoots, drained
   and rinsed, cut into 1-inch (2.5 cm) pieces
   (optional)

2 tsp (10 mL) fresh lemon juice

1 very large mango, peeled and cut in slivers

Put the rice in a pot with 3¼ cups (810 mL) of water and bring to a boil on high heat. Reduce the heat to medium-low. Cover and cook, stirring occasionally, for about 50 minutes or until tender.

In a large frying pan over medium heat, heat the olive oil and sauté the onions, stirring, for about 25 minutes, or until soft. Add the chickpeas, curry powder, and sea salt and pepper to taste and cook for about 3 minutes. Add the cooked rice, bamboo shoots (if using) and lemon juice and cook for about 3 minutes. Add the mango, mix well and heat through before serving.

APPLE INDIAN RICE

Apple Indian Rice

 MAKES
4 servings | TIME
1 hour 30 minutes

A gently flavoured Indian rice that is great either with other Indian dishes or on its own.

1½ cups (375 mL) water

½ cup (125 mL) apple juice

1 cup (250 mL) chopped red cabbage

1 large red apple, peeled, cored and chopped

½ cup (125 mL) brown rice

1 Tbsp (15 mL) dairy-free nonhydrogenated margarine

1 tsp (5 mL) ground cinnamon

½–1 tsp (2–5 mL) whole cumin seeds

sea salt and pepper (for use sodium substitute)

Preheat the oven to 375°F (190°C).

Place everything in a large ovenproof dish and mix well. Cover and bake for about 1½ hours, until the rice is cooked. Check in case you need to add more water.

Vegetable Biryani

MAKES 4 servings

TIME 1 hour 15 minutes

A slightly different take on a classic rice dish from India. This is great for gatherings. And it's high in fibre, antioxidants and healthy oils.

¾ cup (185 mL) long-grain brown rice

¼ cup (60 mL) short-grain brown rice

2 tsp (10 mL) ground turmeric

1 tsp (5 mL) sea salt (for **HD** use sodium substitute)

2 Tbsp (30 mL) first cold pressed extra virgin olive oil

3 cooking onions, chopped

2 tsp (10 mL) ground coriander

2 tsp (10 mL) garam masala

½ tsp (2 mL) chili powder

2 tsp (10 mL) poppy seeds

1 Tbsp (15 mL) black mustard seeds

¼ tsp (1 mL) pepper

1 can (14 oz/398 mL) diced tomatoes, with juice

¼ tsp (1 mL) dried oregano

¼ tsp (1 mL) dried basil

1 cup (250 mL) long green beans, cut into ¼-inch (5 mm) pieces

¼ cup (60 mL) raw, unsalted whole cashews

2 Tbsp (30 mL) brown sesame seeds

2 Tbsp (30 mL) raw, unsalted sunflower seeds

Place both types of rice in a pot with 3 ½ cups (875 mL) of water and cover. Bring to a boil, then reduce heat to low and cook for 50 minutes to 1 hour, or until done. Add the turmeric and sea salt after about 40 minutes.

Meanwhile, in a frying pan over medium-low heat, heat the oil and sauté the onions, stirring, for about 30 minutes, or until they are soft and translucent. Add the coriander, garam masala, chili powder, poppy seeds, black mustard seeds and pepper and stir for 1 minute. Add the tomatoes with their juice, and the oregano and basil. Simmer, covered, for about 10 minutes.

Preheat the oven to 350°F (180°C).

Place the contents of the frying pan, the cooked rice and the green beans in an ovenproof casserole dish. Mix well. Cover and bake for about 20 minutes. Uncover and top with the cashews, sesame seeds and sunflower seeds and return to the oven to heat through for a minute or two.

Red Mango Lentils

MAKES	TIME
2 servings	30 minutes

Sweet and spicy. This is good with rice and steamed greens.

1 cup (250 mL) dried red lentils, washed

2 Tbsp (30 mL) fresh lemon juice

1½ tsp (7 mL) curry powder

1 tsp (5 mL) mango powder

1 tsp (5 mL) first cold pressed extra virgin olive oil

¼ tsp (1 mL) sea salt (for **HD** use sodium substitute)

¼ tsp (1 mL) chili flakes

Place everything in a medium-size pot with 2 ½ cups (625 mL) water. Bring to a boil then reduce the heat to low and cook, stirring, for about 25 minutes. Check the water level. You may need to add more if it starts to dry out.

Spicy Red Lentils with Vegetables

MAKES	TIME
4 servings	35 minutes

Dal is a spicy staple served all over India. Serve this with Indian bread or rice. Instead of sea salt, try using dulse flakes to taste.

2 tsp (10 mL) first cold pressed extra virgin olive oil

1 fresh hot green chili, diced, with seeds

1½ cups (375 mL) dried red lentils, washed

3 small red bell peppers, chopped

2 very large garlic cloves, minced

1 new potato, peeled and diced

¼ small yam, peeled and diced

1 Tbsp (15 mL) black mustard seeds

1 tsp (5 mL) sea salt (for **HD** use sodium substitute)

¼–½ tsp (1–2 mL) chili powder

¼ tsp (1 mL) garam masala

4 cups (1 L) water

In a large soup pot, place the oil and the green chili and sauté for 1 minute on medium heat. Add the lentils, bell peppers, garlic, potato, yam, black mustard seeds, sea salt, chili powder and garam masala. Stir around for 1 or 2 minutes. Add the water, cover and bring to a boil. Reduce the heat to medium-low and cook, covered, stirring now and then, for about 30 minutes. Add more water as it cooks if needed.

Curried Chickpeas with Orzo and Lentils

C   HD   M   MS   OA   RA   V

MAKES	TIME
4 servings	45 minutes

A filling, easy dish with a twist. The orzo pasta is obviously not authentically Indian, but it goes really well here.

> 4 cups (1 L) water
> 1¼ cups (310 mL) canned chickpeas, drained and rinsed
> ¼ cup (60 mL) orzo
> ½ large yam, skin on, quartered and then sliced
> 1 fresh hot chili, diced, with seeds (optional)
> 2 Tbsp (30 mL) dried red lentils, washed
> 1 Tbsp (15 mL) curry powder
> 1 tsp (5 mL) first cold pressed extra virgin olive oil
> 1 vegetable stock cube

Place everything in a large pot and bring to a boil, on medium high heat, stirring frequently. Reduce the heat to low, cover and cook on low heat for about 40 minutes, stirring once in a while. Add more water if it gets too dry. There should be some liquid when it is done, but not too much.

Spicy Chickpeas and Spinach

	MAKES	TIME
	4 servings	45 minutes

Chickpeas are served all over India. This dish is great served with whole wheat naan.

1 tsp (5 mL) first cold pressed extra virgin olive oil

1 large white onion, diced

1 can (19 oz/540 mL) chickpeas, drained and rinsed

1½ cups (375 mL) spaghetti sauce

½ cup (125 mL) water

1 large piece of dried mango, cut up

4 tsp (20 mL) curry powder

¼–½ tsp (1–2 mL) cayenne pepper

2 cups (500 mL) torn-up fresh spinach (you can use baby spinach)

In a large frying pan over medium-low heat, heat the olive oil and sauté the onion, stirring, for about 25 minutes. Add the chickpeas, spaghetti sauce, water, dried mango, curry powder and cayenne and cook, covered, stirring now and then, for about 15 minutes. Add the spinach and cook for another 3 minutes.

Coconut Vegetable Curry

	MAKES	TIME
	4 servings	40 minutes

A dish that tastes sweet, spicy and wonderful. Serve with brown basmati rice and sliced mango or mango salad.

2 Tbsp (30 mL) first cold pressed extra virgin olive oil or dairy-free nonhydrogenated margarine

5 green onions, chopped

1 large red bell pepper, bite-size pieces

1 medium-size orange bell pepper, bite-size pieces

1 medium-size yam, peeled, bite-size pieces

1 large potato, peeled, bite-size pieces

1 large carrot, bite-size pieces

1 can (19 oz/540 mL) chickpeas, drained and rinsed

1½ cups (375 mL) water

sea salt and pepper (for **HD** use sodium substitute)

1 Tbsp (15 mL) curry powder

1–1½ tsp (5–7 mL) chili flakes

1 tsp (5 mL) garam masala

1½ cups (375 mL) coconut milk

In a frying pan over medium heat, heat the oil and sauté the green onions, stirring, for about 10 minutes or until the onions are soft. Add the bell peppers, yam, potato and carrot and cook, stirring, for 5 minutes. Add the chickpeas, water, sea salt and pepper to taste, curry powder, chili flakes and garam masala. Cover and cook for 15 to 20 minutes or until the potato and yam are soft. Stir occasionally and add more water if necessary. Add the coconut milk and heat through for 4 to 5 minutes before serving.

Curried Red Kidney Beans

	MAKES	TIME
	4 servings	35 minutes

A staple eaten all over India. Add Indian rice, bread and a green for a complete meal.

> 1½ cups (375 mL) canned tomatoes, with juice
> 1 Tbsp (15 mL) first cold pressed extra virgin olive oil or dairy-free nonhydrogenated margarine
> 1 large cooking onion, chopped
> 1 can (19 oz/540 mL) red kidney beans, drained and rinsed
> 1 Tbsp (15 mL) curry powder
> 1 tsp (5 mL) ground cumin
> sea salt and pepper (for **HD** use sodium substitute)
> cayenne pepper (optional)

Purée the tomatoes.

In a large frying pan over medium heat, heat the oil and sauté the onion until soft, stirring, about 20 minutes. Add the kidney beans, puréed tomatoes, curry powder, cumin, sea salt and pepper to taste and cayenne (if using) and cook, stirring, for about 15 minutes.

Split Peas and Okra

											MAKES	TIME
C	CA	CD	D	G	HD	M	MS	OA	RA	V	4 servings	1 hour 15 minutes

Spicy and delicious. Okra and split peas turn up in a lot of Indian cooking.

> 1 cup (250 mL) dried yellow split peas, washed
>
> 2 tsp (10 mL) first cold pressed extra virgin olive oil
>
> 2 large cooking onions, chopped
>
> 20 fresh okra, ends removed and sliced in thin rounds
>
> 2 pickled green chilies, finely chopped
>
> 1 Tbsp (15 mL) black mustard seeds
>
> 1½ Tbsp (22 mL) fresh lemon juice
>
> sea salt and pepper (for **HD** use sodium substitute)

Put the split peas in a pot with 5 cups (1.25 L) water. Bring to a boil on high heat. Reduce the heat to medium-low and cover. Cook, stirring occasionally for 45 minutes to 1 hour or until tender. When the split peas are done, drain, reserving 1½ cups (375 mL) of the cooking water.

Meanwhile, in a large frying pan over medium-low heat, heat the oil and sauté the onions, stirring, for about 25 minutes until soft and translucent. Add the okra, chilies and mustard seeds and cook for 2 minutes. Add the reserved cooking water and cook for 15 minutes, stirring. Add the cooked yellow split peas and cook for about 5 minutes. Add the lemon juice and sea salt and pepper to taste. Mix well before serving.

Split Peas and Cauliflower with Spicy Okra

	MAKES	TIME
	4 servings	**1 hour 15 minutes**

Similar to the previous recipe, but with healthy cruciferous cauliflower.

1 cup (250 mL) dried yellow split peas, washed

4 tsp (20 mL) dairy-free nonhydrogenated margarine, divided

18 fresh okra, ends removed and sliced in thin rounds

¼ cup (60 mL) soy milk

2 tsp (10 mL) curry powder

1 tsp (5 mL) ground cinnamon

¼ tsp (1 mL) cayenne pepper

sea salt (for **HD** use sodium substitute)

3 Tbsp (45 mL) fresh lemon juice

1 cup (250 mL) cauliflower florets

Put the split peas in a pot with 2 ¾ cups (685 mL) water. Bring to a boil on high heat. Reduce the heat to medium-low and cover. Cook, stirring occasionally, for about 45 minutes to 1 hour or until tender, and drain if needed.

Meanwhile, in a large frying pan over medium heat, heat 3 tsp (15 mL) of the margarine and sauté the okra, stirring, for a few minutes. Add the soy milk and curry powder and sauté for a few minutes. Add the cinnamon, cayenne and sea salt (to taste) and sauté, covered, until the okra is tender, stirring occasionally. Add the lemon juice and then the cooked yellow split peas, cauliflower and remaining 1 tsp (5 mL) margarine. Heat through for a few minutes before serving.

Curried Tofu

 **C CA CD D G HD M MS OA RA V**

MAKES	TIME
4 servings	10 to 15 minutes

An easy, spicy way of eating tofu.

> 3 Tbsp (45 mL) barbecue sauce (if the sauce
> contains tomatoes, omit for **RA**)
> 1 Tbsp (15 mL) fresh lemon juice
> 2 tsp (10 mL) curry powder
> 1 package (12 oz/350 g) extra-firm tofu, cut into
> ½-inch (1 cm) slices

Preheat the barbecue to medium-low.

Mix the barbecue sauce with the lemon juice and curry powder. Place the tofu in a non-stick grilling basket on the barbecue and brush them with the sauce. Turn the tofu as it cooks, about 10 minutes. It should be slightly crispy.

Asia

Recipes

Asia

ASIAN COUNTRIES ARE HOME TO some of the most vegetarian-friendly cuisines in the world. The meals are often simple to prepare, well balanced and rich in tradition.

Asian cuisine doesn't usually use dairy, so the diets are extremely healthy. They feature many super-veggies like broccoli, cauliflower, cabbage and deep-green leafy vegetables, which are absolutely loaded with nutrients that help to fight just about every disease you can think of; many types of healthy, flavourful mushrooms that are rich in proteins and full of immunity-enhancing nutrients that contribute to overall health; and garlic and onions, also immune-system powerhouses. Other vegetables that feature in these cuisines include bamboo shoots, bean sprouts, snow peas, bell and chili peppers, seaweed, carrots and tree ear fungus.

Soy also stars in these cuisines. This excellent source of protein can be made into anything and everything from a stir-fry to smoothies to pasta sauce and even cheesecake. Soy is an important food for promoting health.

Some countries, including Thailand, use lots of coconut milk and mango in traditional recipes. Coconut milk, tempeh and tofu are popular in Indonesia, home of the "rice table," or *rijsttafel*, which features many veggie dishes. Miso and soy are associated with Japan, and wheat gluten and soy are widely used in China. All the food from these regions tastes incredible, is high in fibre and good fats and helps to promote a healthy weight.

Stir-fries, soups, noodle dishes, rice dishes, vegetable dishes and tofu dishes can be found everywhere in these cuisines. Sauces vary from sweet to spicy. The meal is often, but not always, served all at once, and may be eaten with chopsticks, a fork or a spoon. For the most part, the vegetables are lightly cooked, and therefore are crisp, colourful and bursting with flavours and nutrients. The foods can be made spicy by adding chilies, cayenne or other hot spice, depending on the dish. These hot spices are heart friendly and rich in antioxidants. Ginger also features highly in these cuisines—a tasty spice that not only prevents and treats stomach ailments, like nausea, but also is thought to help in the treatment and prevention of heart disease, cancer, arthritis and memory problems.

Asia has mastered the art of making a dish look gorgeous, smell incredible and taste unique and delicious, all while offering an array of healthy nutrients that contribute to good health and well-being.

STARTERS AND SIDES

Potatoes and Onions in Sesame Oil and Tamari

V	MAKES **4 servings**	TIME **40 minutes**

Sesame oil and tamari are classic Asian ingredients.

2 large white potatoes diced

1 small taro potato, peeled and diced, or a small yam, skin on and diced

1–2 medium-size white onions, peeled and finely chopped

2 Tbsp (30 mL) sesame oil

2 Tbsp (30 mL) tamari

1 Tbsp (15 mL) balsamic vinegar (optional)

black sesame seeds

Place the white potatoes and taro potato/yam in a pot and just cover with cold water. Cover with a lid, bring to a boil, then reduce the heat to low. Add the onions, sesame oil, tamari, balsamic vinegar (if using) and a good sprinkling of black sesame seeds and cook, covered, for about 30 minutes, stirring now and then to prevent sticking.

Mushrooms, Onions and Potatoes

	MAKES	TIME
	4 servings	30 minutes

If you serve this with some greens like bok choy or broccoli, you can make a very healthy complete meal.

4 mini red potatoes, skin on, halved

1 large white onion, diced

2 cups (500 mL) halved button mushrooms

3 Tbsp (45 mL) soy sauce

1 Tbsp (15 mL) sesame oil

1 Tbsp (15 mL) balsamic vinegar

1 Tbsp (15 mL) black sesame seeds

Place everything in a pot on medium heat and just barely cover with water. Cover and cook, stirring now and then, until the potatoes are fork-tender, about 25 minutes.

Ginger-Flavoured Squash

C **CA** **CD** **D** **G** **HD** **M** **MS** **OA** **RA** **V** | MAKES **4 servings** | TIME **50 minutes**

This is a delicious combination of carotene-rich squash and antioxidant-rich ginger and cayenne.

> 1 acorn squash, cut in half lengthwise,
>   seeds removed
> soy sauce for brushing
> ground ginger for sprinkling
> pinch of cayenne pepper (optional)

Preheat the oven to 350°F (180°C).

Place the squash, cut side down, on a cookie sheet and bake until soft, 45 minutes to 1 hour. Remove from the oven and brush the inside well with soy sauce. Sprinkle liberally with ginger and a little cayenne pepper, if using, and roast for a few more minutes.

Bok Choy and Mushrooms

MAKES	TIME
4 servings	10 to 15 minutes

This is an easy, healthy side dish that comes from China. It features nutrient-rich bok choy and shiitake mushrooms—and it tastes great.

1 tsp (5 mL) first cold pressed extra virgin olive oil

3 cups (750 mL) sliced fresh shiitake mushrooms

½-inch (1 cm) piece fresh ginger, grated

a little piece of kudzu root (approx. ½ inch/1 cm) and 1 Tbsp (15 mL) water to thicken the sauce (optional)

3 Tbsp (45 mL) soy sauce

5–6 baby bok choy, chopped

pepper

In a frying pan, warm the oil, then add the mushrooms and ginger and sauté on medium heat for about 5 minutes. Add the piece of kudzu root and water, if using, and soy sauce. Stir for 3 to 5 minutes and allow to thicken. Add the bok choy and pepper to taste. Cook, stirring, for 2 to 3 minutes. The greens should be bright green.

Mango and Arugula Salad

 **C** **CD** **D** **G** **HD** **M** **MS** **OA** **RA** **V** | MAKES **4 servings** | TIME **5 minutes**

A salad with a bite. This is rich in beta-carotenes from the mangos, and other antioxidants from the bell peppers. The arugula, a dark leafy green, is packed with nutrients. Soy sauce, lime and chili are a tasty combination frequently found in Asia.

SALAD

1 medium bunch arugula, torn up

2 medium mangos, peeled, pitted and sliced in thin strips

2 green onions, chopped finely

1 small red bell pepper, cut in thin strips (optional; omit for **RA**)

DRESSING

2 Tbsp (30 mL) first cold pressed extra virgin olive oil

1 Tbsp (15 mL) soy sauce

1 tsp (5 mL) balsamic vinegar

juice of 1 lime

¼ tsp (1 mL) honey (optional; omit for **D** **V**)

¼ tsp (1 mL) chili flakes

pepper

For the salad, arrange the ingredients in the order listed in layers on a platter. Mix together the dressing ingredients and pour over the salad. Serve at room temperature.

Thai Mango Salad

	MAKES	TIME
	4 servings	5 to 10 minutes

This is a healthier version of a classic salad served all over Thailand. I use cane sugar, which is a healthier option than processed sugar. I love the combination of garlic, lime juice, cayenne and soy sauce paired with the sweetness of the mangos—and it's a great source of beta-carotene.

4 medium mangos, peeled, pitted and cut into
  1-inch (2.5 cm) strips

1 medium red bell pepper, cut into thin strips

1½ cups (375 mL) mung bean sprouts

1 large clove garlic, minced

juice of 2 limes

3 Tbsp (45 mL) soy sauce

1 Tbsp (15 mL) brown cane sugar

¼ tsp (1 mL) cayenne pepper or chili flakes

Place the mangos, bell pepper and sprouts in a pretty bowl. Mix together the garlic, lime juice, soy sauce, cane sugar and cayenne or chili flakes and pour over the salad. Toss and serve.

Thai Salad

MAKES	TIME
4 servings	5 minutes

An attractive antioxidant-rich salad that is great for entertaining. In Thailand they would often serve it with a pretty edible flower on the plate.

2 Tbsp (30 mL) fresh lime juice

1 Tbsp (15 mL) soy sauce

1¼ tsp (6 mL) brown cane sugar

⅛–½ tsp (½–2 mL) chili flakes

1 small clove garlic, minced (optional)

2 large mangos, peeled, pitted and cut into bite-size pieces, or 2 cups (500 mL) bite-size pieces of peeled papaya, or half of each

2 green onions, finely chopped

1 small red bell pepper, bite-size pieces

½ green bell pepper, bite-size pieces

½ yellow bell pepper, bite-size pieces

½ cup (125 mL) mung bean sprouts

cilantro sprigs (optional)

Mix together the lime juice, soy sauce, sugar, chili flakes and garlic (if using) to make a dressing. Mix the mangos with the green onions, all of the bell peppers and the bean sprouts in a large bowl and toss with the dressing. Serve with cilantro sprigs if desired.

SOUPS

Shiitake and Adzuki Bean Soup

C **CA** **CD** **D**   **HD** **M** **MS** **OA** **RA** **V**   MAKES | TIME
4 servings | 1 hour 15 minutes

I created this soup, inspired by a recipe from China, for one of my patients who was fighting cancer. It's loaded with anti-cancer nutrients, it tastes amazing and it's easy to digest.

1 cup (250 mL) dried adzuki beans, washed

1 Tbsp (15 mL) first cold pressed extra virgin olive oil

10–12 large whole garlic cloves

½–1 tsp (2–5 mL) grated fresh ginger

25 medium-size fresh shiitake mushrooms

10 cups (2.5 L) water or organic vegetable stock

4 bunches baby bok choy, chopped

2 Tbsp (30 mL) soy sauce

dash of vegan Worcestershire sauce (for **CD** use gluten-free Worcestershire)

Place the adzuki beans in a pot, cover with water and bring to a boil. Reduce the heat to medium-low, cover and cook for about 45 minutes, until tender. Reserve some of the cooking liquid.

In a large soup pot, place the oil and garlic and sauté on medium heat for a few minutes, stirring. Crush the garlic with a potato masher. Add the ginger and cook for a few minutes, stirring. Add the mushrooms and sauté for a few minutes, stirring. Add the water or stock and bring to a boil. Cover and simmer on medium-low heat for about 20 minutes. Add the bok choy, cooked adzuki beans with 2 Tbsp (30 mL) of their cooking water, soy sauce and a dash of Worcestershire sauce and cook for 4 to 5 minutes.

Thai Noodle Veggie Soup

MAKES	TIME
4 servings	15 to 20 minutes

A delicious meal-in-a-bowl soup that is served all over Thailand—and plenty in our house too. The bean sprouts, although modest looking, are powerhouses of nutrition. Rice noodles are used a lot in Thai cooking, so go ahead and use them if you are avoiding gluten or if you simply prefer them.

¼ lb (125 g) uncooked whole wheat spaghetti (for **CD** see above)

1 Tbsp (15 mL) first cold pressed extra virgin olive oil

3 cups (750 mL) button mushrooms, sliced (optional; omit for **CA** **G**)

1 large carrot, cut into matchsticks

1 small napa cabbage, shredded

3 green onions, finely chopped

8 cups (2 L) vegetable stock

1 tsp (5 mL) hot sauce

¼ tsp (1 mL) chili flakes

1½ cups (375 mL) mung bean sprouts

⅓ cup (80 mL) snow peas

sea salt and pepper (for **HD** use sodium substitute)

Cook the pasta according to the package instructions.

In a large soup pot, place the oil and the mushrooms and sauté, stirring, for about 5 minutes. Add the carrot, cabbage and green onions and sauté for 2 minutes. Add the stock, hot sauce and chili flakes and cook for about 5 minutes. Add the sprouts and snow peas, season to taste with sea salt and pepper and cook for 3 minutes. Add the cooked noodles.

Spicy Thai Soup

MAKES
4 servings

TIME
30 minutes

We had versions of this delicious filling soup all over Thailand, and it seems that it's available for breakfast, lunch *and* dinner. It became my favourite breakfast while I was there. They bring hot sauce to your table so you can add as much or as little as you want. I like it hot.

3 oz (90 g) rice vermicelli

1 tsp (5 mL) first cold pressed extra virgin olive oil

½ package (6 oz/175 g) extra-firm tofu, cubed

8 large button mushrooms, sliced (optional; omit for **CA** **G**)

8 cups (2 L) vegetable stock

4 baby bok choy, separated into whole leaves

1 large carrot, cut into matchsticks

1 tsp (5 mL) hot sauce

¼ tsp (1 mL) chili flakes

pepper

1 cup (250 mL) mung bean sprouts

1 cup (250 mL) frozen green peas

Cook the noodles according to the package instructions.

In a frying pan on medium heat, place the oil and the tofu and sauté, stirring, for about 15 minutes or until browned. Add the mushrooms and sauté until they begin to soften, about 5 minutes.

In a large soup pot, place the vegetable stock, bok choy, carrot, hot sauce, chili flakes and pepper to taste. Cook for 3 minutes. Add the sprouts and frozen peas and cook for another 3 minutes. Add the noodles before serving.

Hot and Sour Soup

	MAKES	TIME
	4 servings	25 minutes

This is a Vietnamese version of hot and sour soup, which is served all over parts of Asia. Each country makes it just a little differently. The greens make this spicy soup—basically a healthy meal-in-a-bowl—even healthier, so do use them.

1 tsp (5 mL) sesame oil

10 button or fresh shiitake or mixed mushrooms, sliced (optional; omit for Ⓖ)

2 oz (60 g) extra-firm tofu, cubed

6 cups (1.5 L) vegetable stock

3–4 crushed dried red chilies, less if you find it too hot

¾ cup (185 mL) pineapple juice

8–10 bite-size pineapple pieces

1 large tomato, cut in chunks

1 cup (250 mL) bok choy, cut up

¼ cup (60 mL) chopped broccoli florets

½ medium-size red bell pepper, diced

½ cup (125 mL) mung bean sprouts, or more to taste

¼ cup (60 mL) snow peas, cut up

¼ cup (60 mL) canned bamboo shoots, drained and rinsed, bite-size pieces (optional)

rice vinegar (optional)

In a large soup pot on medium-low heat, place the sesame oil with the mushrooms and tofu and cook for 5 minutes, stirring. Add the stock, the crushed red peppers, the pineapple juice and pineapple pieces, and tomato. Cook for 12 minutes, covered, stirring now and then. Add the bok choy, broccoli, bell pepper, mung bean sprouts, snow peas and bamboo shoots and cook for 3 to 5 minutes, stirring. Add a little rice vinegar to taste at the end of cooking if you like more of a sour taste.

Miso Soup

MAKES	TIME
4 servings	5 minutes

This Japanese soup is a light, nutritious meal that helps the body get rid of the radiation that we absorb every day.

- 4 cups (1 L) water
- 4 baby bok choy, sliced
- 2 green onions, chopped finely
- 1 oz (30 g) extra-firm tofu, cubed
- ¼ cup (60 mL) light miso paste (for **CD** look for gluten-free miso)

Place the water in a soup pot on medium heat and bring to a boil. Add the bok choy, green onions and tofu and cook for 3 to 4 minutes, just until the bok choy is cooked. Stir in the miso paste and remove from the heat.

Miso Soup with Noodles

C **CA** **CD** **D** **G** **HD** **M** **MS** **OA** **RA** **V**

MAKES	TIME
4 servings	10 to 15 minutes

The greens (super-veggies) and the soy make this soup super-healthy. Make it when you want a little something or aren't feeling great and just want some extra nutrition.

2 oz (60 g) brown-rice spaghettini or vermicelli

4 cups (1 L) water

2–3 cups (500–750 mL) torn-up fresh greens, like red and green chard, kale or bok choy

4 green onions, sliced

1-inch (2.5 cm) piece dried kombu

1 oz (30 g) extra-firm tofu, cubed

dulse flakes

4 tsp (20 mL) light miso paste (for **CD** look for gluten-free miso)

Cook the noodles according to the package instructions.

Bring the 4 cups (1 L) water to a boil and add the greens, onions, kombu and tofu. Cook for 4 minutes. Add a sprinkle of dulse flakes and heat through for 1 minute. Remove from the heat and stir in the miso paste. Add the cooked noodles and serve hot.

Incredible Potato and Mushroom Stew

MAKES	TIME
4 servings	45 minutes

This is truly one of the best stews I've ever had. It smells great—of sautéed mushrooms and dark toasted sesame oil—and it tastes incredible.

1 large white onion, diced

3 tsp (15 mL) toasted sesame oil, divided

20 medium-size button mushrooms, sliced

6 small red or white potatoes, skin on, diced

1 large carrot, diced

1 Tbsp (15 mL) soy sauce

1 tsp (5 mL) balsamic or rice vinegar

pepper

Place the onion in a pot with a close-fitting lid on medium-low heat. Add 1 tsp (5 mL) of the sesame oil and sauté for about 10 minutes, stirring and adding a little water, if needed, to prevent sticking. Add the mushrooms, potatoes, carrot and soy sauce. Cover and cook for about 30 minutes, stirring occasionally and checking the water level. Add the vinegar and the remaining 2 tsp (10 mL) sesame oil and cook for a few minutes more. Season to taste with pepper if desired.

Sweet and Sour Tofu

CD   HD M MS OA RA V   MAKES
2 servings   TIME
40 minutes

Another simple and fast dish containing soy, a very healthy food and a good source of protein. Serve with rice and greens for a complete meal.

1 tsp (5 mL) first cold pressed extra virgin olive oil
⅓ package (4 oz/115 g) extra-firm tofu, cubed
1 Tbsp (15 mL) soy sauce
1 Tbsp (15 mL) balsamic vinegar
¾ tsp (4 mL) brown cane sugar
¼ tsp (1 mL) chili flakes

In a frying pan on medium-high heat, heat the olive oil and brown the tofu on all sides, stirring frequently. Mix together the soy sauce, balsamic vinegar, cane sugar and chili flakes in a bowl. Toss the cooked tofu in this marinade to coat on all sides and allow to stand for 20 minutes. Toss again and serve.

Spicy Chop Suey with Tofu

MAKES	TIME
4 servings	30 minutes

A spicy dish from China that adapts to endless variations. Use whatever vegetables you have that need using up. Just remember to put longer-cooking vegetables in first and fast-cooking vegetables in last. Shiitake mushrooms are wonderful immunity enhancers. Serve hot over brown rice.

3 tsp (15 mL) first cold pressed extra virgin olive oil, divided

1 package (12 oz/350 g) extra-firm tofu, cubed

1 cup (250 mL) fresh shiitake mushrooms, chopped (optional; omit for Ⓖ)

3 green onions, finely sliced

½ tsp (2 mL) chili flakes

¼–½ tsp (1–2 mL) cayenne pepper

sea salt and pepper (for HD use sodium substitute)

2 large sticks celery, thinly sliced diagonally

½ large green bell pepper, sliced (optional; omit for RA)

1 cup (250 mL) boiling water with two ½-inch (1 cm) pieces of dried kudzu root dissolved in it

4 baby bok choy, sliced

1 cup (250 mL) broccoli florets

1 cup (250 mL) mung bean sprouts

3 Tbsp (45 mL) soy sauce

2 Tbsp (30 mL) rice vinegar

1 tsp (5 mL) honey

In a frying pan on medium heat, heat 1 tsp (5 mL) of the oil and brown the tofu on all sides, stirring, for about 10 minutes. Add the rest of the oil (2 tsp/10 mL) along with the mushrooms, green onions, chili flakes, cayenne pepper, and sea salt and pepper to taste, and sauté, stirring, for about 5 minutes. Add the celery and bell pepper and sauté, stirring, for 3 minutes. Add the water with the kudzu and allow to thicken. Add the bok choy, broccoli, sprouts, soy sauce, rice vinegar and honey and cook for 3 to 4 minutes.

Curried Noodles with Vegetables

MAKES	TIME
4 servings	25 minutes

A light, delicious dish from China that is served in many restaurants. In China they use rice noodles, which make this taste lighter. The curry spices are wonderful for keeping the immune system strong.

½ lb (250 g) rice vermicelli

2 oz (60 g) extra-firm tofu, cubed (optional)

1 Tbsp + 1 tsp (15 mL + 5 mL) first cold pressed extra virgin olive oil, divided

¾ cup (185 mL) chopped green beans (¼-inch/5 mm pieces)

12 medium-size button mushrooms, sliced

2 large fresh shiitake mushrooms, sliced thinly

1 medium carrot, cut into matchsticks

¼ small red bell pepper, cut into thin strips (optional; omit for **RA**)

1½ cups (375 mL) mung bean sprouts

1 Tbsp (15 mL) curry powder (strength according to taste)

⅛–¼ tsp (0.5–1 mL) cayenne pepper (optional)

sea salt and pepper (for **HD** use sodium substitute)

Cook the noodles according to the package instructions.

If you are using the tofu, heat the 1 tsp (5 mL) of olive oil in a frying pan over medium heat and brown the tofu on all sides, stirring, for about 10 minutes. Set aside.

Place the 1 Tbsp (15 mL) olive oil in the same frying pan over medium heat and cook the green beans, button and shiitake mushrooms, carrot and bell pepper for 4 to 5 minutes, stirring. Add the bean sprouts, curry powder, cayenne pepper (if using), and sea salt and pepper to taste. Cook, stirring, for 1 minute. Add the cooked noodles before serving.

Mung Bean Noodles

C **CA** **CD** **D** **G** **HD** **M** **MS** **OA** **RA** **V**

MAKES	TIME
2 servings	12 minutes

This meal-in-a-bowl is loaded with garlic and ginger, helping to keep the heart—and, in fact, the whole body!—healthy.

7 oz (200 g) dried mung bean threads

1 Tbsp (15 mL) sesame oil

4 cloves garlic, minced

⅓-inch (8 mm) piece fresh ginger, minced

14 green beans, chopped

1 medium-size carrot, julienned

1 Tbsp (15 mL) soy sauce

cayenne pepper

Cook the noodles according to the package instructions.

In a frying pan on medium heat, heat the oil and add the garlic and ginger. Sauté for 2 to 3 minutes, stirring. Add the green beans, carrot, soy sauce and cayenne pepper to taste. Cook for 5 minutes, stirring. Add the cooked noodles, heat through and mix well before serving.

Chinese Noodles with Cabbage and Mushrooms

	MAKES	TIME
	4 servings	35 to 40 minutes

Easy to do and made from healthy, readily available ingredients, like tofu, cabbage and bean sprouts. Use rice pasta for a gluten-free option.

6 oz (175 g) uncooked whole wheat linguine (for **CD** use rice noodles)

1 Tbsp (15 mL) first cold pressed extra virgin olive oil

⅓ package (4 oz/115 g) extra-firm tofu, thinly sliced

1 small white onion, chopped

1 small red bell pepper, cut in strips (optional; omit for **RA**)

2 cups (500 mL) button mushrooms, sliced (optional; omit for **CA** **G**)

2 cups (500 mL) shredded green cabbage

1½ cups (375 mL) mung bean sprouts

¼ cup (60 mL) soy sauce

¼ tsp (1 mL) cayenne pepper

pepper

Cook the noodles according to the package instructions.

In a large frying pan on medium heat, heat the oil and brown the tofu on all sides, about 15 minutes. Add the onion and sauté, stirring, until soft, about 7 minutes. Add the bell pepper, mushrooms and cabbage and sauté for 7 to 10 minutes, stirring. Add the bean sprouts, soy sauce, cayenne pepper and pepper to taste and heat through for 3 minutes. Add the noodles and heat through before serving.

Thai Noodles

   | MAKES 4 servings | TIME 20 to 25 minutes

A delicious, easy way of getting some healthy tofu, cruciferous vegetables and shiitake mushrooms.

½ lb (250 g) uncooked whole wheat spaghetti

2 Tbsp (30 mL) first cold pressed extra virgin olive oil

1 medium-size white onion, cut into slivers

3 large cloves garlic, minced

⅓ package (4 oz/115 g) extra-firm tofu, cubed

10 medium-size fresh shiitake mushrooms, sliced (optional; omit for G)

1 red or green bell pepper, diced (optional; omit for RA)

1 cup (250 mL) broccoli florets

1 cup (250 mL) cauliflower florets

¼ tsp (1 mL) cayenne pepper

chili flakes

juice of 1 large lime

2 Tbsp (30 mL) soy sauce

Cook the noodles according to the package instructions.

In a frying pan, heat the oil and then sauté the onion on medium heat, stirring, for about 7 minutes. Add the garlic and then the tofu, mushrooms and bell pepper and sauté for about 5 minutes, stirring. Add the broccoli, cauliflower, cayenne pepper and a pinch of chili flakes and cook, stirring, for about 4 minutes. Mix the lime juice with the soy, add to the pan and heat through. Add the noodles and heat through again. Add more cayenne to taste before serving.

Vegetable Pad Thai

MAKES	TIME
4 servings	25 minutes

A traditional national dish served all over Thailand. It's sweet and spicy with a hint of tartness thanks to the lime, and features a wide variety of vegetables.

6 oz (175 g) wide brown-rice Thai noodles (or fettuccine)

1 Tbsp (15 mL) first cold pressed extra virgin olive oil

2 oz (60 g) extra-firm tofu, cubed

1 egg, beaten (optional; omit for **D** **MS** **RA** **V**)

2 baby bok choy, chopped

1 medium-size red bell pepper, diced (omit for **RA**)

½ cup (125 mL) broccoli florets

½ cup (125 mL) cauliflower florets

1 cup (250 mL) mung bean sprouts

handful of snow peas

handful of canned baby corn, drained and rinsed

handful of canned bamboo shoots, drained and rinsed

3 Tbsp (45 mL) soy sauce

1 Tbsp (15 mL) rice vinegar

¼ tsp (1 mL) chili flakes

¼ cup (60 mL) crushed unsalted peanuts

lime wedges

Cook the noodles according to the package instructions.

In a large frying pan, heat the oil. Add the tofu and cook, stirring, for about 7 minutes, or until slightly browned. Add the egg (if using) and cook, stirring, for about 2 minutes. Add the bok choy, bell pepper, broccoli and cauliflower and cook, stirring, for 3 to 4 minutes. Add the mung bean sprouts, snow peas, baby corn, bamboo shoots, soy sauce, rice vinegar and chili flakes and cook, stirring, for 3 to 4 minutes. Add the noodles and peanuts and heat through. Serve with lime wedges to garnish.

VEGETABLE
PAD THAI

Bok Choy and Shiitake Mushrooms

| | | | | | | | | | | | MAKES
4 servings | TIME
15 minutes |

A super-delicious and healthy gluten-free meal from China—and the shiitake mushrooms, garlic and ginger are all tasty immunity boosters. Serve hot over brown-rice noodles.

2 tsp (10 mL) sesame oil

5 large cloves garlic, minced

¼ tsp (1 mL) ground ginger

pepper

garlic salt

14 large fresh shiitake mushrooms, sliced

½ small green bell pepper, bite-size pieces
(optional; omit for **RA**)

3 small bok choy, chopped

1 cup (250 mL) snow peas

½-inch (1 cm) piece kudzu root

3 Tbsp (45 mL) soy sauce

In a large frying pan over medium heat, heat the oil. Add the garlic and sauté, stirring, for 30 seconds. Add the ground ginger, pepper to taste and a pinch of garlic salt and then the mushrooms and bell pepper and sauté, stirring, for about 10 minutes. Add the bok choy, snow peas, whole piece of kudzu root and soy sauce and heat through, stirring, for a few minutes.

Spicy Vegetables with Noodles

			MAKES	TIME
			4 servings	15 minutes

We ate this dish near the ancient ruins of Angkor Wat, in Cambodia, at an outdoor restaurant—right near a sign that said "Do not go off the main path: land mine warning"! If you ever get a chance to see Angkor Wat, don't miss it. We arrived early in the morning and saw a family of monkeys walking with each other and picking up their babies just like humans do.

6 oz (175 g) brown-rice vermicelli

1–2 Tbsp (15–30 mL) first cold pressed extra virgin olive oil

4 green onions, chopped

1½ cups (375 mL) button mushrooms, sliced (optional; omit for CA G)

1 cup (250 mL) finely sliced green cabbage

¼ cup (60 mL) finely chopped green beans

1 oz (30 g) extra-firm tofu, cubed

2 cups (500 mL) mung bean sprouts

2–3 Tbsp (30–45 mL) soy sauce

1 tsp (5 mL) hot sauce

Cook the noodles according to the package instructions.

In a frying pan on medium heat, heat the oil. Add the green onions then the mushrooms, cabbage, green beans and tofu and sauté, stirring, for about 7 minutes. Add the bean sprouts, soy sauce and hot sauce and cook, stirring, for about 3 minutes. Add the noodles and mix well. Add more hot sauce to taste before serving.

Mung Bean Noodles with Tofu and Vegetables

MAKES
4 servings

TIME
35 minutes

This is one of my favourite noodle dishes, and it's gluten-free. Mung bean threads can usually be found in Asian supermarkets.

6 oz (175 g) dried mung bean threads

⅓ package (4 oz/115 g) extra-firm tofu, cubed

1 Tbsp (15 mL) first cold pressed extra virgin olive oil

2 cups (500 mL) sliced mushrooms (shiitake, button, oyster, chanterelle or a combination; for **CA** use shiitake)

4 green onions, finely chopped

1 medium carrot, julienned

¾ cup (185 mL) combination of chopped florets of broccoli and cauliflower, and napa cabbage

3 Tbsp (45 mL) soy sauce

1 tsp (5 mL) toasted sesame oil

1 tsp (5 mL) brown-rice vinegar

¼ tsp (1 mL) cayenne pepper

Cook the mung bean threads according to the package instructions.

In a large non-stick frying pan on medium heat, crisp the tofu without oil on all sides, stirring. Add the oil then the mushrooms and cook for about 5 minutes, stirring. Add the green onions, carrot, broccoli, cauliflower and napa cabbage and cook, stirring, for 3 to 4 minutes. Add the soy sauce, sesame oil, rice vinegar and cayenne pepper and stir for 1 minute to heat through. Add the cooked mung bean threads and heat through again. Add more cayenne pepper to taste before serving.

Sesame and Garlic Stir Fry

 C CA CD D G HD M MS OA RA V

MAKES | 4 servings
TIME | 10 to 15 minutes

A gluten-free dish that is light and full of vegetables and adapts well to what you have in the fridge and whatever is in season. Serve hot over brown-rice noodles.

1½ Tbsp (22 mL) sesame oil, more if needed

⅓ package (4 oz/115 g) extra-firm tofu, cubed

4 large cloves garlic, peeled and minced

2 large portobello mushrooms, sliced (optional; omit for CA G)

1 red bell pepper, bite-size pieces (optional; omit for RA)

3 green onions, chopped

1 stick celery, sliced diagonally

1 cup (250 mL) cut-up Chinese broccoli (florets and stalk)

¾ cup (185 mL) snow peas

½-inch (1 cm) piece fresh ginger, finely grated

3 Tbsp (45 mL) soy sauce

In a large wok on medium heat, heat the sesame oil. Add the tofu and garlic and sauté, stirring, for 1 minute. Add the mushrooms and bell pepper and sauté, stirring, for about 4 minutes. Add the green onions, celery, Chinese broccoli, snow peas and ginger and sauté, stirring, for 3 minutes. Add the soy sauce and heat through for 1 minute.

Indonesian Noodles

MAKES
4 servings

TIME
15 minutes

A light, gluten-free pasta dish full of vegetables and with a sweet and spicy kick.

½ lb (250 g) wide brown-rice noodles

1 tsp (5 mL) first cold pressed extra virgin olive oil

3 large garlic cloves, minced

10 snow peas

1 medium-size red bell pepper, cut in strips

1 medium carrot, cut in thin rounds

1 large tomato, cut in wedges, seeds discarded

¾ cup (185 mL) broccoli florets

¾ cup (185 mL) cauliflower florets

2 oz (60 g) extra-firm tofu, cubed

2 cups (500 mL) mung bean sprouts

¼ tsp (1 mL) cayenne pepper

chili flakes

¼ cup (60 mL) pineapple juice

2 Tbsp (30 mL) rice vinegar

1 tsp (5 mL) honey

3 green onions, finely chopped

Cook the noodles according to the package instructions.

In a large frying pan on medium heat, heat the olive oil. Add the garlic and sauté, stirring, for 1 minute. Add the snow peas, bell pepper, carrot, tomato, broccoli, cauliflower and tofu and sauté, stirring, for about 3 minutes. If necessary add 1 to 2 tsp (5–10 mL) of water to prevent the vegetables from sticking as they cook. Add the mung bean sprouts, cayenne pepper and a pinch of chili flakes and sauté for 1 minute. Mix together the pineapple juice, vinegar and honey and add to the pan. Stir and heat through for 1 minute. Add the cooked noodles and green onions. Stir and heat through for 1 minute. Add more cayenne pepper to taste before serving.

Spicy Vegetable Rice

		MAKES	TIME
		4 servings	55 minutes

A delicious rice dish from China that adapts to endless variations using whatever you have in the fridge. Adding the super-food cruciferous vegetables—cauliflower, broccoli, napa cabbage and bok choy—is optional, but it makes this dish a great one for boosting immunity and fighting cancer and heart disease.

1⅓ cups (330 mL) brown rice

1 Tbsp (15 mL) first cold pressed extra virgin olive oil

2 large cooking onions, chopped

2 large sticks celery, sliced diagonally

1 small carrot, cut into matchsticks

1 small green or red bell pepper, or half of each, bite-size pieces (optional; omit for **RA**)

2 eggs, beaten (optional; omit for **D** **MS** **RA** **V**)

1 cup (250 mL) broccoli florets (optional)

1 cup (250 mL) cauliflower florets (optional)

4 baby bok choy, chopped (optional)

½ cup (125 mL) chopped napa (optional)

1 cup (250 mL) mung bean sprouts (optional)

3 Tbsp (45 mL) soy sauce

1 tsp (5 mL) vegan Worcestershire sauce (for **CD** use gluten-free Worcestershire)

1 tsp (5 mL) sesame oil

½–1 tsp (2–5 mL) cayenne pepper

pepper

handful of raw walnuts halves

handful of raw unsalted sunflower seeds

Place the rice in a pot with 4 cups (1 L) of water and bring to a boil on high heat. Reduce the heat to medium-low, cover, then cook for about 50 minutes, stirring occasionally, until tender.

Meanwhile, in a frying pan on medium heat, heat the olive oil then cook the onions, stirring, for 15 to 20 minutes or until soft. Add the celery, carrot and bell pepper and sauté, stirring, for 4 to 5 minutes. Add the eggs and cook for a few minutes, breaking them apart as they cook. Add any other veggies you are using and cook for 4 minutes. Add the cooked rice, soy sauce, Worcestershire sauce, sesame oil, cayenne pepper, pepper to taste, walnuts and sunflower seeds. Heat through. Add more cayenne pepper to taste before serving.

Spicy Thai Rice

C

MAKES	TIME
4 servings	1 hour

Spicy and delicious, with that unique Thai flavour combo of lime, soy sauce, peanuts, garlic and hot spice.

1 cup (250 mL) brown rice

1 Tbsp (15 mL) first cold pressed extra virgin olive oil

1 large white onion, chopped

12 large button mushrooms, sliced

3 large garlic cloves, minced

1 fresh hot chili or jalapeño pepper, diced

1 medium red or green bell pepper, bite-size pieces (optional; omit for **RA**)

2 eggs, beaten (omit for **D** **MS** **RA** **V**)

3–4 baby bok choy, sliced

1½ cups (375 mL) mung bean sprouts

5 Tbsp (75 mL) soy sauce

¼ cup (60 mL) crushed raw, unsalted peanuts

juice of 2 limes

1 tsp (5 mL) cayenne pepper

pepper

Put the rice in a pot with 3¼ cups (810 mL) of water. Bring to a boil on high heat. Reduce the heat to medium-low, cover and cook, stirring occasionally, for about 50 minutes or until tender.

Meanwhile, in a frying pan on medium heat, heat the olive oil. Add the onion and sauté, stirring, for about 20 minutes. Add the mushrooms and sauté, stirring, for 7 minutes. Add the garlic and chili and sauté, stirring, for about 2 minutes. Add the bell pepper and eggs and cook, stirring, for about 5 minutes, allowing the eggs to break apart. Add the bok choy, mung bean sprouts, cooked brown rice, soy sauce, peanuts, lime juice, cayenne and pepper to taste and heat through for 4 to 5 minutes.

Thai Fried Rice

      | MAKES 4 servings | TIME 1 hour

A classic served all over Thailand. This is loaded with healthy cruciferous vegetables and tofu.

1 cup (250 mL) brown rice

1 Tbsp (15 mL) first cold pressed extra virgin olive oil

⅓ package (4 oz/115 g) extra-firm tofu, cubed

1 egg, beaten (optional; omit for **D** **HD** **MS** **RA** **V**)

2 green onions, finely chopped

2 baby bok choy, sliced

1 medium carrot, thinly sliced

1 medium red bell pepper, sliced (optional; omit for **RA**)

1 cup (250 mL) frozen green peas

½ cup (125 mL) canned baby corn, drained and rinsed

½ cup (125 mL) chopped broccoli florets

½ cup (125 mL) chopped cauliflower florets

½ cup (125 mL) chopped napa cabbage

1 cup (250 mL) mung bean sprouts

2–3 Tbsp (30–45 mL) soy sauce

¼ tsp (1 mL) chili flakes

¼ cup (60 mL) crushed raw, unsalted peanuts (optional; omit for **CA**)

lime wedges (optional)

Put the rice in a pot with 3 ¼ cups (810 mL) of water and bring to boil on high heat. Reduce the heat to medium-low and cover. Cook, stirring occasionally, for about 50 minutes or until tender.

In a large frying pan on medium heat, heat the oil. Add the tofu and cook, stirring, for about 7 minutes, or until slightly browned. Add the egg (if using) and cook, stirring, for 2 minutes. Add the green onions, bok choy, carrot, bell pepper, green peas, baby corn, broccoli, cauliflower and napa cabbage and cook, stirring, for about 3 minutes. Add the mung bean sprouts, cooked brown rice, soy sauce and chili flakes and cook, stirring, for 3 to 4 minutes. Add the peanuts and heat through. If desired, serve garnished with lime wedges.

Sweet and Sour Mushrooms and Pineapple

C   **CD**   **HD** **M** **MS** **OA** **RA** | MAKES | TIME
4 servings | 10 to 15 minutes

A light Chinese dish full of immunity-enhancing mushrooms. You can add cubed browned tofu or greens for the last three minutes of cooking time if you like. Serve over rice with more steamed greens.

> 2 tsp (10 mL) sesame oil
> 6 large fresh shiitake mushrooms
> 6 oyster mushrooms
> 1 package (8 oz/220 g) enoki mushrooms
> two ½-inch (1 cm) pieces of kudzu root
> 5 Tbsp (75 mL) soy sauce
> 2 Tbsp (30 mL) pineapple juice
> 1 Tbsp (15 mL) honey
> 1½ cups (375 mL) bite-size pieces fresh pineapple

In a frying pan on medium heat, heat the oil. Add all the mushrooms and sauté for about 7 minutes. Add the pieces of kudzu root, soy sauce, pineapple juice and honey and allow to thicken, stirring frequently. Add the pineapple and heat through.

Black-Eyed Peas with Greens and Rice

MAKES	TIME
4 servings	1 hour

The flavour of this one is kind of Asian—Asian enough to justify the recipe being in this chapter—but many of the ingredients are from the American South, including black-eyed peas.

½ cup (125 mL) brown rice

1 Tbsp (15 mL) first cold pressed extra virgin olive oil

1 small white onion, diced

4 large garlic cloves, minced

½ medium-size red bell pepper, bite-size pieces (optional; omit for **RA**)

1 can (19 oz/540 mL) black-eyed peas, drained and rinsed

3 Tbsp (45 mL) soy sauce

2 Tbsp (30 mL) balsamic vinegar

1 medium bunch bok choy, sliced pepper

¼ cup (60 mL) raw, unsalted sunflower seeds

Put the rice in a pot with 1⅓ cups (330 mL) of water. Bring to a boil on high heat. Reduce the heat to medium-low and cover, cook, stirring occasionally for about 50 minutes or until tender.

Meanwhile, in a large frying pan on medium heat, heat the oil. Sauté the onion, stirring, for about 15 minutes. You may need to add a little water as it cooks to prevent sticking. Add the garlic and bell pepper and sauté, stirring, for about 5 minutes. Add the cooked rice, black-eyed peas, soy sauce and vinegar. Cook, stirring, for about 2 minutes. Add the bok choy and pepper to taste and cook, stirring, for about 5 minutes. Add the sunflower seeds and heat through before serving.

Adzuki Beans and Rice

MAKES
2 servings

TIME
about 2 hours 15 minutes

A great and tasty combination from China of healthy greens, beans and rice. If you use shiitake mushrooms, you will improve not only your immune system but also the taste of the dish.

1½ cups (375 mL) dried adzuki beans, washed

½ cup (125 mL) brown rice

1 Tbsp (15 mL) sesame oil

14 mushrooms, sliced (fresh shiitake are good for this dish; for **CA** use shiitake)

4 sticks celery, sliced diagonally

4 green onions, finely chopped

4 large garlic cloves, minced

¼-inch (5 mm) piece fresh ginger, grated

¼–½ tsp (1–2 mL) chili flakes

2 small bunches baby bok choy, chopped

2–3 Tbsp (30–45 mL) soy sauce

Add the adzuki beans to 5 cups (1.25 L) of cold water in a large pot. Bring to a boil, then reduce the heat to medium-low and cook, partially covered, for about 2 hours or until soft. Add more water if needed—if it seems like it is drying out—and stir as they cook. Once the beans are cooked, drain and set aside. (Save a little cooking water for later.)

Meanwhile, cook the rice by placing in a pot with 1⅓ cups (330 mL) water. Bring to a boil on high heat. Reduce the heat to medium-low and cover, cook, stirring occasionally for aboug 50 minutes or until tender.

In a frying pan, heat the oil. Add the mushrooms and sauté for about 5 minutes. Add the celery, green onions, garlic, ginger and chili flakes, and cook for 3 minutes. Add the bok choy, soy sauce and cooked beans and cooked rice. You can add in a little of the water from the cooked adzuki beans if you like, for extra nutritional value. Heat through, stirring, for about 3 minutes. Add more soy sauce to taste.

Veggie Sushi

MAKES
4 servings

TIME
1 hour 5 minutes

An easy Japanese dish that gets in those healthy, mineral-rich sea vegetables. It's always a crowd-pleaser at parties because it's such a great finger food.

½ cup (125 mL) short-grain brown rice

3–4 nori sheets (you may need more)

1½ tsp (7 mL) soy sauce

1¼ tsp (6 mL) umeboshi plum paste

English cucumber, finely sliced

1 avocado, bite-size pieces

wasabi paste

Put the rice in a pot with 1⅔ cups (410 mL) of water. Bring to a boil on high heat. Reduce the heat to medium-low. Cover and cook, stirring occasionally, for about 50 minutes or until tender.

Mix the cooked rice with the soy sauce. (Lightly rinse the nori sheets under the tap to weaken the seaweed flavour if preferred.) Spread a 1-inch (2.5 cm) wide row of rice along one end of the nori sheet. Place a little umeboshi plum and some cucumber or avocado on top of the rice. Roll, seal and chill for 20 minutes. Cut into serving-size pieces. Serve with wasabi paste and soy sauce.

Red Thai Curry Paste

MAKES
½–¾ cup (125–185 mL)

TIME
10 minutes

Use this wherever and whenever you want a great spicy Thai flavour. You can use the seeds of the chilies if you would like a bit more heat.

4 large fresh hot red chilies, skinned, seeded and diced

3 large cloves garlic, minced

1 small white onion, diced

2 Tbsp (30 mL) first cold pressed extra virgin olive oil

1 Tbsp (15 mL) hot water

2 tsp (10 mL) fresh lime juice

1 tsp (5 mL) thinly sliced lemongrass

1 tsp (5 mL) ground coriander

½ tsp (2 mL) ground cumin

¼ tsp (1 mL) finely chopped fresh ginger

Throw everything in a blender and blend. You can store this in the fridge for about 5 days.

Tofu Red Curry

MAKES	TIME
4 servings	25 minutes

A fiery, delicious Thai dish. The coconut milk adds a wonderful sweetness that pairs perfectly in this dish with the heat of the curry paste. Serve with brown rice.

2 Tbsp (30 mL) first cold pressed extra virgin olive oil

8 long green beans, cut into 1-inch (2.5 cm) pieces

½ package (6 oz/175 g) extra-firm tofu, cubed

1 cup (250 mL) chopped napa cabbage (optional)

½ cup (125 mL) chopped broccoli florets

½ cup (125 mL) chopped cauliflower florets

¼ cup (60 mL) canned bamboo shoots, drained and rinsed

¼ cup (60 mL) canned baby corn, drained and rinsed

½ medium-size red bell pepper, bite-size pieces (optional; omit for **RA**)

½ carrot, thinly sliced

a few snow peas

handful of fresh shiitake mushrooms, sliced (optional; omit for **G**)

1 cup (250 mL) mung bean spouts

1 can (14 oz/400 mL) coconut milk

1 Tbsp (15 mL) red curry paste (store-bought, or see facing page)

fresh basil, chopped (optional)

In a large frying pan on medium heat, heat the oil. Add the beans and tofu and cook, stirring, for about 10 minutes. Add the napa cabbage, broccoli, cauliflower, bamboo shoots, baby corn, bell pepper, carrot, snow peas and shiitake mushrooms (if using) and cook for 5 to 7 minutes. Add the mung bean sprouts, coconut milk, curry paste and fresh basil (if using) and cook, stirring, for 3 to 4 minutes.

Hot Rice Breakfast

MAKES
1 serving

TIME
5 minutes

This dish from China is a delicious way of getting in lots of fibre, from the brown rice and flaxseed, and nutrients from miso. And it's spicy, too! My favourite hot sauce is a Chinese one called Koon Yick Wah Kee chili sauce that is made with yams, vinegar and chili. It's available in Asian markets, and many good restaurants use it.

⅓ cup (80 mL) instant brown-rice cereal

1 cup (250 mL) boiling water

1 Tbsp (15 mL) light miso paste (for **CD** look for gluten-free miso)

1 Tbsp (15 mL) black sesame seeds

1–2 Tbsp (15–30 mL) ground flaxseeds

1 tsp (5 mL) hot sauce

Place the instant rice cereal in a bowl and pour the boiling water over it. Stir in the miso, sesame seeds, flaxseeds and hot sauce to taste. Eat!

Japanese-Style Beans and Cabbage

MAKES
4 servings

TIME
20 minutes

This Japanese dish contains sake, which gives the dish a wonderful light sweetness that pairs perfectly with the garlic. I like it served with kalamata olives, greens, dates and a cucumber salad.

3 Tbsp (45 mL) first cold pressed extra virgin olive oil

1 head garlic, cloves separated and peeled but kept whole

1½ cups (375 mL) sake

3 cups (750 mL) shredded red cabbage

1 large carrot, shredded

1 can (19 oz/540 mL) cooked navy or great northern beans, drained and rinsed

pepper

2 tsp (10 mL) dried thyme, or 2 Tbsp (30 mL) fresh thyme

In a frying pan on low heat, heat the oil. Add the garlic and sauté, stirring, for a few minutes. Add the sake and cook, stirring, for a few minutes. Crush the garlic with a fork. Add the cabbage, carrot and beans. Season to taste with pepper and cover. Cook on medium heat for about 10 minutes, stirring. Add a little water if it's dry. Add the thyme near the end of cooking time.

Adzuki Loaf

			MAKES	TIME
			4 servings	about 1 hour 10 minutes

A great-tasting loaf that you can serve like meat loaf—with rice or potatoes, greens, a salad, etc. Or serve it cold, sliced, in a sandwich with veggies like sprouts or cucumber or whatever you like.

1 can (19 oz/540 mL) adzuki beans, drained
    and rinsed
2 eggs, beaten (for **D** **HD** **MS** **RA** **V** use
    egg replacement)
3 large garlic cloves, minced
5 Tbsp (75 mL) soy sauce
¼ cup (60 mL) brown-rice flour
2 Tbsp (30 mL) chopped chives
1 Tbsp (15 mL) sesame oil
1-inch (2.5 cm) piece fresh ginger, grated (optional)
½ tsp (2 mL) cayenne pepper
pepper
dulse flakes
brown sesame seeds

Preheat the oven to 375°F (190°C). Grease an 8½- × 4½-inch (22 cm × 11 cm) loaf pan.

Place the beans, eggs, garlic, soy sauce, brown-rice flour, chives, sesame oil, ginger, cayenne pepper, pepper to taste and a good sprinkling of dulse flakes in a large bowl and mix well. Press into the prepared loaf tin and press the sesame seeds into the top of the loaf. Bake for about 1 hour or until cooked (a toothpick inserted in the centre should come out clean).

Sesame-Flavoured Amaranth

 **C** **CA** **CD** **D**   **HD** **M** **MS** **OA** **RA** **V**

MAKES	TIME
4 servings	1 hour 5 minutes

A great way of using amaranth, a delicious gluten-free grain from China. This recipe also contains a healthy sea vegetable, kombu.

1½ cups (375 mL) dried shiitake mushrooms

2 cups (500 mL) amaranth

1 small carrot, cut into matchsticks

1-inch (2.5 cm) piece dried kombu

3 Tbsp (45 mL) soy sauce

2 Tbsp (30 mL) dried red lentils, washed

1 Tbsp (15 mL) toasted sesame oil

¼ tsp (1 mL) cayenne pepper

½ cup (125 mL) frozen green peas

Place the mushrooms, amaranth, carrot, kombu, soy sauce, lentils, sesame oil and cayenne pepper in a pot with 4 to 5 cups (1–1.25 L) of water and bring to a boil, stirring. Reduce the heat to medium-low and cook, covered, stirring now and then and checking the water level every so often, for about 1 hour or until everything is cooked. Add the peas during the last 5 minutes of cooking.

Shiitakes with Mustard Greens

C **CA** **D** **HD** **M** **MS** **OA** **RA** **V**

MAKES
4 servings

TIME
about 1 hour

The combination of toasted sesame oil and tamari offers a real taste of Asia. Rich with healthy shiitake mushrooms and mustard greens, a super-veggie.

8 dried shiitake mushrooms
½ cup (125 mL) bulgur wheat
¼ cup (60 mL) dried adzuki beans, washed
3 cups (750 mL) water
1 cup (250 mL) chopped mustard greens
2 tsp (10 mL) tamari
1 tsp (5 mL) toasted sesame oil
½ tsp (2 mL) black sesame seeds
pinch of dulse flakes

In a soup pot, place the shiitake mushrooms, bulgur wheat and adzuki beans in the water and cover. Bring to a boil then reduce the heat to medium and cook, stirring once in a while, for about 1 hour. The beans should be soft. Monitor the water level and add more water as required if it gets too dry. Add the mustard greens, tamari, sesame oil, sesame seeds and a tiny pinch of dulse flakes and cook for 4 to 5 minutes. It should be slightly saucy but the dish should not be swimming.

Grilled Squash

C CA CD D G HD M MS OA RA V

MAKES	TIME
4 servings	15 minutes

A great, easy way of getting beta-carotene-rich squash in your diet.

¼ cup (60 mL) light oil, like sunflower oil

3 Tbsp (45 mL) soy sauce

1 tsp (5 mL) sesame oil

¼ tsp (1 mL) cayenne pepper

1 acorn squash, skin on, cut in strips

Preheat the barbecue to medium.

Mix together the oil, soy sauce, sesame oil and cayenne pepper. Grill the squash strips, brushing both sides with the oil mixture as you turn them, for 10 to 12 minutes.

Grilled Honey-Ginger Tofu and Broccoli

MAKES	TIME
4 servings	45 minutes

An easy, healthy barbecue dish that uses soy and broccoli, both powerhouse foods that will boost your immune system.

SAUCE

2-inch (5 cm) piece fresh ginger

1½ cups (375 mL) boiling water

3½ Tbsp (52 mL) honey

2 Tbsp (30 mL) first cold pressed extra virgin
   olive oil

TOFU

1 package (12 oz/350 g) extra-firm tofu, cubed

1 medium head broccoli, cut into long florets with
   stalk attached

1 large red bell pepper, cut in strips

¼ large red onion, sliced

juice of 1½ large limes

For the sauce, grate the ginger into the boiling water. Cover and let stand for 20 minutes. Add the honey and olive oil.

Preheat the barbecue to high.

Using a large non stick grilling basket, brown the tofu on all sides on the barbecue. Add the broccoli, bell pepper and onion and stir for 1 minute. Add the sauce to the veggies, enough to coat well, and grill, for 3 minutes. Add the rest of the sauce as the veggies grill. Sprinkle with lime juice before serving.

Grilled Tofu

MAKES	TIME
4 servings	15 minutes

An easy, healthy way of eating Asian-flavoured tofu.

1 package (12 oz/350 g) extra-firm tofu, cut into
  ½-inch (1 cm) slices

SAUCE

¼ cup (60 mL) soy sauce

2 garlic cloves, minced

¼-inch (5 mm) piece fresh ginger, minced
  (optional)

¼ tsp (1 mL) cayenne pepper (optional)

1 tsp (5 mL) honey

2 Tbsp (30 mL) first cold pressed extra virgin
  olive oil

1 tsp (5 mL) toasted dark sesame oil (optional)

Preheat the barbecue to medium-low.

Mix all the ingredients for the sauce and brush on all sides of the tofu slices as they cook in a non-stick griller basket, turning them as they cook, until done, about 10 minutes. They should be slightly crispy.

SALAD ROLLS
WITH GRILLED
VEGETABLES

Salad Rolls with Grilled Vegetables

MAKES	TIME
4 servings	30 minutes

You don't often see celiac-friendly rolls made with grilled vegetables. You can find rice paper sheets in the Asian section of your grocery store or at Asian markets.

SAUCE

1 small clove garlic, peeled and minced (optional)

¼ cup (60 mL) soy sauce

2 Tbsp (30 mL) sesame oil

1 Tbsp (15 mL) honey

1 tsp (5 mL) rice vinegar

¼ tsp (1 mL) cayenne pepper

SALAD ROLLS

1 large yellow bell pepper, sliced

1 large red bell pepper, sliced

1 medium-size green bell pepper, sliced

1 large white onion, sliced

1⅓ cups (80 mL) snow peas

1 cup (250 mL) broccoli florets

⅓ package (4 oz/115 g) extra-firm tofu, cubed

rice paper sheets

hot sauce (optional)

Mix the sauce ingredients together. Preheat the barbecue to medium.

Grill the tofu in a non-stick grilling basket for about 7 minutes, or until slightly golden and crispy, brushing with the sauce. Remove and set aside. Grill the peppers, onion, snow peas and broccoli in the basket, brushing with more sauce, for about 5 minutes. Mix the veggies with the tofu.

Moisten the rice paper sheets well using warm water. Place some of the cooked veggies and tofu on one sheet and form into a roll. Repeat with the rest of the filling and rice paper. Serve with hot sauce, if desired, or any other sauce you enjoy.

Grilled Asian Vegetables

C CA CD D G HD M MS OA   V | MAKES | TIME
4 servings | 10 minutes

A delicious way of getting in the super-veggie broccoli.

1 head broccoli, cut into long florets with
stalk attached

1 very large red bell pepper, cut into
medium strips

1 medium white onion, cut into wedges and the
layers separated

2 Tbsp (30 mL) sesame oil (preferably dark)

2 Tbsp (30 mL) soy sauce

1 Tbsp (15 mL) water

pinch of cayenne pepper

handful of brown sesame seeds (optional)

Mix everything together in a large bowl and marinate for a few minutes. Preheat the barbecue to medium.

Remove the veggies from the marinade. Using a grilling basket if desired, grill the veggies for 4 to 5 minutes while brushing with the marinade. The broccoli should be tender-crisp.

Latin America
and the Caribbean

Recipes

Latin America and the Caribbean

THE FOOD FROM THIS VAST region is full of colour and flavour and can be wonderfully spicy. When travelling around this area, I was pretty much assured of finding some tasty—and creative yet simple—form of rice and beans everywhere I went. (Note that in some parts of South America, meat plays a more prominent role in the cuisine.)

Red beans, black beans, kidney beans; other legumes and peas, rice, corn, tomatoes, and hot peppers of all kinds show up in many parts of Mexico, Central and South America and the Caribbean. And quinoa (the super-healthy, complete-protein, gluten-free grain-like seed) and amaranth (another super-healthy, gluten-free grain) show up in Peru, a very vegetarian-friendly place. Peru is also reported to have over a thousand varieties of potatoes, and you can see endless varieties in the markets, from baby-finger-size to fist-size, from white to purple. I rarely eat french fries, but Peru makes the best ones I have ever had.

Spices like cumin, cayenne, chili, cilantro, oregano and garlic and various kinds of hot peppers are a huge part of the Latin American diet. Coriander, cumin and hot peppers are also pillars of the Caribbean diet, along with nutmeg, cinnamon, coconut and ginger. Hot spices, ginger and garlic are great for health and well-being.

Avocados are wonderful in this part of the world. An enduring memory of Guatemala: I was sitting on the back of the local bus, in other words, a pickup truck, and staring at the back of another pickup truck piled high with the biggest avocados I have ever seen. I had the best guacamole ever in that country.

Foods are often served with a little bit of everything on your plate, in your bowl or on your table. The end result is a colourful, wonderful feast sure to please everyone.

Guatemalan Guacamole

C **CA** **CD** **D** **G** **HD** **M** **MS** **OA** **RA** **V**	MAKES 4 servings	TIME 5 to 10 minutes

As mentioned in the chapter opener, the best guacamole I ever had was in Guatemala. The avocados were a sight to behold: green giants that I knew were loaded with minerals and heart-friendly nutrients. In Mexico they use a yellow cheese called *queso chihuahua*, but you can use Jack, Parmesan or aged cheddar. Serve this with nachos.

2 large very ripe avocados, peeled, pitted and mashed

1 large tomato, diced (optional; omit for **RA**)

juice of 1 large lime

1 Tbsp (15 mL) diced red onion (optional)

1 clove garlic, minced (optional)

¼ tsp (1 mL) chili powder (optional)

5 sprigs fresh cilantro, chopped

grated cheese (optional; omit or use for **CA** **CD** **D** **G** **MS** **RA** **V**)

Mix the avocados and tomato with the lime juice, as well as the onion, garlic and chili powder (if using). Sprinkle the cilantro and cheese (if using) overtop of the guacamole.

GUATEMALAN
GUACAMOLE

Spicy Black Bean Dip/Spread

MAKES
4 servings

TIME
5 minutes

A well-flavoured spicy spread that's easy to make. Serve in a sandwich or wrap, on crackers or little breads, or with nachos.

1 can (19 oz/540 mL) black beans, drained
   and rinsed

½ small white onion, diced

1–1½ fresh hot chilies, diced

1 large tomato, chopped (optional; omit for **RA**)

1 small red bell pepper, diced (optional; omit for **RA**)

1 Tbsp (15 mL) first cold pressed extra virgin
   olive oil

handful of fresh cilantro

sea salt and pepper (for **HD** use sodium substitute)

½ cup (125 mL) fresh corn kernels (optional)

Place the beans, onion, chili peppers, tomato, bell pepper and olive oil in a food processor with a handful of cilantro and sea salt and pepper to taste. Blend until fairly smooth. Mix in the corn (if using) by hand.

Spicy Red Bean Spread/Dip

C **CA** **CD** **D**   **HD** **M** **MS** **OA** **RA** **V** | MAKES | TIME |
| 4 servings | 5 minutes |

These delicious red beans seem to show up everywhere in Honduras. They are often available in Latin American stores, but if you can't track them down, just use red kidney beans, which are larger. This dish is good either way. Serve in a sandwich or wrap, or with crackers, nachos or little breads.

1 can (19 oz/540 mL) red beans, drained and rinsed

¼ cup (60 mL) grated cheese, like Parmesan
   (for **CA** **CD** **D** **MS** **RA** **V** use vegan cheese)

1 large tomato, chopped (optional; omit for **RA**)

1 large clove garlic, very finely minced

1 small white onion, chopped

1–2 Tbsp (15–30 mL) hot sauce

1 Tbsp (15 mL) first cold pressed extra virgin
   olive oil

Place everything in a food processor and blend until fairly smooth.

Spiced Chickpeas

			MAKES	TIME
			4 servings	5 to 10 minutes

A spicy Mexican side dish that's rich in garlic to help boost your immune system.

3 Tbsp (45 mL) dairy-free nonhydrogenated
  margarine
7–8 large garlic cloves, minced
1 can (19 oz/540 mL) chickpeas, drained and rinsed
¼–½ tsp (1–2 mL) cayenne pepper

In a frying pan over medium heat, heat the margarine and sauté the garlic, stirring, for a couple of minutes. Add the chickpeas and cayenne and cook, stirring, for a few minutes.

Spicy Potatoes

| | MAKES
4 servings | TIME
35 minutes |

A wonderful, easy Mexican dish that takes everyday ingredients and turns them into a delicious fiery food.

> 2 Tbsp (30 mL) first cold pressed extra virgin olive oil
>
> 1 large white onion, chopped
>
> 2 fresh hot green chilies, diced, with seeds
>
> 4 large red potatoes, peeled and diced
>
> 2 cups (500 mL) raw greens, like spinach, but you can use whatever you've got (for **G** do not use spinach)
>
> 2 Tbsp (30 mL) balsamic vinegar
>
> sea salt and pepper (for **HD** use sodium substitute)

In a frying pan over medium heat, heat the oil and sauté the onion, stirring, for 15 to 20 minutes. Add the chilies and then the potatoes and sauté, stirring, for about 10 minutes. Add some water if it starts to stick. Add the spinach and vinegar and cook for 3 minutes. Season to taste with sea salt and pepper before serving.

Avocado Salad with Quinoa

MAKES	2 servings	
TIME	25 minutes	

A beautiful, filling salad from Peru that makes use of gluten-free quinoa. Quinoa is a complete protein and is really a seed, not a grain as many people believe. Be careful when you scoop the flesh out of the avocados. You need to keep the skins intact, like little bowls.

½ cup (125 mL) uncooked quinoa

1 cup + 2 Tbsp (280 mL) of water

2 large avocados, sliced lengthwise, flesh diced, reserve the skins

1 cup (250 mL) finely chopped tomatoes (optional; omit for **RA**)

2 green onions, finely chopped

¼ cup (60 mL) cooked black beans, from a can, drained and rinsed (optional; omit for **G**)

1 Tbsp (15 mL) first cold pressed extra virgin olive oil

juice of 2 limes

sea salt and pepper (for **HD** use sodium substitute)

Place the water and the quinoa in a pot, cover and boil over high heat, then turn the heat to low and simmer for about 15 minutes, stirring occasionally.

Combine the cooked quinoa with the avocados, tomatoes, green onions and black beans. Add the oil and lime juice and season to taste with sea salt and pepper. Divide this mix evenly between the four avocado skins. Serve at room temperature.

Zippy, Tangy Kidney Bean Salad

MAKES
4 servings

TIME
5 minutes

I had a version of this salad in Guatemala at a gorgeous hillside restaurant where tourists could eat raw food with no concerns because they used purified water to wash the vegetables. The view was spectacular: flowers everywhere, the lake at Panajachel below, and the surrounding mountains emerging from the mist.

The olives in this dish are an example of how tourism has influenced the regional cuisine.

1 very large ripe avocado, peeled, pitted and sliced thinly

1 can (19 oz/540 mL) red kidney beans, drained and rinsed

12 kalamata olives

5 green onions, finely chopped

2–4 pickled hot peppers, diced (jalapeños work well here)

2 Tbsp (30 mL) apple cider vinegar or fresh lime juice

1 tsp (5 mL) first cold pressed extra virgin olive oil

sea salt and pepper (for **HD** use sodium substitute)

Mix everything together well and serve. You can use more peppers for more spice if you like.

Kidney Bean and Salsa Salad

MAKES	TIME
4 servings	5 minutes

Easy and spicy, and flavoured with the salsa, cayenne and green onions that show up often in Mexican cooking. Garlic chives work well in this dish; they have a stronger flavour than regular chives.

1 can (19 oz/540 mL) red kidney beans, drained
and rinsed

4–5 green onions, chopped

3 Tbsp (45 mL) salsa

2 Tbsp (30 mL) chopped garlic chives

1 Tbsp (15 mL) first cold pressed extra virgin olive
oil or flaxseed oil

1 Tbsp (15 mL) fresh lemon juice

pinch of cayenne pepper

sea salt and pepper (for **HD** use sodium substitute)

Mix everything well and serve.

Mexican Black Bean Soup

C   **HD** **M**   **OA**

MAKES	TIME
4 servings	about 3 hours

I first had this soup on a chilly night after a day at the jungle ruins of Cobá in the steamy rain. Serve this hot with some chopped fresh cilantro and feta cheese in each bowl and lime wedges on the side. In Mexico they use *queso fresco,* which tastes like feta. Since feta is readily available, you can use that instead of trying to track down the real thing. The feta and oregano add a Greek influence.

2 cups (500 mL) dried black beans, washed

3 Tbsp (45 mL) first cold pressed extra virgin olive oil

1 red onion, diced

2 tsp (10 mL) dried oregano

¼–½ tsp (1–2 mL) chili flakes

sea salt and pepper (for **HD** use sodium substitute)

5 large garlic cloves, minced

2 large white onions, diced

1 red bell pepper, diced

½ cup (125 mL) feta cheese, crumbled

fresh cilantro for garnish

lime wedges

In a large soup pot place the beans in 10 to 12 cups (2.5–3 L) of water. Cover and bring to a boil on high heat. Reduce the heat to medium-low and simmer, covered, for 2½ to 3 hours or until tender. Stir occasionally. Add more water if necessary as the beans cook.

Meanwhile, in a frying pan over medium heat, heat the olive oil and sauté the onion, stirring often, for 15 to 20 minutes or until soft. Add a little water rather than more oil if it starts to stick. Add the oregano, chili flakes, and sea salt and pepper to taste, then add the garlic, onions and bell pepper. Sauté for 7 to 10 minutes, stirring often. Add a little water if necessary. Add this mixture to the beans and their cooking water. Heat through for 5 minutes on medium, stirring. Serve topped with crumbled feta cheese and cilantro and a lime wedge on the side.

Spicy Black Bean Soup

	MAKES	TIME
	4 servings	about 4 hours

Bean soups show up everywhere in Central America and are healthy and filling. The kombu in this soup provides healthy minerals as well as more flavour.

2 Tbsp (30 mL) first cold pressed extra virgin olive oil

1 large white onion, chopped

3 large garlic cloves, minced

3 sticks celery, diced

1 large carrot, diced

1½ cups (375 mL) dried black beans, washed

three 1-inch (2.5 cm) pieces dried kombu

1 bay leaf

12 cups (3 L) vegetable stock (or part water, part stock)

½–1 tsp (2–5 mL) cayenne pepper

juice of 2 lemons

2 tsp (10 mL) dried oregano

In a large soup pot over medium heat, heat the olive oil and sauté the onion, stirring, for about 10 minutes. Add the garlic, celery and carrot and sauté, stirring, for about 1 minute. Add the black beans, kombu and bay leaf, then the stock and cayenne pepper, and bring to a boil. Cover and reduce the heat to medium-low. Cook for 3 ½ hours, stirring and checking now and then to see if it needs more stock or water as it cooks. Add the lemon juice and oregano, mix well and cook for a few more minutes before serving.

Chilled Avocado Soup

C **CA** **CD** **D** **G** **HD** **M** **MS** **OA** **RA** **V** | MAKES
4 servings | TIME
5 minutes

A cooling Guatemalan soup that is rich in soy. Serve it right away to prevent discoloration.

> 2 very large avocados, stoned and peeled
> 2 ¾ cups (685 mL) chilled soy milk
> 1 ½ Tbsp (22 mL) fresh lemon juice
> chili flakes
> sea salt and pepper (for **HD** use sodium substitute)
> 2 Tbsp (30 mL) chopped chives

Place the avocados in a blender with the chilled soy milk, lemon juice, a large pinch of chili flakes, and sea salt and pepper to taste. Blend until smooth. Sprinkle with chives to serve.

Squash or Pumpkin Stew

MAKES	TIME
4 servings	2 hours 45 minutes

A colourful stew that's great when it's brought to the table in a clay dish. This is a very festive Mexican dish.

2 cups (500 mL) onion soup stock

2 cups (500 mL) acorn squash or pumpkin, peeled, bite-size pieces

2 large white onions, diced

1 stick celery, chopped

¾ cup (185 mL) frozen or fresh corn kernels

1 cup (250 mL) canned chickpeas, drained and rinsed

½ cup (125 mL) canned black beans, drained and rinsed

5 Tbsp (75 mL) first cold pressed extra virgin olive oil

½–1 tsp (2–5 mL) cayenne pepper

sea salt and pepper (for **HD** use sodium substitute)

Preheat the oven to 350°F (180°C).

Place everything in an ovenproof clay dish, mix and cover. Bake for 2 ½ hours. Everything should be tender.

Spicy Black Beans and Greens

| MAKES | TIME |
| 4 servings | 30 minutes |

You can use whatever mixed greens you have on hand for this super-healthy, spicy Central American meal.

3 Tbsp (45 mL) first cold pressed extra virgin
   olive oil

1 large cooking onion, diced

½ small red onion, diced

3–5 small- to medium-size fresh hot green chilies,
   diced, with seeds

4 medium-size red potatoes, peeled and diced

4 very large button mushrooms, sliced

1 red bell pepper, diced

3 cups (750 mL) mixed greens (red and green chard
   and kale work well)

1 can (19 oz/540 mL) black beans, drained
   and rinsed

1 tsp (5 mL) dried oregano

sea salt and pepper (for **HD** use sodium substitute)

¼ cup (60 mL) balsamic vinegar

In a frying pan over medium heat, heat the oil and sauté the white and red onions, stirring, for 10 minutes. Add the spicy peppers and then the potatoes, mushrooms and bell pepper and sauté, stirring, for another 10 minutes. You may need to add a little water if it starts to stick. Add the greens, black beans, oregano, and sea salt and pepper to taste. Sauté for 2 minutes then add the vinegar. Cook, stirring, for 3 to 4 minutes.

Black Bean Chili

	MAKES	TIME
	4 servings	about 3 hours 45 minutes

An easy Mexican dish. Just add a salad with lots of greens.

2 cups (500 mL) dried black beans, washed

1 cup (250 mL) brown rice

2 Tbsp (30 mL) first cold pressed extra virgin olive oil

2 large white onions, chopped

2 large garlic cloves, minced

1 medium carrot, quartered lengthwise and sliced

1 large stick celery, sliced

¼ large green bell pepper, diced

2 cups (500 mL) vegetable stock

1 can (5.5 oz/156 mL) tomato paste

1–2 tsp (5–10 mL) chili powder

1 tsp (5 mL) dried oregano

sea salt and pepper (for **HD** use sodium substitute)

handful of raw, unsalted sunflower seeds

In a large pot over medium heat, cook the beans in 10 cups (2.5 L) water, covered, for about 3½ hours or until soft. Add more water, if necessary, and stir occasionally as they cook.

Put the rice in a separate pot with 3¼ cups (810 mL) water and bring to a boil on high heat. Reduce the heat to medium-low and cover. Cook, stirring occasionally, for about 50 minutes or until tender.

Meanwhile, in a frying pan over medium heat, heat the oil and sauté the onions, stirring, for about 20 minutes. Add the garlic, carrot, celery and bell pepper and cook for 5 to 7 minutes. Add the cooked beans (drain them first if they are sitting in a lot of cooking liquid) cooked rice, stock, tomato paste, chili powder, oregano, and sea salt and pepper to taste. Cook for about 5 minutes. Serve with sunflower seeds sprinkled overtop.

Black Bean Chili with Mushrooms

	MAKES	TIME
	4 servings	1 hour

This Mexican chili is very easy to make and contains the sweet and mild cubanelle pepper.

¾ cup (185 mL) brown rice

1 Tbsp (15 mL) first cold pressed extra virgin
   olive oil

1 large white onion, diced

12 large button mushrooms, sliced

½ medium-size green bell pepper, bite-size pieces

½ cubanelle pepper, chopped

½–1 tsp (2–5 mL) chili powder

1 can (19 oz/540 mL) black beans, drained
   and rinsed

1½–2 cups (375–500 mL) tomato juice

2 tsp (10 mL) dried oregano

Place the rice in a pot with 2¾ cups (685 mL) of water and bring to a boil on high heat. Reduce the heat to medium-low, cover and simmer, stirring now and then, for about 50 minutes.

Meanwhile, in a large frying pan over medium heat, heat the oil and sauté the onion, stirring, until tender, about 15 minutes. Add the mushrooms, bell pepper and cubanelle pepper and sauté for 5 minutes, stirring. Add the chili powder and sauté for 5 minutes, stirring. Add the black beans, tomato juice and oregano and cook, stirring, for about 7 minutes. Mix with the hot rice.

Honduran Black Bean Chili

MAKES	TIME
4 servings	3 hours 30 minutes

A wonderful, sweet-tasting chili from Honduras that cooks itself in one pan. A complete meal if you add some greens or a salad.

¾ cup (185 mL) brown rice

2 Tbsp (30 mL) first cold pressed extra virgin olive oil

2 very large white onions, diced

6 large garlic cloves, minced

2–3 fresh hot green chilies, diced, with seeds depending on how hot you like it

1¼ cups (310 mL) dried black beans, washed

2 large red bell peppers, bite-size pieces

2 large tomatoes, chopped small

2 tsp (10 mL) dried oregano

sea salt and pepper (for **HD** use sodium substitute)

Place the rice in a pot with 2¾ cups (685 mL) of water and bring to a boil on high heat. Reduce the heat to medium-low, cover and simmer, stirring now and then, for about 50 minutes.

Meanwhile, in a large frying pan with a lid, heat the oil and sauté the onion, stirring, on medium heat for about 5 minutes. Add the garlic and green chilies and cook for 1 minute. Add the black beans and enough water to cover them by 1 inch (2.5 cm) or so, and cover with a lid. Bring to a boil, then reduce the heat to medium. Cook, stirring occasionally and adding more water as needed, for about 3 hours or until the beans are soft. Add the bell peppers, tomatoes, cooked rice, oregano, and sea salt and pepper to taste, and cook for about 20 minutes.

Black Bean, Rice and Yam Casserole

MAKES	TIME
4 servings	about 2 hours

A spicy colourful dish from Jamaica that's rich in lycopene and high in fibre.

3 cups (750 mL) water

1 can (28 oz/796 mL) chopped tomatoes, with juice

1 can (19 oz/540 mL) black beans, drained and rinsed

1 cup (250 mL) short-grain brown rice

¼ cup (60 mL) gluten-free textured vegetable protein

¼ cup (60 mL) first cold pressed extra virgin olive oil

1 medium yam, skin on, bite-size pieces

1 small hot banana or jalapeño pepper, diced, with seeds

1 tsp (5 mL) dried oregano

1 tsp (5 mL) dried basil

¼ tsp (1 mL) cayenne pepper

sea salt and pepper (for **HD** use sodium substitute)

Preheat the oven to 350°F (180°C).

Place everything in an ovenproof dish, mix well and bake for 2 hours or until everything is soft. Check the water level as it cooks and add more if necessary.

Lentil, Amaranth, Spinach and Wild Rice Casserole

MAKES
4 servings

TIME
about 2 hours 30 minutes

This dish makes use of the amazing grain amaranth from Peru. This recipe is easy to prepare and is a complete meal.

1 can (28 oz/796 mL) chopped tomatoes, with juice

3 cups (750 mL) water

1¾ cups (435 mL) chopped fresh spinach

1 cup (250 mL) dried green lentils, washed

1 cup (250 mL) amaranth

¼ cup (60 mL) wild rice

¼ cup (60 mL) first cold pressed extra virgin olive or sunflower oil

2 cooking onions, sliced

1 large carrot, sliced

handful of currants

1 Tbsp (15 mL) dried basil

sea salt and pepper (for **HD** use sodium substitute)

Preheat the oven to 375°F (190°C).

Place everything in a 9- × 13-inch (23 × 33 cm) ovenproof dish and cover with aluminum foil. Bake for 2½ hours, checking once in a while to see if it needs more water as it cooks. It is done when everything is tender.

Huevos with Black Beans and Salsa

CA **CD** **OA**

MAKES	TIME
1–2 servings	5 minutes

An easy breakfast served all over Guatemala. Serve with toast and/or nachos.

2 eggs

1 tsp (5 mL) dairy-free nonhydrogenated margarine

6 Tbsp (90 mL) salsa

¼ cup (60 mL) cooked black beans
(canned are fine)

In a frying pan, fry the eggs in the margarine on medium heat until set but still a little loose. Put each egg on a plate (or both on one plate if you're super-hungry!) and cover with salsa and cooked beans.

Red Lentil, Kidney Bean and Vegetable Stew

MAKES 4 servings	**TIME** 1 hour 15 minutes	

A colourful Caribbean dish loaded with healthy ingredients that are high in fibre and antioxidants. It even sneaks in a healthy sea vegetable—kombu. Sea vegetables are rich in minerals.

2 Tbsp (30 mL) first cold pressed extra virgin olive oil

2 large white onions, peeled and chopped

1 fresh hot green chili, finely chopped

1 yellow bell pepper, bite-size pieces

1 small yam, skin on, diced

2 cups (500 mL) water

½ cup (125 mL) dried red lentils, washed

⅓ cup (80 mL) amaranth

2-inch (5 cm) piece dried kombu

2 tsp (10 mL) ground cumin

sea salt and pepper (for **HD** use sodium substitute)

1 can (28 oz/796 mL) chopped tomatoes, drained

1 can (19 oz/540 mL) red kidney beans, drained and rinsed

In a frying pan over medium heat, heat the oil and sauté the onions, stirring, for 20 minutes. Add the chili, bell peppers and the yam and cook for 3 minutes. Add the water, lentils, amaranth, kombu, cumin, and sea salt and pepper to taste and cook, stirring, for 30 minutes, or until everything is soft. You may need to add some more water. Add the tomatoes and kidney beans. Cook, stirring, for another 20 minutes.

Kidney Bean and Amaranth Chili

MAKES	TIME
4 servings	about 1 hour 10 minutes

A very filling one-dish chili that is wonderfully different because of the amaranth, a staple grain in Peru. And it is gluten-free.

2 Tbsp (30 mL) first cold pressed extra virgin olive oil

1 large cooking onion, chopped

3 large garlic cloves, minced

½ large yellow bell pepper, bite-size pieces

½ large green bell pepper, bite-size pieces

1½ tsp (7 mL) chili powder

¼ tsp (1 mL) cayenne pepper

sea salt (for **HD** use sodium substitute)

1 cup (250 mL) amaranth

1 can (19 oz/540 mL) kidney beans, drained and rinsed

1 can (14 oz/398 mL) canned chopped tomatoes, with juice

1 cup (250 mL) frozen corn

In a frying pan over medium heat, heat the oil and sauté the onion, stirring, for about 25 minutes. Add the garlic and bell peppers and sauté for a couple of minutes, stirring. Add the chili powder, cayenne and sea salt to taste.

Meanwhile, in another pot, place the amaranth in 4 cups (1 L) of water and bring to a boil. Reduce the heat to low and cook for ½ hour or until soft. Drain if there is a lot of excess liquid, and add to the frying pan. Add the beans and tomatoes with their juice and cook for 10 minutes. Add the corn during the last 3 minutes of cooking.

KIDNEY BEAN, PUMPKIN AND POTATO PIE

Kidney Bean, Pumpkin and Potato Pie

MAKES 4 servings **TIME** 1 hour 15 minutes

An attractive and tasty pie from Jamaica, flavoured with coriander, cumin, garlic and cayenne. This is great for company. Serve with a salad.

3 medium-size white potatoes, peeled and diced

2 ½ cups (625 mL) peeled, cubed pumpkin

1 ¾ tsp (9 mL) ground coriander, divided

sea salt and pepper (for **HD** use sodium substitute)

1 cooking onion, chopped

1 Tbsp (15 mL) first cold pressed extra virgin olive oil

5 garlic cloves, minced

2 medium-size tomatoes, chopped

1 medium-size red bell pepper, bite-size pieces

1 can (14 oz/398 mL) red kidney beans, drained and rinsed

¾ tsp (3 mL) ground cumin

¼ tsp (1 mL) cayenne pepper

Preheat the oven to 350°F (180°C). Grease a 9-inch (23 cm) pie plate.

Steam the potatoes and pumpkin in a steamer basket until tender. Mash and add 1 tsp (5 mL) of the coriander and sea salt and pepper to taste. Spread in the prepared pie plate like a crust.

In a large frying pan, sauté the onion in the oil over medium heat, stirring, for about 25 minutes. Add the garlic, tomatoes and bell pepper and cook for 5 minutes. Add the kidney beans and cook for another 2 minutes. Add the remaining ¾ tsp (4 mL) coriander, and the cumin, cayenne, and sea salt and pepper to taste. Mix and heat through. Spread this over the potato-pumpkin crust and bake for 30 minutes.

Caribbean Stew

MAKES	TIME
4 servings	about 2 hours 15 minutes

A spicy dish that tastes of the islands. I like to finish this off with a fruit salad for dessert.

4 cups (1 L) water

1 can (19 oz/540 ml) red kidney beans, drained and rinsed

1 can (5.5 oz/156 ml) tomato paste

12 button mushrooms, halved

5 medium-size cloves garlic, minced

1 large sweet onion, sliced

1 medium-size white or yellow yam, skin on, bite-size pieces

½ medium-size yellow or green bell pepper, bite-size pieces

¼ cup (60 ml) gluten-free textured vegetable protein

¼ cup (60 ml) first cold pressed extra virgin olive oil

2 ½ tsp (12 ml) ground cumin

2 tsp (10 ml) vegetable stock

pepper

Preheat the oven to 375°F (190°C).

Place everything in an ovenproof dish, cover and bake for about 2 hours. You may need to add more water as it cooks.

Pinto Bean and Amaranth Chili

      | MAKES | TIME
| 4 servings | 45 minutes

This chili uses Mexico's pinto bean and Peru's amaranth. And it's gluten-free.

⅓ cup (80 mL) amaranth

1 Tbsp (15 mL) first cold pressed extra virgin olive oil

3 large garlic cloves, minced

1 green bell pepper, diced

1 can (19 oz/540 mL) pinto beans, drained and rinsed

¼–½ tsp (1–2 mL) chili powder

pepper

1¼ cups (310 mL) salsa

1 cup (250 mL) frozen corn

1 tsp (5 mL) dried oregano

¾ cup (185 mL) grated aged cheddar (optional; omit or use vegan cheddar for **CA** **CD** **D** **MS** **V**)

Place the amaranth in 2 cups (500 mL) of boiling water and soak for 10 minutes.

In a large frying pan over medium heat, heat the oil and sauté the garlic, stirring, for 2 minutes. Add the bell pepper and sauté, stirring, for 4 minutes. Add the beans, chili powder and pepper to taste and stir around for 1 minute. Add the amaranth and its soaking water. Cook on medium heat for 30 minutes, stirring, and adding more water if needed. Add the salsa, corn and oregano and cook, stirring, for 5 minutes. Add the cheese if you are using it and heat through before serving.

Mexican White Beans

MAKES **4 servings**	TIME about 3 hours 30 minutes

This dish from Mexico cooks itself while you do other things. Serve with a salad.

6 cups (1.5 L) water

2 cups (500 mL) dried navy beans, washed

1 cup (250 mL) chopped canned tomatoes

¼ cup (60 mL) first cold pressed extra virgin olive oil

2 very large white onions, chopped

2–3 pickled jalapeño peppers, diced

1 large clove garlic, minced

½ small yam, skin on, diced

2 tsp (10 mL) dried oregano

sea salt and pepper (for **HD** use sodium substitute)

Preheat the oven to 350°F (180°C).

Place everything in a large ovenproof dish and cover. Bake for about 3½ hours until the beans are soft. You may need to add more water as it cooks.

Chickpeas in a Spicy Peanut Sauce

C **CD** **HD** **M** **MS** **OA** **RA** **V** | MAKES 4 servings | TIME 5 to 10 minutes

I invented this easy dish on the little island of Tobago. We were in a gorgeous, quiet cottage on a beautiful bay, surrounded by stunning mountains of green that reached out like fingers—covered in yellow and purple flowers—into the botanical gardens below. These ingredients are what I had to cook with that day.

1 can (19 oz/540 mL) chickpeas, drained and rinsed

1 cup (250 mL) mango, orange or grapefruit juice

¼ medium-size red onion, sliced

1–3 Tbsp (15–45 mL) hot sauce

1 Tbsp (15 mL) natural peanut butter (crunchy or smooth)

Place everything in a pot, cover and bring to a boil. Reduce the heat to low and cook, stirring now and then, for about 5 minutes.

Potato and Chickpea Roti

MAKES
5–6 rotis

TIME
about 30 minutes

We first had these made by a man named Jaba, who sold his food from a little wooden hut on the main street in Charlotteville, Tobago. They were so good that Ted would wait each day, sometimes for half an hour or more, to get one of these delicious creations. If you're unsure about which greens to use, I can thoroughly recommend bok choy for this.

2 medium-size potatoes, peeled and diced

½ white onion, sliced

1 can (19 oz/540 mL) chickpeas, drained and rinsed

1 cup (250 mL) mango or apple juice

3–4 Tbsp (45–60 mL) garlic chili hot sauce

3–4 tsp (15–20 mL) curry powder

1 cup (250 mL) chopped greens

whole-wheat tortillas (for **CD** use brown-rice tortillas)

In a pot, place the potatoes and onion and just enough water to cover. Bring to a boil and cover. Reduce the heat to medium-low and cook for about 15 minutes. Reduce the heat further to low and add the chickpeas, juice, garlic chili hot sauce and curry powder and cook for about 10 minutes, partially covered, stirring now and then. Add the greens and cook, stirring now and then, for another 5 minutes.

Place some of this mixture in a tortilla and roll it up. Serve hot or cold.

Red Bean, Potato and Mushroom Roti

MAKES
about **7 rotis**

TIME
about 30 minutes

Another fantastic roti. You should have seen the size of the pumpkin-like squashes they had on Tobago. These huge giants would show up once a week on the back of pickup trucks that stopped everywhere for the locals to buy produce. As with the previous roti recipe, I can thoroughly recommend bok choy for this.

2 medium-size potatoes, peeled and diced

1½ cups (375 mL) mixed mushrooms, chopped

1 cup (250 mL) peeled and diced squash (optional)

½ white onion, sliced

1 can (19 oz/540 mL) red kidney beans, drained and rinsed

1 cup (250 mL) mango or apple juice

3–4 Tbsp (45–60 mL) garlic chili hot sauce

3–4 tsp (15–20 mL) curry powder

1½ cups (375 mL) chopped greens

whole-wheat tortillas (for CD use brown-rice tortillas)

In a pot, place the potatoes, mushrooms, squash (if using) and onion and just cover with water. Bring to a boil and cover. Reduce the heat to medium-low and cook for about 15 minutes. Reduce the heat further to low and add the kidney beans, juice, garlic chili hot sauce and curry powder. Cook for about 10 minutes, partially uncovered, stirring now and then. Add the greens and cook, stirring now and then, for about 5 minutes.

Place some of this mixture in a tortilla and roll it up. Serve hot or cold.

Red Beans and Rice

C **CA** **CD** **D**   **HD** **M** **MS** **OA**   **V**

MAKES
4 servings

TIME
about 3 hours 15 minutes

A spicy dish served in different versions all over Central America. We practically lived on it when we were there.

1 cup (250 mL) dried small red beans, washed

1 cup (250 mL) brown rice

1 Tbsp (15 mL) first cold pressed extra virgin olive oil

2 large white onions, chopped

1 fresh jalapeño pepper, diced, with seeds

2 large tomatoes, diced

1 small green bell pepper, diced

1 tsp (5 mL) ground cumin

½ tsp (2 mL) chili powder

¼–½ tsp (1–2 mL) cayenne pepper

1 tsp (5 mL) sea salt (for **HD** use sodium substitute)

pepper

2 Tbsp (30 mL) spaghetti sauce

1 Tbsp (15 mL) fresh lemon juice

In a pot, place the beans in 6 cups (1.5 L) of cold water. Cover and bring to a boil, then reduce the heat to medium-low and cook for 2 ½ to 3 hours or until soft. Drain the beans, reserving about 1 cup (250 mL) of the cooking liquid.

Meanwhile, in a separate pot, place the rice in 3 ¼ cups (810 mL) of water. Cover and bring to a boil, then reduce the heat to medium-low and cook for about 50 minutes.

In a large frying pan over medium heat, heat the oil and cook the onions and jalapeño pepper, stirring now and then, for about 20 minutes. Add the tomatoes and bell pepper and cook, stirring, for about 5 minutes. Add the cumin, chili powder and cayenne pepper. Add up to 1 tsp (5 mL) sea salt. Add pepper to taste, then the spaghetti sauce and lemon juice and cook for 1 minute.

Add the beans with their reserved cooking liquid and the cooked rice to the frying pan. Cook, stirring now and then, for about 15 minutes to warm through.

Vegetables and Beans with Rice

MAKES	TIME
4 servings	1 hour

A fabulous rice dish that I first had in Belize. The coconut milk makes the dish taste slightly sweet, and the hot sauce gives it the perfect bite.

1⅓ cups (310 mL) brown rice

1 Tbsp (15 mL) first cold pressed extra virgin olive oil

¼ large red onion, diced

1 medium-size tomato, diced (optional; omit for **RA**)

6 mushrooms (your choice), sliced

2 green onions, chopped

1 cup (250 mL) chopped broccoli florets

1 cup (250 mL) chopped cauliflower florets

1 can (19 oz/540 mL) red beans, drained and rinsed

1½ cups (375 mL) canned coconut milk

1–2 tsp (5–10 mL) hot sauce

sea salt (for **HD** use sodium substitute)

juice of 1 lime

Place the rice in a pot with 4 cups (1 L) of water and bring to a boil. Reduce the heat to medium-low heat and cover. Cook for about 50 minutes, stirring now and then.

Meanwhile, in a frying pan over medium heat, heat the oil and sauté the onion, stirring, for about 3 minutes. Add the tomato and cook for 2 minutes. Add the mushrooms and green onions and cook for 2 minutes. Add the broccoli and cauliflower and cook for 3 minutes. Add the cooked brown rice, beans, coconut milk, hot sauce and sea salt to taste, and cook for another few minutes, stirring. Serve hot with lime juice sprinkled overtop.

Red and Black Bean Chili

MAKES	**TIME**
4 servings	**1 hour**

Hearty and filling. Loaded with healthy fibre and antioxidants. And very tasty.

⅔ cup (160 mL) brown rice

1 Tbsp (15 mL) first cold pressed extra virgin olive oil

1 large white onion chopped

3 large garlic cloves, minced

1 large red bell pepper, bite-size pieces

1 can (19 oz/540 mL) red kidney beans, drained and rinsed

1 can (19 oz/540 mL) black beans, drained and rinsed

1 can (28 oz/796 mL) diced tomatoes, with juice

1½ cups (375 mL) tomato juice

2–3 tsp (10–15 mL) chili powder

1 tsp (5 mL) ground cumin

sea salt and pepper (for **HD** use sodium substitute)

1½ cups (375 mL) frozen corn

chopped fresh cilantro (optional)

Place the rice in a pot with 2¼ cups (560 mL) water. Bring to a boil then reduce the heat to low. Cover, and cook, stirring now and then, for about 1 hour.

Meanwhile, in a large frying pan over medium-low heat, heat the oil and sauté the onion, stirring now and then, for about 20 minutes. Add the garlic and cook for 1 minute, stirring. Add the bell pepper and cook for a few minutes, stirring. Add the red and black beans then the tomatoes with their juice, tomato juice, chili powder, cumin, cooked rice, and sea salt and pepper to taste. Cook for about 5 minutes, stirring. Add the corn and heat through for 3 minutes. Garnish with some chopped cilantro if desired.

Tofu Rancheros

	MAKES	TIME
	4 servings	30 minutes

Versions of this dish are served everywhere all over Mexico, probably to accommodate people's increasing desire to not eat eggs and to get more healthy soy in their diets. Shiitake mushrooms are good in this dish. Like the tofu, they are not authentically Mexican, but they make the dish delicious and increase its health benefits. If desired, you can add some cooked black or red beans.

1 tsp (5 mL) first cold pressed extra virgin olive oil

½ package (6 oz/175 g) extra-firm tofu, cubed

6 large mushrooms (your choice; for **CA** use shiitake), diced

¼ large red bell pepper, diced

pepper

1 cup (250 mL) salsa

1 cup (250 mL) canned black or red beans, drained and rinsed (optional)

In a frying pan over medium heat, heat the oil and brown the tofu on all sides, stirring. Add the mushrooms, bell pepper and pepper to taste, and cook, stirring, for 4 minutes. Add the salsa and beans (if using) and cook, stirring, for 4 minutes.

SPICY TOFU VEGGIE
STIR-FRY

Spicy Tofu Veggie Stir-Fry

MAKES	TIME
4 servings	25 minutes

This one really is made by the spicy hot cactus pear sauce. You will find it in Latin American supermarkets, but if it's too difficult to track down, you can use regular hot sauce. Green habanero sauce is a good alternative.

1 tsp (5 mL) first cold pressed extra virgin olive oil

1 package (12 oz/350 g) extra-firm tofu, cubed

2 cups (500 mL) chopped broccoli florets

1 medium-size red bell pepper, bite-size pieces

½ large green bell pepper, bite-size pieces

½ large red onion, diced

2 tsp (10 mL) spicy hot cactus pear sauce

1 tsp (5 mL) regular hot sauce

juice of 1 lime

In a wok over medium heat, heat the oil and brown the tofu on all sides, stirring. Add the broccoli, bell peppers, onion and the hot sauces and cook, stirring, for about 5 minutes. Sprinkle the lime juice overtop and serve hot.

Tofu Burritos

     MAKES **4 servings**   TIME **30 minutes**

Guatemalan burritos are a little different from the Mexican kind. Serve with guacamole, either right in it or on the side.

1 tsp (5 mL) first cold pressed extra virgin olive oil

½ package (6 oz/175 g) extra-firm tofu, cubed or crumbled

5 large button mushrooms, sliced

¼ medium-size green bell pepper, diced

¼ small red onion, diced

1–3 tsp (5–15 mL) hot sauce

1 can (14 oz/398 mL) black beans, drained and rinsed

1 cup (250 mL) chopped broccoli florets

1 cup (250 mL) salsa

whole wheat tortillas (for use rice paper sheets or corn tortillas)

In a frying pan over medium heat, heat the oil and lightly brown the tofu, stirring, on all sides. Add the mushrooms, bell pepper, onion and hot sauce and sauté for 4 minutes, stirring. Add the beans, broccoli and salsa, and cook for 4 minutes, stirring.

Heat the tortillas. Heap the filling into a tortilla and roll to eat.

Chili Rellenos

MAKES	TIME
2 servings	1 hour 15 minutes

I first had this festive dish in a traditional outdoor market in Peru. This version does not cook in the traditional batter, so it is healthier. Stuffed foods are ideal for company as they look impressive.

1 Tbsp + 1 tsp (15 mL + 5 mL) first cold pressed
    extra virgin olive oil, divided

1 medium-size white onion, cubed

3 cups (750 mL) finely chopped
    button mushrooms

⅓ package (4 oz/115 g) extra-firm tofu, diced

2 green bell peppers

1½ cups (375 mL) grated cheese, a combination of
    Jack, cheddar and mozzarella (for **C** **CD** **D** **HD** **M**
    MS **V** use vegan cheese)

In a frying pan over medium heat, heat the 1 Tbsp (15 mL) oil and sauté the onion, stirring, for about 25 minutes. Add the mushrooms and sauté, stirring for about 5 minutes.

In a separate pan over medium heat, warm the 1 tsp (5 mL) oil and brown the tofu on all sides, stirring. Add to the mushrooms.

Preheat the oven to 350°F (180°C).

Cut the tops off the bell peppers and remove the seeds. Stuff the peppers with the mushroom mixture. Replace the caps. Place in an ovenproof dish and place 1 Tbsp (15 mL) of water in the bottom of the pan. Cover the peppers with the cheese and bake for about 30 to 40 minutes, or until tender.

Caribbean Stuffed Red Peppers

MAKES | TIME
4 servings | 1 hour 45 minutes

Festive and colourful, and a rich source of carotenes. When I was in the Caribbean, I noticed a lot of coriander seed, tomatoes and red peppers being used in the cooking.

1 cup (250 mL) brown rice

4 Tbsp (60 mL) first cold pressed extra virgin olive oil, divided

2 white onions, chopped

1 cup (250 mL) peeled, cubed pumpkin

3 large tomatoes, diced

2 tsp (10 mL) ground coriander

¼ tsp (1 mL) cayenne pepper (optional)

sea salt and pepper (for **HD** use sodium substitute)

5 red bell peppers

Place the rice in a pot with 3 ¼ cups (810 mL) water and bring to a boil. Reduce the heat to medium-low, cover and cook for about 50 minutes, stirring now and then.

Meanwhile, in a frying pan over medium heat, heat 2 Tbsp (30 mL) of the oil and sauté the onions and pumpkin, stirring, for 20 minutes. Add a little water if they start to stick to the pan.

Preheat the oven to 350°F (180°C).

Mix together the remain 2 Tbsp (30 mL) olive oil with the cooked rice, onion-pumpkin mix, tomatoes, coriander, cayenne, and sea salt and pepper to taste. Cut the peppers in half lengthwise and remove the seeds. Stuff each half with some of the vegetable mixture. Place each stuffed half on a cookie sheet, stuffed side up. Drizzle with a little olive oil and bake for 35 to 40 minutes, or until the peppers are cooked.

North America

Recipes

North America

IT'S DIFFICULT TO SAY WHAT North American cuisine is. Some say it is convenience food or fast food, some say it's barbecue and others say it's a blend of everybody else's cuisines—and, to a great degree, these descriptions are all accurate. North America is home to people from all over the world who brought their cuisines with them. So, you find influences from the British Isles, Central and Eastern Europe, Asia, India, Latin America, the Caribbean, Africa and everywhere else you care to name. This means we have access to foods and spices from all over the world. We have even hijacked foods like Italian pizza, for example, so that they are now almost synonymous with North American cuisine.

The personality of North American cooking also includes the way we eat. Many of us are on the go, so we often find ourselves eating in front of the computer or the TV, or at a street vendor. And then we switch it up and eat in a nice restaurant, or around a campfire—using ample amounts of barbecue sauce on everything. We eat at the cottage, at friends' houses and of course at our own houses, whether it's at the kitchen table, outside if we have a patio, and in the dining room on special occasions.

We tend to like our salads and to borrow from our favourite international cuisines. In some of the Southern states and California, you find influences from Mexico and Cuba, with chilies and cumin and other spices figuring more prominently. In Louisiana, a unique blend of cooking combines Acadian cooking from Nova Scotia, with okra via the African slaves and sassafras from the First Nations people. They also use a lot of cayenne in their dishes. Quebec features many dishes that originated from France but have developed a flavour of their own over time. In Toronto, where I live, you get all kinds of Asian, Indian, Mexican, Italian, Greek, Thai, Ethiopian—just about every known food on the planet, and this is true of most big North American cities. The products available in grocery stores, the fast food, the frozen foods and the food in people's kitchens represent this variety.

So what is North American cuisine? Almost anything you want, any way you want.

Chickpea Spread

MAKES	TIME
4 servings	5 minutes

Like the recipe that follows this one, this is kind of like a healthy egg salad that's completely egg- and dairy-free. Serve on whole wheat or gluten-free bread, with lettuce and alfalfa sprouts.

1 can (19 oz/540 mL) chickpeas, drained and rinsed

1 medium stick celery, diced

¼ small white onion, diced

3 Tbsp (45 mL) vegan mayonnaise

2 Tbsp (30 mL) fresh dill, chopped

pepper

Place everything in a food processor and blend until smooth.

Avocado Spread

C **CA** **CD** **D** **G** **HD** **M** **MS** **OA** **RA** **V**

MAKES	TIME
4 servings	5 to 10 minutes

My husband, Ted, thinks this makes a good alternative to egg salad, and it's so much healthier. Serve as is or on crackers or toast.

2 ripe medium-size avocados, mashed

1 large tomato, diced (optional; omit for **RA**)

¼ small white onion, diced

juice of 1 lemon

pepper

pinch of cayenne pepper (optional)

Mix everything together, adding a pinch of cayenne pepper for a bit of spice if you like.

Delicious Tofu Spread

MAKES 4 servings	TIME 10 minutes (chill overnight)

This spread is great on whole-grain bread with sprouts, or served with crackers. It is loaded with immunity-boosting tofu, onions and almonds and healthy oils from the walnuts and flax. It's also filling and makes a great lunch. (Note that you have to prepare it a day in advance.)

1 package (12 oz/350 g) extra-firm tofu

2½ large sweet onions, diced

1 stick celery, chopped (optional)

½ red bell pepper, diced (optional; omit for **RA**)

1 cup (250 mL) almonds

¼ cup (60 mL) walnuts

2 tsp (10 mL) soy sauce

1 tsp (5 mL) medium-hot paprika

1 tsp (5 mL) flaxseed oil or first cold pressed extra virgin olive oil

Blend everything very well in a food processor, then transfer to an airtight container and refrigerate for 1 day before using. Keeps for a week or more in the fridge.

Exotic Woodsy Mushrooms

MAKES	TIME
4 servings	20 minutes

This dish tastes and smells incredible. It is very good as is or over pasta, grains or a vegetable crêpe.

1 Tbsp (15 mL) dairy-free
   nonhydrogenated margarine

2½ cups (625 mL) medium-size button
   mushrooms, halved

4–5 fresh shiitake mushrooms, chopped

4–5 oyster mushrooms, chopped

4–5 chanterelle mushrooms, chopped

2 medium garlic cloves, minced

1 green onion, chopped

3 Tbsp (45 mL) soy sauce

1½ Tbsp (22 mL) fresh lemon juice

1 Tbsp (15 mL) sesame oil

⅛ tsp (½ mL) ground ginger

pepper

cayenne pepper

In a frying pan over medium-low heat, heat the margarine and sauté all the mushrooms, stirring, for about 5 minutes. Add the garlic, green onion, soy sauce, lemon juice, sesame oil, ground ginger, and pepper and cayenne to taste. Sauté, stirring, for about 10 minutes.

Brown-Rice-Flour Bread with Herbs

	MAKES an 8- × 4-inch (1.5 L) loaf	TIME 1 hour 25 minutes

This one took me a while to perfect. It's a great-tasting bread for those who are celiac and can't eat gluten—or, in fact, for anyone. It just tastes good. The small amount of sugar used in this bread to activate the yeast can be tolerated by most people with candida, but if you cannot tolerate it, or you've been advised to avoid breads made with yeast, do not make this.

> 1 cup (250 mL) hot water
>
> 1½ Tbsp (22 mL) active dry yeast
>
> 1 tsp (5 mL) brown cane sugar
>
> 1 tsp (5 mL) sea salt (for **HD** use sodium substitute)
>
> 1 tsp (5 mL) crushed dried rosemary or basil
> (optional)
>
> ⅓ cup (80 mL) tapioca flour
>
> ¼ cup (60 mL) potato flour
>
> 1¼ cups (310 mL) brown-rice flour
>
> 2 Tbsp (30 mL) first cold pressed extra virgin
> olive oil

Thoroughly oil an 8- × 4-inch (20 × 10 cm) loaf pan.

Mix together the hot water, yeast, sugar, sea salt and rosemary or basil (if using). Add the three flours and mix well. Add the olive oil and mix well again. Shape the dough into a loaf and place in the prepared loaf pan. Cover with a dry, light kitchen towel and allow to stand over a warm oven for 20 minutes to activate the yeast, or place in a warm, draft-free area for 20 minutes.

Preheat the oven to 375°F (190°C).

Bake for 50 minutes. Insert a toothpick in the centre to make sure it is cooked through. Allow to cool in the pan for a few minutes before transferring to a cooling rack.

Light Brown-Rice-Flour Bread

| | MAKES
an 8- × 4-inch
(1.5 L) loaf | TIME
1 hour 5 minutes |

Another light and delicious version of brown-rice bread that is great for celiacs. Read the intro to the previous recipe about the sugar and yeast in the bread.

2½ cups (625 mL) brown-rice flour

¾ cup less 1 Tbsp (170 mL) tapioca flour

2 tsp (10 mL) cream of tartar

1 tsp (5 mL) sea salt (for **HD** use sodium substitute)

2 tsp (10 mL) active dry bread yeast

1¼ tsp (6 mL) brown cane sugar

1¼ cups (310 mL) hot water

flaxseeds or brown sesame seeds

Lightly oil an 8- × 4-inch (20 × 10 cm) loaf pan.

Mix together the two flours, cream of tartar and sea salt.

In a separate bowl, mix the yeast and sugar with the hot water. Add to the dry mixture and mix well. Knead on a lightly floured surface for 5 minutes. Shape the dough into a loaf and place in the prepared loaf pan. Sprinkle with flax and/or brown sesame. Press the seeds gently into the bread. Cover with a dry light kitchen towel and allow the bread to stand on top of a hot oven, or place in a warm, draft-free area, for 30 minutes to activate the yeast.

Preheat the oven to 425°F (220°C).

Bake for 30 to 40 minutes. Insert a toothpick in the centre to make sure it is cooked through. Allow to cool in the pan for a few minutes before transferring to a cooling rack.

Potato-Rice-Flour Buns

| | MAKES
approx 6 small buns | TIME
about 30 minutes |

Buns made with celiac-friendly grains and no yeast.

¾ cup (185 mL) potato flour

½ cup (125 mL) brown-rice flour

1 Tbsp (15 mL) baking powder

1 tsp (5 mL) sea salt (for **HD** use sodium substitute)

dried dill or other aromatic herbs (optional)

⅓ cup (80 mL) first cold pressed extra virgin
olive oil

1 egg, beaten (for **D** **HD** **MS** **RA** **V** use
egg replacement)

Preheat the oven to 350°F (180°C).

Mix both flours, baking powder, sea salt and a pinch of dried herb (if using). Add the olive oil and egg, mix well and then add enough water to make a medium-wet dough. Form into small- to medium-size buns. Place the buns on a lightly oiled cookie sheet.

Bake for about 15 to 20 minutes. Insert a toothpick to check that the buns are cooked through.

SALADS

Basic Healthy Salad Dressing

MAKES
2 servings

TIME
about 5 minutes

This dressing is a staple in our house as it is rich in essential fatty acids, which are crucial to good health. They keep your whole body strong and your skin healthy.

2 Tbsp (30 mL) flaxseed oil, chili-flavoured flaxseed oil or hempseed oil

1 Tbsp (15 mL) balsamic vinegar or apple cider vinegar

sea salt and pepper (for **HD** use sodium substitute)

Mix everything well and use on any salad, from a green one to a bean one. It's great on steamed vegetables too.

ADDITIONS

½–1 tsp (2–5 mL) Dijon mustard for a spicy mustard taste (especially good on green salad)

¼ tsp (1 mL) cayenne pepper for a spicy taste

a little freshly grated ginger, or a pinch of ground ginger, for a gingery taste

some minced garlic for a garlicky taste

1 Tbsp (15 mL) tamari for an Asian taste

some freshly chopped or dried herbs

1 tsp (5 mL) tahini for an earthy taste (use lemon juice instead of vinegar, and add some minced garlic if you like)

SUBSTITUTION

freshly squeezed lime or lemon juice instead of the vinegar

Simple Green Salad

 | MAKES 2 servings | TIME 5 to 10 minutes

I include so many options here because I want to get across the importance of eating all kinds of raw vegetables every day, any way you like them. Try to make at least 50 to 75 percent of your diet raw food. Feel free to experiment. I often add raw, unsalted pumpkin seeds to the salad, and sometimes raw, unsalted sunflower seeds.

DRESSING

2 Tbsp (30 mL) flaxseed oil, hemp oil or
   first cold pressed extra virgin olive oil

1 Tbsp (15 mL) balsamic vinegar or
   fig vinegar

1 tsp (5 mL) Dijon mustard (optional)

sea salt and pepper (for **HD** use
   sodium substitute)

freshly chopped herbs (optional)

dulse flakes (optional)

Mix together all the dressing ingredients, then toss them over a combination of the following veggies:

4 cups (1 L) torn-up mixed fresh greens

chopped cauliflower florets

chopped broccoli florets

sliced radishes

any kind of sprout

tomato wedges (omit for **RA**)

red, yellow or green bell pepper slices
   (omit for **RA**)

carrot slices

celery slices

cucumber slices

cut-up green beans

snow peas

chopped onions

chopped green onions

chopped chives

avocado slices

mango slices (omit for **CA**)

pear slices

apple slices

Fresh Greens

| | | MAKES
4 servings | TIME
10 minutes |

This delicious light salad is packed full of vitamins, minerals and, of course, antioxidants. We grow everything in our garden and reap the rewards all summer long.

3 cups (750 mL) torn-up red leaf lettuce

1 cup (250 mL) torn-up green leaf lettuce

large handful of arugula, torn up

small handful of fresh dill, finely chopped

handful of fresh basil, finely chopped

large handful of baby red chard leaves, torn up

large handful of baby kale leaves, torn up

2 Tbsp (30 mL) first cold pressed extra virgin olive oil or flaxseed oil

2 Tbsp (30 mL) balsamic vinegar

sea salt and pepper (for HD use sodium substitute)

Place all the ingredients in a large salad bowl, mix well and serve right away.

Caesar Salad with a Twist

C **CA** **CD** **D** **HD** **M** **MS** **OA** **RA** **V**

MAKES	TIME
4 servings	10 minutes

A more filling version of Caesar salad that is great for picnics too. The beans add more fibre to this classic salad and make it a more complete meal.

1 can (19 oz/540 mL) red kidney beans, drained and rinsed

4 green onions, chopped small

4 garlic cloves, minced

1 medium-size romaine lettuce, torn into bite-size pieces

¼ large red bell pepper, sliced into thin strips (optional, but omit for **RA**)

4–5 Tbsp (60–75 mL) grated Parmesan cheese (for **CA** **CD** **D** **MS** **RA** **V** use vegan Parmesan)

3 Tbsp (45 mL) first cold pressed extra virgin olive oil

3 Tbsp (45 mL) balsamic vinegar

sea salt and pepper (for **HD** use sodium substitute)

Mix everything well in a large bowl and let stand a few minutes. Serve at room temperature.

Spring Salad

 MAKES
4 servings

TIME
about 45 minutes

A great way of combining early spring asparagus with leftover winter root vegetables.

3 medium-size beets with leaves, chopped

1 small turnip, peeled and diced

12–15 spears asparagus, chopped

5 green onions, finely chopped

4 large garlic cloves, minced

3 Tbsp (45 mL) fresh lemon juice

1 Tbsp (15 mL) first cold pressed extra virgin olive oil or flaxseed oil

1 tsp (5 mL) ground cumin

chili flakes

sea salt and pepper (for **HD** use sodium substitute)

Cook the beets and the turnip separately in boiling water over medium heat until tender, about 20 to 30 minutes, depending on how small you chop them. Allow to cool. Steam the asparagus in a steamer basket for 4 minutes then allow to cool. Mix all the cooked veggies with the onions, garlic, lemon juice, oil, cumin, chili flakes to taste, and sea salt and pepper to taste in a large salad bowl and allow to stand for a few minutes before serving.

SPRING
SALAD

Avocado, Tomato and Cheese Salad

C   **HD** **M**   **OA**

MAKES	TIME
4 servings	10 minutes

A simple yet delicious salad that's great for lunch or dinner.

3 large tomatoes, cut in wedges

2 large avocados, cut in thin strips

2 green onions, chopped

½ cup (125 mL) Edam cheese, thinly sliced

2 large garlic cloves, minced

2 Tbsp (30 mL) first cold pressed extra virgin
   olive oil

1 Tbsp (15 mL) fresh lemon juice

sea salt and pepper (for **HD** use sodium substitute)

On a large platter, place the tomatoes, avocados, green onions and cheese. Mix the garlic with the oil, lemon juice, and sea salt and pepper to taste and pour over the vegetables. Serve immediately.

Pear and Asiago Cheese Salad

C **HD** **M** **OA**

MAKES	TIME
4 servings	10 minutes

I first had this at a dinner party at a friend's house. This is my version. The pear is perfect with the Asiago and the walnuts.

2 medium-size tomatoes, cut into wedges

1 small to medium romaine lettuce, torn into bite-size pieces

1 cup (250 mL) radicchio, bite-size pieces

2 medium-size pears, skin on, cored and cut into strips

½ cup (125 mL) grated Asiago cheese

½ cup (125 mL) walnut pieces

2 Tbsp (30 mL) first cold pressed extra virgin olive oil

1 Tbsp (15 mL) fresh lemon juice

sea salt and pepper (for **HD** use sodium substitute)

In a large bowl, place the tomatoes, romaine, radicchio, pears, Asiago cheese and walnuts. Mix together the oil, lemon juice, and sea salt and pepper to taste and pour over the salad. Toss well before serving.

Mango Veggie Salad

MAKES	TIME
4 servings	10 minutes

A colourful salad that is sweet and tangy with a hint of heat.

- 1 tsp (5 mL) brown cane sugar
- ¼–½ tsp (1–2 mL) chili flakes
- 1 Tbsp (15 mL) orange juice
- 2 tsp (10 mL) fresh lemon juice
- 3 green onions, finely chopped
- 2 medium-size mangos, peeled and thinly sliced
- ⅓ medium-size English cucumber, peeled and diced
- ⅓ medium-size red bell pepper, diced (optional; omit for **RA**)
- 1 cup (250 mL) green seedless grapes, sliced in half

Mix the brown sugar and chili flakes with the orange juice and lemon juice. Place the green onions, mango, cucumber, bell pepper and grapes in a bowl. Add the dressing then let stand for a few minutes before serving.

Sweet Dill Potato Salad

 **C** **CA** **CD** **D** **G** **HD** **M** **MS** **OA** **V** | MAKES
4 servings | TIME
about 1 hour

A wonderful picnic salad, flavoured with fresh dill, green onions and pickles.

> 5–6 large potatoes, any kind, peeled and
>   roughly chopped
>
> ½ large yam, peeled and roughly chopped
>
> 6 green onions, finely chopped
>
> 3 large dill pickles, finely chopped
>
> 2–3 Tbsp (30–45 mL) vegan mayonnaise
>
> 1½ Tbsp (22 mL) finely chopped fresh dill or
>   1½ tsp (7 mL) dried dill
>
> sea salt and pepper (for **HD** use sodium substitute)

In a medium-size pot over medium heat, boil the potatoes and yam until tender, about 25 minutes. Cut into small dice. Mix them with the rest of the ingredients in a large bowl and chill for at least ½ hour. Serve cool.

Potato Salad

MAKES	TIME
4 servings	1 hour 20 minutes

A vegan version of potato salad that is healthier and tastier than the traditional version. The artichokes add a really nice texture and flavour.

6 large red potatoes, peeled and roughly chopped

8–10 pickled artichokes, cut up

1 small white onion, diced

¼ cup (60 mL) green relish

1–2 Tbsp (15–30 mL) vegan mayonnaise

sea salt and pepper (for **HD** use sodium substitute)

small handful of fresh dill, finely chopped

In a large pot over medium-high heat, boil the potatoes until tender, about 20 minutes. Cool and dice. Mix the potatoes with the rest of the ingredients in a large bowl and chill for 1 hour. Serve cool.

Red Potato, Onion and Celeriac Salad

	MAKES	TIME
	4 servings	about 1 hour

The celeriac provides a great twist on an old favourite. This is dairy-free.

4–5 large red potatoes, peeled, bite-size pieces

1 medium-size celeriac, peeled, bite-size pieces

1 small white onion, diced

¼ cup (60 mL) fresh dill, finely chopped

2–3 Tbsp (30–45 mL) sweet pickle relish (optional;
    omit or use chopped pickle for **C** **CA** **D** **G**)

1–2 Tbsp (15–30 mL) vegan mayonnaise

sea salt and pepper (for **HD** use sodium substitute)

In a large pot over medium-high heat, boil the celeriac and potato until tender, 20 to 25 minutes. Allow to cool and dice. Mix with the onion, dill, relish (if using), mayonnaise, and sea salt and pepper to taste. Chill for ½ hour. Serve cool.

Summer Bean Salad

										MAKES	TIME
C	CA	CD	D	HD	M	MS	OA	RA	V	4 servings	15 minutes

Perfect for when you don't feel like cooking because of the heat but want something easy to make and filling. The high fibre content of this salad is great for your health.

> 2 cans (each 19 oz/540 mL) mixed beans, drained
> and rinsed
> 1 large tomato, diced (optional; omit for **RA**)
> 2 green onions, diced
> 1½ Tbsp (22 mL) first cold pressed extra virgin
> olive oil or flaxseed oil
> 1½ Tbsp (22 mL) balsamic vinegar
> ½ tsp (2 mL) prepared yellow mustard
> large handful of fresh basil, torn up
> small handful of fresh summer savory, torn up
> sea salt and pepper (for **HD** use sodium substitute)

Place everything in a large salad bowl, mix and chill for a few minutes before serving.

Kidney Bean and Onion Salad

MAKES
4 servings

TIME
35 minutes

Simple and good, and travels well for picnics.

1 can (19 oz/540 mL) red kidney beans, drained and rinsed
1 large white onion, thinly sliced
1 large clove garlic, minced
3 Tbsp (45 mL) canola oil or sunflower oil
1 Tbsp (15 mL) apple cider vinegar
½ tsp (2 mL) prepared yellow mustard
¼ tsp (1 mL) garlic salt
pepper
dash of vegan Worcestershire sauce (for **CD** use gluten-free Worcestershire)
a few sprigs of fresh parsley, finely chopped

Place all the ingredients in a large salad bowl, mix well and chill for half an hour. Serve cool.

Romano Bean Salad

| | | | | MAKES
4 servings | TIME
10 minutes |

An easy salad that adds more protein and fibre to a meal. Or add a whole-grain roll to this and you'll have a complete protein. The soy sauce, green onions and cayenne combine to make a wonderful flavour.

1 can (19 oz/540 mL) romano beans, drained and rinsed

3 green onions, finely chopped

1 stick celery, chopped

¼ large red bell pepper, diced (optional; omit for **RA**)

¼ cup (60 mL) chopped fresh parsley

4 tsp (20 mL) first cold pressed extra virgin olive oil

2 tsp (10 mL) apple cider vinegar

1 tsp (5 mL) soy sauce

¼–½ tsp (1–2 mL) cayenne pepper

pepper

Mix everything well in a large bowl and allow to marinate for a few minutes. Serve at room temperature.

Cabbage, Bean and Rice Soup

| | MAKES
4 servings | TIME
2 hours |

A hearty kind of soup. Just add crusty bread and a salad for a complete meal.

1½ Tbsp (22 mL) first cold pressed extra virgin olive oil

3 large cooking onions, roughly chopped

10–12 cups (2.5–3 L) water

1 can (19 oz/540 mL) kidney beans, drained and rinsed

5 cups (1.25 L) green cabbage, chopped

1 large carrot, sliced

1 medium-size red bell pepper, roughly chopped

½ cup (125 mL) brown rice

2 vegetable stock cubes

sea salt and pepper (for **HD** use sodium substitute)

1 can (28 oz/796 mL) diced tomatoes, with juice

In a large soup pot over medium heat, heat the oil and sauté the onions, stirring, for 20 minutes. Add the water, beans, cabbage, carrot, red pepper, brown rice, stock cubes and sea salt and pepper to taste, and bring to a boil. Cover, reduce the heat to low and cook for about 45 minutes, stirring occasionally. Add the tomatoes with their juice and cook, still covered, for another 45 minutes, stirring occasionally.

White Bean Soup

 **V**

MAKES	TIME
4 servings	3 hours 20 minutes

A hearty soup that is rich in lycopene and health-boosting nutrients. Serve with a large green salad and whole-grain bread.

¼ cup (60 mL) first cold pressed extra virgin olive oil

2 large white onions, chopped

4 large garlic cloves, chopped

12 cups (3 L) water

2 cups (500 mL) dried white beans, washed

6 baby carrots, diced

pepper

1 can (5.5 oz/156 mL) tomato paste

¼ cup (60 mL) soy sauce

1 Tbsp (15 mL) balsamic vinegar

1½ tsp (7 mL) honey (optional; omit for **CA** **D** **V**)

In a large soup pot over medium heat, heat the oil and sauté the onions, stirring, for about 5 minutes. Add the garlic and sauté, stirring, for a few minutes. Add the water, beans, carrots and pepper to taste. Cover and bring to a boil. Reduce the heat to medium-low and cook, partially covered, for about 3 hours, or until soft, stirring from time to time. You may need to add more water. Add the tomato paste, soy sauce, balsamic vinegar and honey and cook, stirring, for about 10 minutes.

Lentil Soup

MAKES
4 servings

TIME
about 1 hour 45 minutes

Chock full of vegetables along with garlic, ginger and onions for optimum health.

2 large potatoes, skin on,
   roughly chopped

1 medium beet, skin on,
   roughly chopped

1 large yam, skin on, roughly chopped

8 cups (2 L) water

1 tsp (5 mL) first cold pressed extra
   virgin olive oil

2 large onions, roughly chopped

4 garlic cloves, minced

½-inch (1 cm) piece fresh ginger, minced

1½ cups (375 mL) dried red lentils,
   washed

1 Tbsp (15 mL) medium-hot paprika

1 tsp (5 mL) ground cumin

¼ tsp (1 mL) chili flakes

sea salt and pepper (for **HD** use
   sodium substitute)

1 bunch beet greens, cut up

1 medium-size tomato, diced

In a large pot over medium heat, boil the potatoes, beet and yam in the water, covered, for about 1 hour, until fork-tender. Strain and reserve the cooking liquid.

In another pot, heat the oil and sauté the onions, stirring, for about 20 minutes. Add the garlic and the ginger and sauté for 1 minute, stirring. Add the lentils, paprika, cumin, chili flakes, sea salt and pepper to taste and the reserved cooking liquid. Bring to a boil, reduce the heat to medium-low and simmer, covered, for about ½ hour, stirring occasionally. You may need to add more liquid as it cooks. Add the beet greens and tomato with the cooked potato, beet and yam. Cook, stirring, for 15 minutes.

Potato and Kale Soup

V | MAKES
4 servings | TIME
1 hour 5 minutes

This soup is truly one of my favourites. It was one of the first ways I thought of how to use super-healthy kale. Everyone always loves it and asks for more.

2 Tbsp (30 mL) butter, olive oil or dairy-free
nonhydrogenated margarine
(for **CA CD D G MS V** use oil or margarine)

2 large white onions, roughly chopped

4–5 very large white or red potatoes, peeled
and diced

10 cups (2.5 L) vegetable stock

1 medium bunch of kale

1 tsp (5 mL) dried or 1 Tbsp (15 mL) fresh dill
(optional)

sea salt and pepper (for **HD** use sodium substitute)

In a large soup pot over medium heat, heat the butter and sauté the onions until soft, 20 to 25 minutes. Add the potatoes and stir for 1 minute. Add the stock and bring to a boil. Reduce the heat to medium, cover and cook, stirring now and then, for about 30 minutes.

Meanwhile, chop the kale and steam it for 15 to 20 minutes in a steamer basket until soft. Drain and discard the cooking water. Add the kale to the soup pot and heat through. You may need to add more stock.

Transfer to a blender and purée until smooth. Season with dill (if using) and sea salt and pepper to taste. Heat through for a couple of minutes before serving.

Potato and Celeriac Soup

 **V** | MAKES 4 servings | TIME 55 minutes

A silky-smooth celeriac-flavoured soup that people love.

> 1 Tbsp (15 mL) dairy-free nonhydrogenated margarine
>
> 1 very large white onion, roughly chopped
>
> 4 large potatoes, red or white, peeled and diced
>
> 1 large celeriac, peeled and diced
>
> 12 cups (3 L) vegetable stock
>
> pepper

In a large soup pot over medium heat, heat the margarine and sauté the onion, stirring, for about 20 minutes. Add the potatoes and celeriac and sauté for 1 minute. Add the stock and bring to a boil. Reduce the heat to medium-low and cook, covered, for 25 to 30 minutes, stirring occasionally. You may need to add more stock. Add pepper to taste, and purée and heat through before serving.

Potato, Garlic and Cabbage Soup

MAKES
4 servings

TIME
about 50 minutes

An excellent way to get immunity-enhancing garlic and vitamin C into your diet, not to mention a healthy cruciferous vegetable if you use the cabbage. (Note that cooking the wine evaporates most of the alcohol, so this recipe is fine for people with gout.)

2–3 Tbsp (30–45 mL) first cold pressed extra virgin olive oil

2 bulbs garlic (about 24 whole garlic cloves, separated and peeled)

1 cup (250 mL) chanterelle mushrooms, chopped (optional; omit for **CA** **G**)

1 cup (250 mL) red wine

10 cups (2.5 L) vegetarian chicken-flavour stock

4 medium-size red potatoes, peeled and diced

1 cup (250 mL) chopped red cabbage (optional)

pepper

In a large soup pot over medium heat, heat the oil and sauté the garlic cloves with the chanterelle mushrooms (if using) for 2 to 3 minutes, stirring. Add the wine and sauté for 2 minutes. Crush the garlic with a potato masher or fork. Add the stock and potatoes and bring to a boil, stirring. Reduce the heat to low and cook for about 20 minutes. Add the cabbage (if using) and cook for about 15 minutes, or until the cabbage is soft. Season to taste with pepper.

Carrot, Garlic and Ginger Soup

	MAKES	TIME
	4 servings	25 to 30 minutes

A delicious soup loaded with carotenes, antioxidants and disease-fighting nutrients. This recipe would be beneficial for cancer patients, who especially do not need extra toxins, so use organic stock.

1 Tbsp (15 mL) first cold pressed extra virgin
    olive oil
6 very large whole garlic cloves
6 cups (1.5 L) organic vegetable stock
4 large carrots, roughly chopped
1 tsp (5 tsp) freshly grated ginger
pepper

In a large soup pot over medium heat, heat the oil and add the garlic cloves. Cover and cook, stirring occasionally, until done on all sides. It only takes a few minutes. Mash with a potato masher or fork. Add the stock, carrots, ginger and pepper to taste and bring to a boil. Cover, reduce the heat to low and simmer for about 20 minutes, until the carrots are tender. Purée and heat through before serving.

Root Vegetable Soup with Shallots and Dill

MAKES	TIME
4 servings	45 minutes

A hearty, flavourful soup.

1 Tbsp (15 mL) butter or first cold pressed extra
   virgin olive oil (for **CA** **CD** **D** **G** **MS** **V** use oil)

3 large shallots, roughly chopped

10–12 cups (2.5–3 L) vegetarian chicken-
   flavour stock

4 large potatoes, peeled and diced

1 large yam, peeled and diced

1 medium-size celeriac, peeled and diced

sea salt and pepper (for **HD** use sodium substitute)

½ cup (125 mL) chopped fresh dill

In a large soup pot over medium heat, heat the butter and sauté the shallots, stirring, until soft, about 10 minutes. Add the stock, potatoes, yam, celeriac, and sea salt and pepper to taste and bring to a boil. Reduce the heat to medium-low and simmer, stirring, for about ½ hour. Add the dill and cook for another 5 minutes. Purée and heat through before serving.

Clay Pot Vegetable Stew

MAKES	TIME
4 servings	3 hours 10 minutes

A fragrant stew that's high in fibre and needs no attention once you've put it in the oven. In it are veggies often used in North American cuisine: carrots, button mushrooms, yams, celery and green beans. The clay pot helps to marry the flavours together, so do try to track one down if you're making this.

6 cups (1.5 L) water

1 cup (250 mL) dried green lentils, washed

½ cup (125 mL) brown rice

½ cup (125 mL) wild rice

¼ cup (60 mL) currants

⅓ medium-size yam, skin on, roughly chopped

8 green beans, cut in 1-inch (2.5 cm) pieces

8 button mushrooms, quartered

2 baby carrots, sliced

1 stick celery, sliced

2 Tbsp (30 mL) first cold pressed extra virgin olive oil

2 Tbsp (30 mL) soy sauce

pepper

Preheat the oven to 350°F (180°C).

Place everything in a large ovenproof clay dish and cover. Bake for about 3 hours, until everything is tender. You may need to add more water as it cooks.

Rice, Lentil and Vegetable Bake

MAKES	TIME
4 servings	about 1 hour 40 minutes

When you cook this, the antioxidant-rich thyme, onions and mushrooms smell wonderful. And each person gets their own little soufflé dish. Just add a salad for a complete meal.

1 cup (250 mL) brown rice

6 cups (1.5 L) vegetable stock

½ cup (125 mL) dried red lentils, washed

2 large yams, peeled and cubed

1 Tbsp (15 mL) first cold pressed extra virgin olive oil

2 large white onions, roughly chopped

2 cups (500 mL) button mushrooms, sliced

1 tsp (5 mL) dried thyme

¼–½ tsp (1–2 mL) cayenne pepper

In a pot, add the rice to the vegetable stock and bring to a boil. Reduce the heat to medium-low, cover and simmer, stirring frequently, for 30 minutes. Add the lentils and cook for another 30 minutes. Drain if necessary.

Meanwhile, in a separate pot, boil the yams until soft, about ½ hour. Drain and mash with some vegetable stock from the potato pot.

In a large frying pan over medium heat, heat the oil and sauté the onions until soft, stirring, about 15 minutes. Add the mushrooms and sauté for a few minutes. Add the thyme and cayenne pepper.

Preheat the oven to 325°F (160°C).

In each of four mini soufflé dishes, place some of the cooked brown rice and lentils, some mashed yam and some onion-mushroom mixture. Cover with aluminum foil and bake for 15 minutes, then uncover and bake for another 15 minutes.

Rice with Vegetables

												MAKES	TIME
C	**CA**	**CD**	**D**	**G**	**HD**	**M**	**MS**	**OA**	**RA**	**V**		4 servings	50 minutes

An easy one-dish supper that is overflowing with healthy foods.

1 cup (250 mL) brown rice

1 Tbsp (15 mL) first cold pressed extra virgin
   olive oil

4 large sticks celery, sliced diagonally

1 large red bell pepper, roughly chopped
   (optional; omit for **RA**)

1 oz (30 g) extra-firm tofu, cubed

2 cups (500 mL) bok choy, chopped

1 cup (250 mL) cauliflower florets

¼ cup (60 mL) walnut halves

small handful of brown sesame seeds

2 Tbsp (30 mL) soy sauce

½–1 tsp (2–5 mL) hot sauce

Place the rice in a pot with 3¼ cups (810 mL) water and bring to a boil.
Reduce the heat to medium-low, cover and cook for about 50 minutes,
stirring now and then.

   In a frying pan over medium heat, heat the oil and cook the celery,
bell pepper and tofu for a few minutes, stirring. Add the bok choy and
cauliflower and cook for 3 minutes. Add the cooked brown rice, walnuts,
sesame seeds, soy sauce and hot sauce, and heat through for a couple
of minutes.

Barley with Vegetables, Red Lentils and Plum

MAKES	TIME
4 servings	2 hours 35 minutes

A wine-, plum- and barley-flavoured dish that requires little attention. Just add a mixed green salad for a complete meal. Use a clay pot for authenticity and to help bring the flavours together.

1 cup (250 mL) white wine—vinho verde works well

1 large white onion, roughly chopped

1 medium-size carrot, roughly chopped

1 medium-size red potato, skin on, diced

1 cup (250 mL) whole-grain barley

½ cup (125 mL) dried red lentils, washed

1 fresh large red plum (look for Chinese plum if possible), diced

sea salt and pepper (for **HD** use sodium substitute)

Preheat the oven to 375°F (190°C).

Place everything in a large ovenproof clay dish and cover with 4 to 5 cups (1–1.25 L) water. Cover and bake for about 2 ½ hours or until everything is soft. You may need to add more water as it cooks.

Rice Pasta with Veggies and Romano Beans

C   **CD** **D**   **HD** **M** **MS** **OA**   **V** | MAKES **4 servings** | TIME **55 minutes**

Mushrooms, basil and tomato flavour this pasta. It has a great bite to it.

6 oz (175 g) long brown-rice pasta or 1½ cups
(375 mL) short brown-rice pasta (any shape)

1 can (19 oz/540 mL) romano beans, drained
and rinsed

1 can (19 oz/540 mL) diced tomatoes, with juice

1¼ cups (310 mL) sliced mushrooms, any type

⅔ cup (160 mL) cubed brick or mozzarella cheese
(for **C** **CD** **D** **HD** **M** **MS** **V** use vegan cheese)

½ cup (125 mL) spaghetti sauce

3–6 pickled hot peppers, diced

3 Tbsp (45 mL) grated Parmesan cheese (for **CD** **D**
MS **V** use vegan Parmesan)

2 Tbsp (30 mL) first cold pressed extra virgin
olive oil

1 tsp (5 mL) dried basil

sea salt and pepper (for **HD** use sodium substitute)

Preheat the oven to 375°F (190°C).

Cook the pasta according to the package instructions.

Place the pasta and the rest of the ingredients in a large ovenproof casserole dish. Mix to combine and bake, covered, for about 40 minutes.

Veggies and Buckwheat Noodles

	MAKES	TIME
	4 servings	15 to 20 minutes

A soupy dish loaded with antioxidants. And it's gluten-free. You should be able to find buckwheat noodles in the health food section or at any Japanese grocery store. If you have celiac disease, make sure the brand you are buying is not cut with any wheat flour.

6 oz (175 g) long buckwheat noodles or 1½ cups
   (375 mL) short buckwheat noodles (any shape)
   (for **CD** see note above)

1 Tbsp (15 mL) sesame oil

5 large garlic cloves, minced

3 Tbsp (45 mL) soy sauce

2 Tbsp (30 mL) rice vinegar

1 tsp (5 mL) honey (optional; omit for **CA** **D** **V**)

1¼ cups (310 mL) broccoli florets

1 cup (250 mL) torn-up and tightly packed fresh
   spinach (optional; omit for **G**)

½ cup (125 mL) frozen peas

½ cup (125 mL) grated pumpkin

¼ tsp (1 mL) ground ginger

pepper

2 cups (500 mL) vegetable stock

Cook the noodles according to the package instructions.

In a large frying pan over medium-low heat, heat the sesame oil and sauté the garlic, stirring, for about 1 minute. Add the soy sauce, rice vinegar and honey (if using), then the broccoli, spinach, peas, pumpkin, ground ginger and pepper and to taste and cook, stirring, for about 3 minutes. Add the stock and heat through for 3 minutes. Serve hot over the noodles.

Extra-Healthy Macaroni

MAKES	TIME
4 servings	1 hour 15 minutes

A great comfort food, but a very healthy version with lentils, whole wheat macaroni, onions, garlic and tomatoes.

½ cup (125 mL) dried green lentils, washed

1½ cups (375 mL) whole wheat macaroni
(for **CD** use brown-rice macaroni)

1 Tbsp (15 mL) first cold pressed extra virgin
olive oil

2 large white onions, roughly chopped

3 large garlic cloves, minced

1 can (28 oz/796 mL) diced tomatoes, with juice

pepper

1 slice whole wheat bread, toasted, bite-size
pieces (for **CD** use gluten-free bread)

dulse flakes

Place the lentils in a pot with 1 ½ cups (375 mL) of water and bring to a boil on high heat. Reduce the heat to medium-low, cover and cook, stirring occasionally, for 45 minutes to 1 hour, until tender.

Meanwhile, cook the pasta according to the package instructions.

In a large frying pan over medium heat, heat the oil and cook the onions, stirring, for about 25 minutes. Add the garlic and cook, stirring, for about 1 minute. Add the cooked macaroni, cooked lentils, tomatoes with their juice, and pepper to taste, and cook, stirring, for about 5 minutes. Add the bread and dulse to taste and heat through, stirring, before serving.

Honey Mustard Tofu

MAKES	TIME
4 servings	25 minutes

This tofu dish is excellent for health and well-being—and it delivers a complete protein. Serve with steamed veggies, rice and a salad.

> 1 Tbsp (15 mL) first cold pressed extra virgin
>   olive oil
> 1 package (12 oz/350 g) extra-firm tofu, cut in
>   ¼-inch (0.5 cm) thick slices
> 2 Tbsp (30 mL) honey
> 2 Tbsp (30 mL) yellow or Dijon mustard

In a frying pan over medium-high heat, heat the olive oil and brown the tofu on both sides. Flip frequently, being careful not to burn it. Mix together the honey and mustard and brush on both sides of the browned tofu. Reduce the heat to medium and cook for 1 minute on each side.

Tofu in Lemon Horseradish Sauce

MAKES	TIME
4 servings	25 minutes

Simple and quick, this can be an appetizer, or a main meal if you add a salad and rice or potatoes.

> 1 package (12 oz/350 g) extra-firm tofu, 1-inch (2.5 cm) cubes
>
> 1 Tbsp (15 mL) first cold pressed extra virgin olive oil
>
> 2 Tbsp (30 mL) vegan mayonnaise
>
> 2 tsp (10 mL) white horseradish
>
> 2 tsp (10 mL) fresh lemon juice
>
> sea salt and pepper (for **HD** use sodium substitute)

In a frying pan over medium heat, brown the tofu on all sides in the oil, stirring. Mix together the mayonnaise, horseradish, lemon juice, and sea salt and pepper to taste and serve over the tofu.

Vegetable and Bean Stew

	MAKES	TIME
	4 servings	2 hours 40 minutes

An easy vegetable and bean stew. Serve with steamed broccoli or Brussels sprouts.

1 can (28 oz/796 mL) diced tomatoes, with juice

3 cups (750 mL) water

1 can (19 oz/540 mL) romano beans, drained
   and rinsed

2 large white onions, roughly chopped

4 baby carrots, sliced

1 large yam, skin on, cubed

1 large red potato, skin on, cubed

10 large button or cremini mushrooms, quartered

⅓ cup (80 mL) first cold pressed extra virgin
   olive oil

1½ tsp (7 mL) dried thyme

sea salt and pepper (for **HD** use sodium substitute)

Preheat the oven to 375°F (190°C).

Place everything in a 13- × 9-inch (33 × 23 cm) glass dish, mix and cover. Bake for about 2 ½ hours until everything has cooked down and blended. You may need to add more water as it cooks. Serve hot.

Soy Bean, Tomato and Artichoke Casserole

V

MAKES
4 servings

TIME
1 hour 35 minutes

A great way of including healthy soy in your diet. You can substitute your favourite mushrooms for the button mushrooms if you like. Serve with a salad.

1 can (28 oz/796 mL) diced tomatoes, with juice

1 can (19 oz/540 mL) soy beans, drained and rinsed

1 can (19 oz/540 mL) artichoke hearts, drained and chopped

2 cups (500 mL) sliced button mushrooms (for **CA** use shiitake)

½ cup (125 mL) frozen corn

1 small yam, skin on, diced

¼ cup (60 mL) first cold pressed extra virgin olive oil

1 tsp (5 mL) dried basil

¾ tsp (4 mL) dried dill

Preheat the oven to 350°F (180°C).

Place everything in a large ovenproof dish, cover and bake for about 1 ½ hours until everything has cooked down and blended. You may need to add more water as it cooks.

Chili with Portobello Mushrooms

MAKES
4 servings

TIME
55 minutes to 1 hour

Portobello mushrooms kick this delicious Louisiana chili up a notch.

1 Tbsp (15 mL) first cold pressed extra virgin olive oil

1 large white or sweet onion, diced

4–5 large portobello mushrooms, bite-size pieces

1 large clove garlic, minced

1 medium-size carrot, diced

1 medium-size red bell pepper, diced

1 can (28 oz/796 mL) tomatoes, drained and puréed in a blender

1 can (19 oz/540 mL) mixed beans, drained and rinsed

1 can (19 oz/540 mL) red kidney beans, drained and rinsed

1½ tsp (7 mL) chili powder

1 tsp (5 mL) Louisiana hot sauce

pepper

1 cup (250 mL) plain soy yoghurt (optional)

1 small (7 oz/198 g) can chipotle peppers, drained (optional)

In a large frying pan over medium heat, heat the olive oil and cook the onion, covered, stirring now and then, for about 20 minutes. Add a little water if it starts to stick. Add the mushrooms, garlic, carrot and bell pepper and cook, covered, stirring now and then, for about 10 minutes. Add the tomatoes, mixed beans and kidney beans, chili powder, hot sauce and pepper to taste and cook for about 20 minutes, covered, and stirring now and then.

If desired, blend the yoghurt and chipotle peppers and add a dollop to each bowl of chili.

Spicy Potato Bean Pie

	MAKES	TIME
	4 servings	1 hour 20 minutes

Wonderful individually layered dishes of deliciousness. Serve with a green salad.

8 large potatoes, peeled and roughly chopped

3 Tbsp (45 mL) first cold pressed extra virgin olive oil

2 large cooking onions, roughly chopped

12 medium-size button mushrooms, sliced

1 fresh hot chili, chopped with a few of the seeds

1 tsp (5 mL) dried oregano

½ tsp (2 mL) garlic powder

½ tsp (2 mL) ground cumin

½ tsp (2 mL) medium-hot paprika, plus more for dusting

¼ tsp (1 mL) cayenne pepper

1 can (19 oz/540 mL) red kidney beans, drained and rinsed

1 can (19 oz/540 mL) diced tomatoes, with juice

sea salt and pepper (for **HD** use sodium substitute)

Boil the potatoes until tender. Drain. Reserve in the pot.

Meanwhile, in a frying pan over medium heat, heat the oil and sauté the onions until soft, about 25 minutes. Add the mushrooms and hot chili and sauté for 2 to 3 minutes. Add the oregano, garlic powder, cumin, paprika and cayenne. Add the kidney beans and tomatoes with their juice and sauté, stirring, for about 5 minutes. Season to taste with sea salt and pepper. To the pot with the potatoes, add just some of the tomato mixture and mash until they are smooth and lump-free.

Preheat the oven to 350°F (180°C).

Rub the inside of four mini soufflé dishes with a little margarine. Then layer each with some mashed potatoes, some of the tomato mixture and then more potatoes. Smooth the tops with a spoon and dust with paprika. Bake for about 40 minutes until golden on top.

Mushroom Potato Bean Casserole

C **HD** **M** **OA**

MAKES
4 servings

TIME
1 hour 40 minutes

An easy one-dish meal. Just add a huge green salad.

> 5 large potatoes, peeled, halved lengthwise and
>   thinly sliced
>
> pepper
>
> 10 button mushrooms, sliced
>
> 1 can (19 oz/540 mL) romano or pinto beans,
>   drained and rinsed
>
> 1 can (10 oz/284 mL) condensed cream of
>   mushroom soup
>
> 1½ onion-flavoured stock cubes
>
> 2 Tbsp (30 mL) soy sauce
>
> 3 cup (750 mL) soy milk

Preheat the oven to 375°F (190°C). Grease a 11- × 7-inch (28 × 18 cm) ovenproof dish.

Layer everything in the order listed in the prepared dish and cover. Bake for 1 ½ hours until tender.

Potato and Broccoli Bake

MAKES	TIME
4 servings	about 1 hour 10 minutes

Comfort food, but with healthy broccoli and soy milk.

1½ cups (375 mL) soy milk

2 eggs, beaten

4 large potatoes, peeled and grated

½ large head broccoli, chopped into small pieces

½ cup (125 mL) grated aged cheddar cheese (for
    C CA CD M V use vegan Parmesan)

½ cup (125 mL) grated mozzarella cheese (for
    C CA CD M V use vegan mozzarella)

pepper

Preheat the oven to 350°F (180°C). Grease a 13- × 9-inch (33 × 23 cm) baking dish.

Mix everything together and place in the prepared baking dish. Bake for 50 to 60 minutes or until golden.

KALE AND
RED PEPPER
IN PHYLLO
PASTRY

Kale and Red Pepper in Phyllo Pastry

      **V** | MAKES 4 servings | TIME about 1 hour

A delicious pastry that is great for entertaining. It makes use of kale, a super-veggie, and it tastes great.

1 Tbsp (15 mL) first cold pressed extra virgin olive oil

4 cups (1 L) bite-size pieces kale

1 large red bell pepper, cut into strips that are then halved

1¾ cups (435 mL) grated aged white cheddar cheese (for **C** **CA** **G** **HD** **M** **MS** **V** use vegan cheddar)

1½ tsp (7 mL) dried dill

sea salt and pepper

first cold pressed extra virgin olive oil, for brushing

10 sheets phyllo pastry, thawed

Preheat the oven to 400°F (200°C). Brush the bottom of an 8-inch (20 cm) square ovenproof dish with a little olive oil.

In a frying pan over medium heat, heat the 1 Tbsp (15 mL) olive oil and sauté the kale and bell pepper, stirring, for 5 minutes. Remove from the heat and mix in the cheese, dill, and sea salt and pepper to taste.

Place 5 phyllo sheets, one on top of the other, in the pan, brushing each sheet lightly on one side with olive oil. You will have to fold them over to fit the pan. Place the filling over the phyllo and spread out evenly. Layer the next five sheets overtop the filling in the same way, again brushing each layer with olive oil. Bake for 30 to 35 minutes or until golden. Cut in squares to serve.

Potato and Kale with Hot Peppers

 **C** **CA** **CD** **D** **G** **HD** **M** **MS** **OA**   **V**

MAKES	TIME
4 servings	40 minutes

A spicy dish loaded with kale to help keep your bones strong, and your heart and every other part of you healthy too.

2 Tbsp (30 mL) first cold pressed extra virgin olive oil

1 very large white onion, roughly chopped

2 large garlic cloves, minced

1 large habanero pepper, diced, with some of the seeds

4 medium-size potatoes, peeled and diced

6–8 large tender kale leaves, cut up, stalks discarded

2 Tbsp (30 mL) balsamic vinegar

1 tsp (5 mL) dried oregano

sea salt and pepper (for **HD** use sodium substitute)

In a large frying pan over medium heat, heat the oil and sauté the onion for about 10 minutes. Add the garlic and habanero (including seeds to taste) then the potatoes and sauté for 1 minute. Add 2 cups (500 mL) water and cook, stirring, for about 20 minutes or until the potatoes are soft. The water should be evaporated. Add the kale then the balsamic vinegar, oregano, and sea salt and pepper to taste and cook for 4 minutes.

Potatoes, Spinach, Tomatoes and Cheese

        **V** | MAKES **4 servings** | TIME **40 minutes**

Comfort food made healthier by fresh spinach and tomatoes, both of which are loaded with antioxidants.

3 Tbsp (45 mL) first cold pressed extra virgin olive oil

3 large white potatoes, peeled and thinly sliced

4 medium-size tomatoes, small dice

2 cups (500 mL) torn-up fresh spinach

sea salt and pepper (for **HD** use sodium substitute)

3 Tbsp (45 mL) grated Parmesan cheese (for **CA** **CD** **D** **MS** **V** use vegan Parmesan)

In a frying pan over medium heat, heat the olive oil and sauté the potatoes, stirring, for about 20 minutes or until soft. Add the tomatoes and cook for about 10 minutes, stirring. Add the spinach and sea salt and pepper to taste and heat through, stirring, for 2 minutes. Add the cheese, heat through and serve.

Kale, Broccoli, Cheese and Walnut Pie

OA

MAKES	TIME
4 servings	1 hour 15 minutes

A walnut- and thyme-flavoured pie with a hint of heat and bursting with two super-veggies—kale and broccoli.

4 green onions, finely chopped

4 medium to large kale leaves, chopped, stalks discarded

1¼ cups (310 mL) chopped broccoli florets

¼–½ tsp (1–2 mL) chili flakes

2 tsp (10 mL) dried thyme

½ tsp (2 mL) sea salt

pepper

10 walnut halves, broken up

¾ cup (185 mL) grated aged cheddar cheese

⅔ cup (160 mL) grated kefalotiri cheese

1 cup (250 mL) whole rye or whole wheat flour

3 eggs, beaten

2 cups (500 mL) soy milk

Preheat the oven to 350°F (180°C). Grease a 9-inch (23 cm) pie plate.

In a bowl, mix everything together in the order listed and pour into the prepared pie plate. Bake for 60 to 70 minutes or until a toothpick inserted in the centre comes out clean.

Pumpkin Fritters

  ⓖ Ⓜ 🅞🅐

MAKES	TIME
4 servings	about 50 minutes

A great-tasting fritter loaded with healthy carotenes. Serve with soup and a salad for a complete meal. If you don't want too much heat, use ground cumin, ground cinnamon or curry powder instead of the cayenne.

> 1 Tbsp (15 mL) dairy-free nonhydrogenated margarine
> 1 large onion, roughly chopped
> 2 cups (500 mL) grated pumpkin (peeled)
> 1 cup (250 mL) grated potatoes (peeled)
> 1 tsp (5 mL) dried parsley
> sea salt and pepper (for 🅗🅓 use sodium substitute)
> 3 Tbsp (45 mL) whole wheat flour
> 2 eggs, beaten
> cayenne pepper

In a frying pan over medium heat, heat the margarine and sauté the onion, stirring, for 20 minutes. Mix the onion with the other ingredients, in the order listed, in a large bowl. Form into small patties, and brown in a frying pan over medium heat in about 1 Tbsp (15 mL) hot olive oil per batch until golden and crispy, about 10 to 20 minutes.

Alternatively, place the patties on a greased cookie sheet and bake at 375°F (190°C) until golden on both sides, 20 to 25 minutes.

Cook on both sides, whether baking or frying.

Gumbo

MAKES
4 servings

TIME
50 minutes

From the southern states, this is an easy vegetarian version of gumbo that is high in lycopene from the tomatoes. Some cultures credit okra as being good for digestion. You can usually find *filé* powder in specialty spice stores.

1 can (28 oz/796 mL) diced tomatoes

2 ½ cups (625 mL) chopped fresh okra

1 cup (250 mL) vegetable stock

pepper

2–3 dashes of Louisiana hot sauce (optional)

1 can (19 oz/540 mL) lima beans, drained
   and rinsed

1 cup (250 mL) frozen corn

½–1 tsp (2–5 mL) filé powder

In a large soup pot over medium heat, place the tomatoes, okra, stock, pepper to taste and a few dashes of hot sauce. Cover and cook, stirring now and then, for about 30 minutes. Add the lima beans and frozen corn and cook, stirring now and then, for about 10 minutes. Add the filé and heat through for a few minutes.

GUMBO

Sloppy Joes

MAKES	**TIME**
4 servings	40 minutes

An easy classic made healthy by leaving out the meat and loading up on the soy and veggies. Serve hot, with or without the hot sauce, over toast, or use in lasagna or over pasta.

1 Tbsp (15 mL) first cold pressed extra virgin
   olive oil
1 large cooking onion, diced
2⅓ cups (580 mL) sliced button mushrooms
1 medium-size green bell pepper, diced
1 jar (19 oz/540 mL) spaghetti sauce
1 package (12 oz/340 g) veggie ground round
¼–1 tsp (1–5 mL) chili flakes
hot sauce (optional)
4 slices whole wheat toast (for **CD** use
   gluten-free toast)

In a frying pan over medium heat, heat the oil and sauté the onion, stirring, for about 25 minutes. Add the mushrooms and bell pepper and sauté for 5 minutes. Add the spaghetti sauce, ground round, chili flakes and hot sauce (if using), and cook for about 5 minutes (or according to the ground round package instructions). Serve over the toast.

Easy Supper

MAKES	TIME
4 servings	20 to 25 minutes

A dish for supper or brunch: eggs or tofu with some healthy additions in the form of mushrooms and peas. Shiitake mushrooms are loaded with immunity-enhancing properties, and they taste awesome.

1 Tbsp (15 mL) dairy-free
  nonhydrogenated margarine

6 fresh shiitake mushrooms, bite-size pieces

6 fresh oyster mushrooms, bite-size pieces

2 slices meatless bologna, diced

3 eggs, beaten or diced extra-firm tofu (for **C** **D**
  HD **M** **MS** **RA** **V** use tofu)

1 cup (250 mL) frozen peas

2 Tbsp (30 mL) soy sauce (optional)

½–1 tsp (2–5 mL) hot sauce

one 3½-inch (9 cm) square slice of vegan cheese,
  diced

In a frying pan over medium heat, heat the margarine and sauté the two mushrooms, stirring, for about 5 minutes. Add the meatless bologna and cook, stirring, until crisp. Add the beaten eggs, frozen peas, soy sauce (if using), hot sauce and vegan cheese and cook, stirring, for 5 minutes.

Tofu Scrambler

MAKES
4 servings

TIME
40 minutes

A tasty way of making an unhealthy breakfast—scrambled eggs—healthy. It's really catching on in many restaurants. Serve hot with a mixed green salad.

1 tsp (5 mL) first cold pressed extra virgin olive oil

1 medium-size white onion, diced

2 cups (500 mL) sliced mushrooms, various kinds (optional; omit for **CA** **G**)

1 package (12 oz/350 g) extra-firm tofu, cut into 1-inch (2.5 cm) cubes

1 large red bell pepper, bite-size pieces (optional; omit for **RA**)

3–4 cups (750 mL–1 L) mixed greens (red and green chard, kale, bok choy are all good)

1½ cups (375 mL) vegetable stock

2 Tbsp (30 mL) balsamic vinegar

hot sauce

pepper

1 tsp (5 mL) soy sauce (optional)

In a large frying pan over medium heat, heat the oil and sauté the onion and mushrooms (if using) for a few minutes, stirring. Add the tofu and stir, browning a little on all sides. Add the bell pepper and sauté, stirring, for a few minutes. Add the greens, stock, vinegar, a few drops of hot sauce and pepper to taste and bring to a low boil. Reduce the heat to medium-low for a few minutes until the stock is absorbed. Add the soy sauce, if you are using it, before serving.

Blueberry Pancakes

MAKES	TIME
4 servings	15 to 20 minutes

These wonderful, fruity blue pancakes are nice and light, and they can be made gluten-free. And, of course, blueberries are loaded with anthocyanidins, which are powerful antioxidants. To make this gluten-free, use 1¼ cups (310 mL) brown-rice flour and ¼ cup (60 mL) potato or tapioca flour.

1½ cups (375 mL) whole wheat or spelt flour
   (for **CD** see above)

1 tsp (5 mL) baking powder

1 Tbsp (15 mL) first cold pressed extra virgin
   olive oil

⅛ tsp (0.5 mL) sea salt (for **HD** use
   sodium substitute)

ground cinnamon

1 egg, beaten (for **HD** **MS** **RA** **V**)

¼ cup (60 mL) blueberry juice

¾–1 cup (185–250 mL) soy milk

1 cup (250 mL) fresh wild blueberries

In a large bowl, mix together the flour and baking powder. Add the oil, sea salt and a pinch of cinnamon and mix well. Mix in the beaten egg and blueberry juice and then just enough soy milk to make a smooth batter. Mix until smooth. Fold in the blueberries.

Grease and heat a griddle over medium heat. Pour on the batter in small batches and cook on each side until slightly golden, about 2 to 3 minutes on each side. You may need to experiment with the amount of oil you use.

Stuffed Grilled Portobello Mushrooms

MAKES	TIME
4 servings	20 minutes

A wonderful combination of thyme and aged cheddar stuffed into delicious portobello mushrooms. For a gluten-free version, use brown-rice bread.

4–6 medium portobello mushrooms

first cold pressed extra virgin olive oil for brushing

2 slices whole wheat bread, diced
   (for **CD** see above)

1 cup (250 mL) grated extra-aged cheddar cheese
   (for **C CD D HD M MS RA V** use vegan cheddar)

1–2 Tbsp (15–30 mL) soy sauce

1 tsp (5 mL) dried thyme

Remove the stems from the mushrooms and reserve them for another time. Brush the mushrooms all over, inside and out, with a little olive oil. In a small bowl, mix together the bread, cheese, soy sauce and thyme.

Preheat the barbecue to medium-low.

Grill the mushrooms on each side for 3 to 4 minutes, with the barbecue lid closed. Remove from the grill. Stuff the mushrooms with the bread and cheese mixtures. Return the mushrooms to the barbecue, stuffing side up. Close the lid and cook for about 4 minutes, checking to make sure they don't burn.

Grilled Eggplant with Parmesan

C **CA**   **M**   **OA**

MAKES
4 servings

TIME
about 1 hour 25 minutes

Use a vegetable grilling basket for this one. For a wheat-free version use brown-rice flour.

> 1 medium eggplant, sliced in ¼-inch-thick (5 mm) rounds
>
> 2 eggs, beaten
>
> 1½ tsp (7 mL) dried oregano
>
> sea salt and pepper
>
> 1½ cups (375 mL) whole wheat flour
>
> 2 cups (500 mL) spaghetti sauce
>
> 1 cup (250 mL) grated Parmesan cheese (for **C** **CA** **M** use vegan Parmesan)

Place the eggplant rounds in a large bowl and just cover with hot water. Add 1 tsp (5 mL) sea salt to the water and soak the eggplant for 1 hour. Drain and rinse.

Preheat the barbecue to medium.

Place the beaten eggs, oregano, and sea salt and pepper to taste in a shallow bowl and the flour in another shallow bowl. Dip each slice of eggplant in the egg and then the flour. Place the coated slices in a regular or non-stick grilling basket. Barbecue on medium heat, with the barbecue lid closed, for up to 10 minutes, flipping them once in a while. Brush some spaghetti sauce on one side of the eggplant and top with cheese. Place cheese side up in the basket and barbecue until the eggplant is hot and cuts easily.

Orange-Flavoured Grilled Tofu

MAKES	TIME
2 servings	15 minutes

Healthy orange-flavoured tofu. Serve with a salad and rice.

2 Tbsp (30 mL) orange juice

¼ tsp (1 mL) orange zest

2 Tbsp (30 mL) honey

1 Tbsp (15 mL) fresh lemon juice

2 Tbsp (30 mL) first cold pressed extra virgin
   olive oil

1 package (12 oz/350 g) extra-firm tofu, cut into
   ½-inch (1 cm) slices

Preheat the barbecue to medium-low.

Mix together the orange juice, orange zest, honey, lemon juice and olive oil in a small bowl. Brush the tofu slices as you grill them in a regular or non-stick grilling basket. Close the barbecue lid, turning occasionally until done, about 10 minutes. They should be slightly crispy.

Layered Potatoes and Kale on the Grill

	MAKES	TIME
	4 servings	25 to 30 minutes

Bring this super-veggie dish to the next barbecue.

4–5 large red potatoes, skin on, thinly sliced

8 large tender kale leaves, bite-size pieces

1 large white onion, very thinly sliced

¾ cup (185 mL) soy milk

¾ cup (185 mL) grated vegan Parmesan

sea salt and pepper (for **HD** use sodium substitute)

Preheat the barbecue to medium.

Place a layer of potatoes on a double layer of aluminum foil and top with a layer of kale then onion. Repeat with the remaining potatoes, kale and onion.

Mix together the soy milk, vegan Parmesan, and sea salt and pepper to taste and pour overtop the veggies. Seal the foil well, keeping in the liquid, and place on the grill, sealed side up. Cook with the lid closed until the potatoes are soft, about 20 minutes.

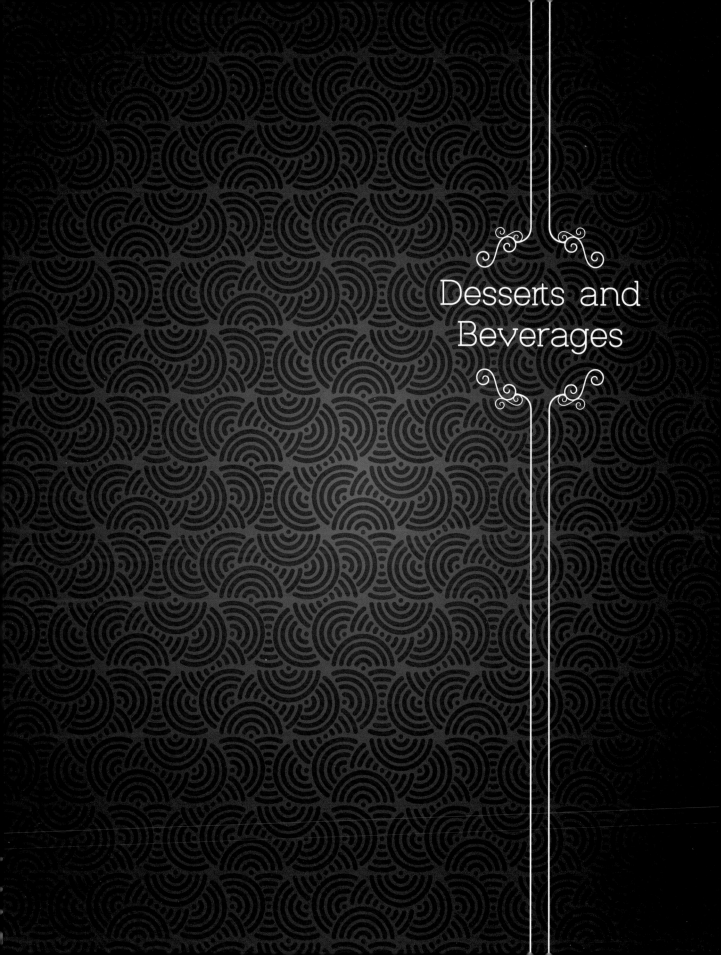

Desserts and Beverages

Recipes

Pop 'Em Balls

MAKES
about 14 balls

TIME
10 to 15 minutes

This is a new version of the tasty, healthy treat that was featured in my last cookbook. It contains flaxseeds with their essential fatty acids that prevent and treat a whole host of health problems. Take these on your next hike, keep them on hand as a healthy snack or serve them at parties. Pop 'Em Balls will stay fresh in the fridge for at least a week. (Pictured on page 402.)

6 dried dates, pitted

1¼ cups (310 mL) Thompson raisins

½ cup (125 mL) shredded unsweetened coconut

½ cup (125 mL) whole almonds

¼ cup (60 mL) sunflower seeds

¼ cup (60 mL) walnut pieces

1 Tbsp (15 mL) milled (ground) flaxseed

1 Tbsp (15 mL) apple juice

Place the dates, raisins, coconut, almonds, sunflower seeds, walnut pieces and flaxseed in a food processor, and blend until fairly smooth. Add just enough apple juice to make everything stick together. Form into balls, using 1 to 2 Tbsp (15–30 mL) of mix for each. Allow to harden in the fridge. Enjoy!

BLUEBERRY
AND COCOA
POP 'EM BALLS

Blueberry and Cocoa Pop 'Em Balls

MAKES	TIME
about 10 balls	10 to 15 minutes

Bursting with antioxidants and blueberries full of anthocyanidins.

¼ cup (60 mL) whole almonds

¾ cup (185 mL) dried blueberries

½ cup (125 mL) unsalted peanuts

½ cup (125 mL) shredded unsweetened coconut

1 tsp (5 mL) pure cocoa powder

apple juice as needed

Place the almonds, blueberries, peanuts, coconut and cocoa powder in a food processor and blend until fairly smooth. Add just enough apple juice to make everything stick together. Form into balls, using 1 to 2 Tbsp (15–30 mL) of mix for each. Allow to harden in the fridge. Enjoy!

Spicy Chocolate Pop 'Em Balls

MAKES	TIME
about 10 balls	10 to 15 minutes

Spicy and good. The antioxidant-rich cocoa powder and the heart-friendly cayenne give these balls quite a health punch for a dessert. And they are rich in almonds too.

1 cup (250 mL) pitted dried dates
½ cup (125 mL) whole almonds
½ cup (125 mL) shredded unsweetened coconut
1 tsp (5 mL) pure cocoa powder
¼ tsp (1 mL) cayenne pepper
apple juice as needed

Place the dates, almonds, coconut, cocoa powder and cayenne pepper in a food processor, and blend until fairly smooth. Add just enough apple juice to make everything stick together. Form into balls, using 1 to 2 Tbsp (15–30 mL) of mix for each. Allow to harden in the fridge. Enjoy!

Date, Fig and Coconut Squares

MAKES
4 servings

TIME
about 45 minutes

A tasty treat made with oats, so it's a healthy option. And if you use the stevia instead of the sugar, this recipe is free of an unhealthy sugar. Many diabetics use stevia.

¼ cup (60 mL) dairy-free
   nonhydrogenated margarine

2 cups (500 mL) quick-cooking oats

¾ cup (185 mL) brown cane sugar
   (for **C** **G** use ¾ tsp/3 mL stevia)

¾ cup (185 mL) shredded unsweetened coconut

1¼ tsp (6 mL) ground cinnamon

¼ tsp (1 mL) sea salt (for **HD** use sodium substitute)

1½ cups (375 mL) pitted dried honey dates

4 fresh figs, chopped small

2 Tbsp (30 mL) fresh lemon juice

¼ cup (60 mL) apple juice

Preheat the oven to 375°F (190°C). Grease an 8-inch (20 cm) square baking dish.

Melt the margarine in a saucepan on low heat, stirring. Remove from the heat. Mix in the oats, brown cane sugar, coconut, cinnamon and sea salt. Mix well and press half the mixture into the prepared pan. Blend the dates, figs and lemon juice in a food processor, and spread over the oatmeal mixture. Top with the other half of the oatmeal mixture. Pour the apple juice overtop and bake for 30 minutes.

Peach Crisp

MAKES 4 servings

TIME about 1 hour

Like apple crisp but with peaches. This one is good with vanilla ice cream (or soy or rice ice cream).

7–8 peaches, peeled, quartered, thinly sliced

1 tsp (5 mL) ground cinnamon, plus more
   for sprinkling

1½ cups (375 mL) quick-cooking oats

½ cup (125 mL) firmLy packed brown cane sugar
   (for **C** **G** use ½ tsp/2 mL stevia)

¼ cup (60 mL) whole wheat flour (for **CD** use
   brown-rice flour)

2 Tbsp (30 mL) dairy-free nonhydrogenated
   margarine

2 Tbsp (30 mL) apple juice

Preheat the oven to 350°F (180°C). Butter an 8-inch (20 cm) square baking dish.

Layer the peaches in the prepared baking dish. Mix the 1 tsp (5 mL) cinnamon with the oats, brown cane sugar, flour and margarine and press firmly over the peaches. Sprinkle with more cinnamon. Pour the apple juice overtop and cover with aluminum foil. Bake for 45 minutes. Remove the foil for the last 7 minutes of baking. Serve hot.

Peach Tofu "Mousse"

MAKES	TIME
4 servings	40 minutes

A healthy mousse-like dessert, rich in healthy genistein from the soy.

1 package (12 oz/350 g) silken tofu

5 large peaches, peeled, roughly chopped

1 Tbsp (15 mL) honey (optional; for **V** use
   ¼ tsp/1 mL stevia)

1 Tbsp (15 mL) peach or mango juice

½ tsp (2 mL) ground cinnamon (optional)

Place everything in a food processor and blend until smooth. Chill for at least ½ hour and serve cool.

Mango Tofu Dessert

MAKES **4 servings**	TIME 15 minutes

A healthy dessert packed with healthy tofu, rich in genistein and carotenes.

> 4 large mangos, peeled, pitted and frozen
> 1 package (12 oz/350 g) silken tofu
> 1 Tbsp (15 mL) mango juice
> 1 Tbsp (15 mL) honey (optional; for
>   use ¼ tsp/1 mL stevia)

Blend everything in a food processor until smooth. Chill for a few minutes before serving.

Apricot and Coconut Squares

MAKES
4 servings

TIME
about 45 minutes

An apricot-coconut treat made with fruit and oats, so it's a healthy option. Again, if you use the stevia instead of the cane sugar, it's free of unhealthy sugar. Many diabetics use stevia.

¼ cup (60 mL) dairy-free
    nonhydrogenated margarine

2 cups (500 mL) quick-cooking oats

¾ cup (185 mL) brown cane sugar
    (for **C** **G** use ¾ tsp/3 mL stevia)

¾ cup (185 mL) shredded unsweetened coconut

1 tsp (5 mL) ground cinnamon

¼ tsp (1 mL) sea salt (for **HD** use sodium substitute)

1½ cups (375 mL) dried apricots

2 Tbsp (30 mL) fresh lemon juice

¼ cup (60 mL) cranberry juice

Preheat the oven to 375°F (190°C). Grease an 8-inch (20 cm) square baking dish.

    Melt the margarine in a saucepan on low heat, stirring. Remove from the heat and mix in the oats, brown cane sugar, coconut, cinnamon and sea salt. Mix well and press half the mixture into the prepared dish. Blend the apricots and lemon juice in a food processor, and spread over the oatmeal mixture. Top with the other half of the oatmeal mixture. Pour the cranberry juice overtop and bake for 30 minutes.

High-Fibre Muffins

C   

MAKES	TIME
about 8 muffins	about 40 minutes

Delicious, healthy muffins that give a boost to your body.

1¼ cups (310 mL) whole wheat flour

¾ cup (185 mL) wheat bran

2 tsp (10 mL) baking powder

½ cup (125 mL) dried cranberries, unsweetened

⅓ cup (80 mL) walnut pieces, more if desired

¼ cup (60 mL) flaxseeds

¾ cup (185 mL) pomegranate or orange juice

3 Tbsp (45 mL) unsweetened apple sauce

2 eggs (for **HD** **MS** **RA** **V** use egg replacement)

2 medium-size oranges, peeled and chopped small

1 Tbsp (15 mL) orange rind, grated (optional)

2 tsp (10 mL) first cold pressed extra virgin olive oil

Preheat the oven to 375°F (190°C). Lightly grease the cups of a muffin tin, or use a non-stick muffin tin.

Place everything in a food processor and blend for a few minutes. If the mix seems dry, add a splash more juice. Fill the muffin cups three-quarters full. Bake for 23 to 28 minutes or until a toothpick inserted in the centre comes out clean.

Banana Walnut High-Fibre Muffins

MAKES	TIME
about 12 medium muffins	about 40 minutes

A delicious fibre-rich muffin with healthy essential fatty acids. For a gluten-free version you can use 1¾ cups (435 mL) brown-rice flour plus ¼ cup (60 mL) tapioca flour instead of the whole wheat flour.

2 cups (500 mL) whole wheat flour
   (for **CD** see above)

2 tsp (10 mL) baking powder

¼ tsp (1 mL) sea salt (for **HD** use sodium substitute)

2 large ripe bananas, peeled and mashed

¾ cup (185 mL) walnut pieces

⅓ cup (80 mL) raisins or dried cranberries

¼ cup (60 mL) flaxseed

¼ cup (60 mL) sunflower seeds (optional)

2 eggs, beaten (for **HD** **MS** **RA** **V** use
   egg replacement)

3 Tbsp (45 mL) first cold pressed extra virgin
   olive oil

¾ cup (185 mL) grapefruit juice

Preheat the oven to 350°F (180°C). Grease the cups of a muffin tin, or use a non-stick muffin tin.

Mix together the flour, baking powder and sea salt. Add the bananas, walnuts, raisins, flaxseed and sunflower seeds (if using). Mix well. Add the eggs and olive oil. Gradually add the grapefruit juice and mix well to make a smooth batter. Fill the muffin cups three-quarters full. Bake for 25 to 30 minutes or until a toothpick inserted in the centre comes out clean.

No Sugar-Added Blueberry Muffins

	MAKES	TIME
	about 12 muffins	about 40 minutes

These blueberry-flavoured muffins are loaded with anthocyanidins (a powerful antioxidant). Celiacs can use 2 cups (500 mL) brown-rice flour plus ½ cup (125 mL) tapioca flour instead of the whole wheat flour.

2 ½ cups (625 mL) whole wheat flour
(for **CD** see above)

2 ¼ tsp (11 mL) baking powder

1 tsp (5 mL) ground cinnamon

1 tsp (5 mL) stevia

¼ tsp (1 mL) sea salt (for **HD** use sodium substitute)

¾–1 cup (185–250 mL) plain or vanilla soy milk (for
C **CA** **D** **G** use plain)

¼ cup (60 mL) first cold pressed extra virgin
olive oil

2 eggs beaten (for **D** **HD** **MS** **RA** **V** use
egg replacement)

1 ½ cups (375 mL) fresh blueberries (or frozen if
fresh are out of season)

Preheat the oven to 375°F (190°C). Lightly grease the cups of a muffin tin, or use a non-stick muffin tin.

Mix together the flour, baking powder, cinnamon, stevia and sea salt. Then add the soy milk (beginning with ¾ cup/185 mL and adding more as necessary), oil and eggs. Mix well and add one third of the blueberries. Blend in a food processor. Fold in the rest of the blueberries. Fill the muffin cups three-quarters full. Bake for 22 to 25 minutes or until a toothpick inserted in the centre comes out clean.

Veggie Juice

MAKES	TIME
about 2 cups (500 mL)	10 minutes

Loaded with nutrients, sweet and delicious. Kind of like a healthy store-bought juice.

4 large sticks celery

3 red chard leaves

3 green chard leaves

3 large carrots

2 large tomatoes

1 red bell pepper

Cut up all the veggies so they fit through the juicer and juice.

Ted's Favourite Vegetable Juice

MAKES	TIME
1 serving	about 5 minutes

A very healthy way of getting in extra nutrients. This is tasty, refreshing and packs quite a punch. Good for the heart and just about everything else.

2 large carrots

1 large Mutsu, Granny Smith, Gala or Empire apple

1 clove garlic

1 stick celery

1-inch (2.5 cm) piece fresh ginger, more if you like it spicy

small handful of fresh parsley

handful of fresh spinach (optional; omit for Ⓖ)

Cut up all the veggies so they fit through the juicer and juice.

Vegetable Beet Juice

MAKES	TIME
1 serving	about 5 minutes

A wonderful way of getting in your vegetables with lots of extra nutrients and energy. And it tastes great with the ginger.

3 large carrots

2 sticks celery

1 small- to medium- size beet with leaves

a large handful of fresh spinach

½-inch (1 cm) piece fresh ginger, more if you like it spicy

Cut up all the veggies so they fit through the juicer and juice.

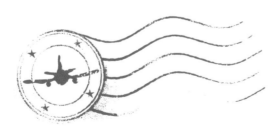

Real Iced Tea

MAKES	TIME
7 cups (1.75 L)	about 1 hour

Easy and refreshing on a hot day. This tea is especially lovely if you use very fresh herbs. The alfalfa is an effective internal cleanser and rich in minerals, the chamomile is good for digestion and nervousness and rich in calcium, and the peppermint is also a good digestive.

7 cups (1.75 L) boiling water

1 Tbsp (15 mL) fresh alfalfa herb

1 tsp (5 mL) dried or 1 Tbsp (15 mL)
    fresh chamomile flowers

1 tsp (5 mL) dried or 1 Tbsp (15 mL)
    fresh peppermint

juice of 1 large lime

1 Tbsp (15 mL) honey (for **CA** **D** **V** use stevia)

spearmint leaves for serving

Pour the boiling water over the herbs and cover. Allow to stand for 20 minutes to infuse and then strain. Add the lime juice and honey and chill. Serve cold with spearmint leaves and ice.

REAL
ICED
TEA

Springtime Green

											MAKES	TIME
C	CA	CD	D	G	HD	M	MS	OA	RA	V	1 serving	about 5 minutes

A refreshing, cooling, cleansing summer drink. Good for the heart and high blood pressure.

> 2 large sticks celery
> 1 lime, peeled
> ⅓ large English cucumber, peeled

Cut up all the ingredients so they fit through the juicer and juice.

Healthy Quick Start Smoothies

| | | MAKES
1 serving | TIME
about 5 minutes |

Smoothies are healthy drinks and can be a snack or a meal. They are particularly good for anyone who needs extra nutrition, especially if you use the options given below. They are wonderful for everyone: athletes, people in a hurry, those who don't like breakfast and those who are recovering from an illness. You can use rice milk or hemp milk instead if you prefer.

2 cups (500 mL) plain, vanilla or chocolate soy milk
(for **C** **CA** **D** **G** use unsweetened)

1 small banana, peeled, you can freeze it if you
like, or use other fruit to taste, like berries and
mango (for **CA** use berries)

1 scoop protein powder (whey, rice or soy;
plain, vanilla or chocolate; for **C** **CA** **D** **G**
look for sugar-free protein powder)

Place everything in a blender and blend until smooth.

For extra nutrition you can sneak in the following (in any combination that takes your fancy):

1 tsp–1 Tbsp (5–15 mL) or more of spirulina
powder, or 1 to 2 frozen wheat grass packets

1 Tbsp (15 mL) flaxseeds

1 dose probiotics

1 dose multivitamin/mineral

1 dose herbs like astragalus, or 2 g packet of
instant ginseng tea

Mango Smoothie

	MAKES	TIME
	1 serving	about 5 minutes

A refreshing, fruity drink loaded with essential fatty acids from flax, as well as calcium, magnesium and carotenes. This is one of my favourite smoothies.

> 1 cup (250 mL) chilled vanilla soy milk
>   (for **C** **D** G use unsweetened or plain)
> 1 mango, peeled
> 1 Tbsp (15 mL) flaxseed oil
> 1 Tbsp (15 mL) fruit-flavoured liquid calcium/
>   magnesium, vitamin D and zinc supplement

Place everything in a blender and blend until smooth.

Chocolate Nut Smoothie

MAKES
1 serving

TIME
about 5 minutes

This is Ted's favourite drink, and one he put together. It is high in calcium (the tahini) and other nutrients, gives energy and boosts immunity—and tastes incredible. I drink it for breakfast, and it keeps me going for hours. If you can't find unsweeted chocolate soy milk and are avoiding sugar, you may have to skip this smoothie.

1¼ cups (310 mL) chocolate soy milk
   (for **C** **D** **G** use unsweetened)

⅓ cup (80 mL) plain soy milk

½ banana

1 Tbsp (15 mL) milled (ground) flaxseed

1 tsp (5 mL) almond butter

½ tsp (2 mL) tahini, made from brown
   sesame seeds

¼–1 tsp (1–5 mL) spirulina

2 g packet of instant ginseng tea

Place everything in a blender and blend until smooth.

Fig, Date and Chocolate Shake

	MAKES	TIME
	1–2 servings	about 5 minutes

A totally vegan drink that is sweet and delicious.

2 cups (500 mL) plain, vanilla or chocolate soy milk
   (for **C** **G** use plain or unsweetened)

4 fresh dark figs, skin on

4 pitted dried dates

½ tsp (2 mL) pure vanilla extract

2 tsp (10 mL) cocoa powder (minimum 70% cocoa),
   use less if using chocolate soy milk

Place everything in a blender and blend until smooth.

Chocolate Peanut Butter Shake

	MAKES	TIME
	1 serving	about 5 minutes

A delicious version of a healthy chocolate peanut butter cup in drink form. It's rich in healthy soy milk and anthocyanidins from the blueberries. If you can't find unsweetened chocolate soy milk and are avoiding sugar, you may have to skip this shake.

1¼ cups (310 mL) chocolate soy milk

2 Tbsp (30 mL) fresh or frozen blueberries

1 Tbsp (15 mL) organic peanut butter

1 very small banana, peeled

Place everything in a blender and blend until smooth.

Iced Green Tea with Lime

	MAKES	TIME
	4 servings	about 1 hour 30 minutes

A great energy-building, immune-system-enhancing, antioxidant-rich, refreshing iced tea from China! You could use stevia instead of honey if you prefer.

> 5 cups (1.25 L) boiling water
> 3–4 tsp (15–20 mL) green tea leaves with
>   jasmine flowers
> 2 tsp (10 mL) broken up ginseng sticks
> juice of 1 large lime
> honey (optional; omit or use stevia for **C** **CA** **D** **V**)

Pour the water over the tea leaves and ginseng sticks. Let stand for 1 hour then strain through a tea strainer. Let cool and add the lime juice and sweetener if you are using it. Serve with ice.

Iced Green Tea with Lemon

C **CA** **CD** **D** **G** **HD** **M** **MS** **OA** **RA** **V** | MAKES
4 servings | TIME
about 1 hour 30 minutes

This cooling, refreshing drink from China also happens to be
an energy builder.

> 6 cups (1.5 L) boiling water
>
> 1½–2 tsp (7–10 mL) green tea leaves with
>   jasmine flowers
>
> one 2 g packet of instant ginseng; you can use
>   two, if desired
>
> juice of 1 lemon

Place everything in a bowl and let stand for 1 hour. Strain through a tea
strainer and refrigerate. Serve with ice.

Index